F

WEAVING

WEAVING

A MANUAL OF TECHNIQUES

Rosemary Bridgman

The Crowood Press

First published in 1991 by
The Crowood Press Ltd
Gipsy Lane, Swindon
Wiltshire SN2 6DQ

British Library Cataloguing in Publication Data

Bridgman, Rosemary
  Weaving : a manual of techniques.
  1. Handicrafts : Weaving
  I. Title
  746.14

  ISBN 1 85223 444 X

To Frank, with my most grateful thanks for his patience and understanding over the years since the textile bug bit me – even to the extent of teaching himself to cook so that we didn't starve (greater love hath no man, surely)

Acknowledgements

All photographs by the author unless otherwise credited.
Line-drawings by David Joffe.
Photographs and computer graphics by the author.

Typeset by Inforum Typesetting, Portsmouth
Printed and bound in Great Britain by BPCC Hazell Books, Aylesbury

Contents

Preface

I once heard someone say that the true mark of a craftsman is how he describes himself on his passport. If so, I am afraid I rate nowhere. Perhaps it is easier for a man to say 'silversmith', 'woodworker', 'metalworker' (though 'weaver' might raise a few eyebrows – 'A bit archaic, surely . . .'). However, for a woman of my generation the cover-all word 'housewife' is quite difficult to discard – probably because it is impossible to ignore the fact that, as with most women, that role fills at least half of my life. Nor do I resent this, except in so far as I much prefer weaving to some of my housewifely tasks, such as cleaning the house. But perhaps I should describe myself in future as 'housewife/designer-weaver' and so acknowledge the happy conjunction between the role I played for the first part of my adult life and its subsequent combination with my work as a professional maker of textiles.

Out of the decision to bring together an orchardful of uncut grass and a flock of Shetland sheep has evolved a whole new world – a world of relooking and learning, of like-minded friends and shared experiences and, finally, of the rather daunting yet irresistible challenge of being asked to write this book. And of trying to get my ideas as well as my technical know-how down on paper without allowing the whole thing to get quite out of hand. A book of 75,000 words sounded plenty, but to cover a subject which started at the dawn of time – well, it has been a very tight squeeze, and I can only apologize for any omissions obvious to my fellow weavers. They are entirely my fault and in no way that of all those friends who have contributed, directly or indirectly, to the words on these pages. Without their help and encouragement, writing the book would not have been half as easy, or as enjoyable.

I would particularly like to thank Itsuko Alford for her help with the photographs; my teaching colleague, Geoffrey Glover, for checking the chapters on design; Cate Mack, for making me free of Norwood Farm and its rare breeds of domestic livestock; and Jo Tether, for letting me photograph both past and current work.

TOOLS AND MATERIALS

1
Origins

It is probably safe to say that weaving is one of the oldest crafts practised by man. It has been defined as the interlacing together of one set of flexible threads at right angles through another set of flexible threads, using some form of framework to hold and tension the threads.

Most of our great artistic endeavours – Stone Age cave paintings of man the hunter and his prey animals, for instance – have been made both for a serious purpose, as a 'good luck' invocation to the gods in the case of the paintings, and to satisfy the artistic and creative urge. I find it difficult to believe that such quality of line was not made as much out of love as out of religious opportunism.

So with textiles, I think. No doubt the first men didn't need much in the way of body covering in the heat of the African sun, and the skins of the animals they killed must have kept our forefathers reasonably warm as they slowly moved north. Anthropological studies of tribes who still practised a 'Stone Age' lifestyle within living memory, tribes such as the Bushmen of the Kalahari desert in southern Africa, have shown that the urge to decorate the body is every bit as great as the need to cover it from the elements. So

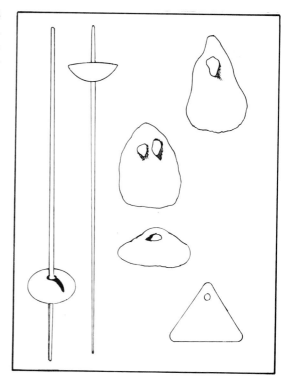

Stone or pottery spindle whorls and loom weights are found in archaeological digs.

it seems reasonable to suppose that men, both for religious and for personal reasons, not only painted their skin with natural pigments but also embellished

7

themselves with feathers, grasses and flowers 'woven' into 'garments'.

Unfortunately, textiles and the various fibres from which they are made are very perishable. So even the technically expert present-day archaeologist seldom comes across traces of the textiles themselves in man's early settlements. It is only by finding the tools with which the textiles were made (spindle whorls, loom weights) that we can be sure that the spinning and interlacing of fibres to form baskets, mats and clothing goes back to early neolithic times, probably 12,000 to 15,000 years ago, after the end of the last ice age.

What must be one of the oldest finds of an actual textile, dating back to *circa* 6000 BC, was discovered in excavations at the Stone Age settlement of Catal Huyuk in Anatolia – the huge central plain of Turkey across which man and his animals have moved out of central Asia since time began. It is desperately delicate, carbonized by age, but still recognizable as a piece of plain-weave cloth, either flax or wool, woven at 30 × 38 threads per inch. Certainly those weavers were not beginners – theirs was a fine, quality cloth. So it can surely be said that man was a weaver ten thousand years ago.

This fact fires me with a sense of excitement and challenge which I want to share in this book. The idea that, as weavers, we can wrap ourselves in the comfort of a traditional craft, both necessary and beautiful, while at the same time we challenge ourselves to reinterpret it for today, and for our own personal satisfaction.

HOW IT ALL STARTS

Textiles start with the yarn, and the yarn starts with the fibre. A fibre is the smallest visible unit from which textiles are made; take apart a thread of yarn from a fabric, untwist it and tease it out, and you will see the fibres that have gone into its making. There are many naturally fibrous materials, those produced without the aid of any chemical process, most of which are, or have been at one time or another, used for yarn making. And equally there are many differences in the way these fibres are prepared and then made into a yarn, from the spinning (twisting) of relatively short-stapled wool to the reeling off from the cocoon of a continuous single filament of silk.

Natural fibres fall into two categories: cellulose and protein. Cellulose fibres are of vegetable origin and are produced from seeds and stems – cotton, linen, jute, hemp, sisal, ramie, nettle, raffia. Protein fibres are of animal origin, such as sheep's wool and the hair fibres (which do not have the crimp and resilience of wool) from various breeds of goats, dogs, cats, rabbits, members of the camelid family – camel, llama, alpaca – and some species of wild cattle such as the musk ox of North America. Asbestos is a natural mineral fibre, now known to be dangerous and so restricted in its use today, while glass is a man-made substance, categorized as mineral, which can be spun out into fibres and used in textile manufacture.

Most of these are 'staple' or 'staple length' fibres; that is to say, they are measured by the limit of their growth length, such as the height of the flax (linen) or nettle (ramie) plant, or the year's growth of the sheep's fleece (wool) or the angora goat's hair (mohair). And because of the relative shortness of the staple length these fibres are spun together, in order to give a yarn of sufficient strength to serve the purpose for which it is intended.

A continuous monofilament fibre, which in the case of man-made ones can be several miles long, is produced by the extrusion of a chemical solution which is hardened by various means, chemical and otherwise, into a long, fine filament. Several of these lightly twisted together give the basic fibre, which can then be *plied* (retwisted) into the required quality and thickness of yarn.

A fibre is found wrapped round the cocoon of the many species of silk moths, particularly *Bombyx mori*, the mulberry silk moth, domesticated by the Chinese nearly 5,000 years ago. These are reeled off to produce a natural monofilament fibre. Waste lengths such as silk filament from damaged cocoons, and silk taken from the cocoons of wild silk moths, are combined, chopped to length and spun together as for staple fibres. Silk has properties allied to both cellulose and protein fibres and so belongs to both groups.

There are also numerous man-made fibres, mostly manufactured nowadays as by-products of the petroleum industry, as are many synthetic dyes. They all tend to have specific properties designed for specific purposes and/or manufacturing processes, so this allows handweavers to discount many and concentrate on those which will enhance the quality of their work. Among the best-known and most useful to the handweaver are rayon and acetate, acrylic, polyester, nylon and, to add 'lift' and excitement, metallic yarns.

FROM SIMPLE FRAMES TO SOPHISTICATED FABRICATORS

In his *The Book of Looms* (required reading for anyone wanting to put their work into

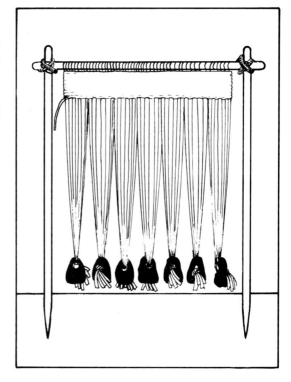

A warp-weighted loom. The warp threads, bunched and weighted, hang from the cross-bar. Weaving is from top to bottom.

its historical context) Eric Broudy tells us that the word loom comes from the Old English word *geloma*, meaning a tool or utensil. And that is exactly what a loom is: it is a tool for tensioning yarns at right angles to each other, so that a fabric may be created more easily.

As such, it can take many forms. For instance, it may be a simple supported crossbar, from which hang the *warp* threads, the ones which run from end to end of the fabric. These warp threads are tensioned by being gathered into bunches and weighted down with a stone or something similar. This allows easier passage of the *weft* thread, from edge to edge of the fabric, at right angles to the warp.

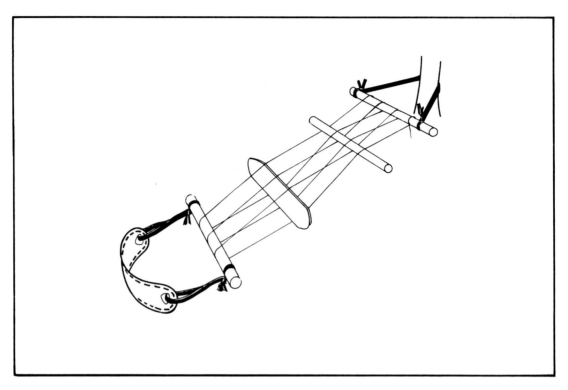

A diagrammatic representation of a backstrap loom. One end is fastened to a firm stay (a tree or post), the other round the weaver's body.

This warp-weighted loom of the ancient Greeks is still used today both in Scandanavia and in North America – a tool which has truly proved its value. And there is a clearly visible line of development from this loom, which appears to be the originator of the principle of vertical warp threading, and today's upright tapestry looms – sturdy and simple yet sophisticated frames for the weaving of heavy fabrics such as rugs and tapestries.

One more weaving tool which has proved its worth through the ages is another simply tensioned device, the backstrap loom. At the beginning of his chapter on the backstrap and other primitive looms, Eric Broudy quotes a fellow American, H. Ling Roth: 'The loom is after all only the frame upon which a principle, weaving, is worked out, and . . . there is considerable reason for the supposition that it may have been invented more than once.'

With yarns, local availability and climatic conditions dictated what was used. So too with looms. The yarn used, the materials available, and the life led by the weavers dictated their choice of looms. Tightly spun coarse wool or hair fibres are not broken by the heavy vertical pull of weights on the warp yarns. But for short-staple cotton or other fine vegetable fibres such as ramie Asian weavers needed, and still need, the greater control over tensioning which a device such as the backstrap loom gives.

The backstrap loom is actually incredi-

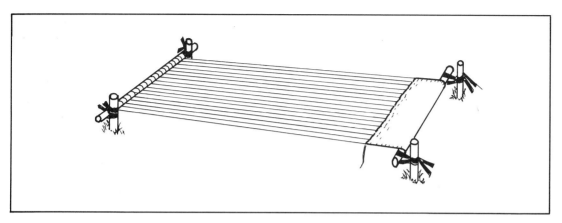

A ground loom. Warp and front beam are secured to pegs driven in to the ground.

bly clever in its apparent simplicity. The warp beam, the back one of the two pieces of wood between which the warp threads are tied, is secured to a tree or some such, while the front one, the cloth beam, is attached to a belt which runs round the weaver's body. Leaning back a little is all that is needed to tension the warp, and the weaver can lean as hard or as lightly as the strength of the warp yarn allows.

This pattern of warp threads being tensioned horizontally between a back or warp beam and a front or cloth beam (the one nearest to the weaver) is echoed in other simple weaving devices, such as the ground loom or mat loom. There are pictorial records in Egyptian tombs, dating back to around 2000 BC, of weavers working on a loom of this kind. The warp beam is secured to pegs driven into the ground and, the proper distance away for the length of cloth required, the cloth beam is similarly pegged down. The weaver actually sits on the cloth he has woven, so he is in effect moving down the loom as he weaves from front beam to back beam. Today's north African tribesman uses a similar two-bar horizontal loom, some-

times sitting beside the *selvedge* (the warp threads on either edge of the cloth) or, as with the ancient Egyptian, sitting on the woven portion. Either way he moves bodily down the warp until all is woven. This loom also has one great virtue, most important to nomadic tribes; it is easily transportable. When they move to the next watering-hole, the pegs securing the two beams are pulled out of the ground and the work is rolled up round the beams and tied onto the back of the pack camel with the other household goods.

Long ground looms pegged down under shady trees may be fine for Africa but are somewhat impracticable in wetter and colder Europe. However, the horizontal position for warp threads has become, in fact, the most commonly used format for cloth weaving and it was probably east Asian weavers who developed a more compact and sophisticated frame to hold warp threads horizontal – what we now call the *treadle loom*. And it must have been the need to speed up the weaving process which led to this development. Backstrap looms, for instance, allow a skilled weaver to construct anything from

11

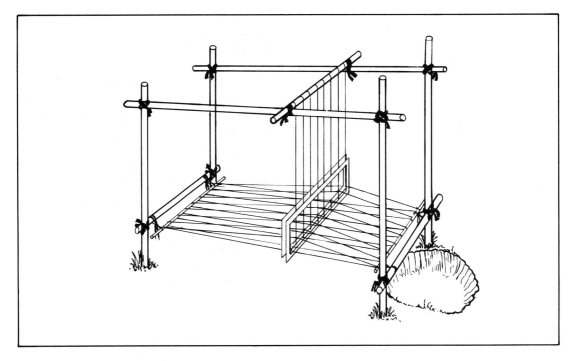

An Indian 'pit' loom – a two-shaft treadle loom. The weaver sits in a pit to bring him level with the warp, just above ground level.

simple plain-weave everyday fabrics to the most intricate brocaded ceremonial cloths, but it is a slow process. The use of treadles, depressed by the feet, to lift the *harnesses* and form the *shed* through which the hands were now free to pass the weft thread, considerably speeded up the process.

There does not appear to be any logical pattern in this development of the tools of the craft; again, it seems probable that availability of materials, population growth which necessitated increased production, personal preferences and the many other factors which control all the developments of civilizations played their part here too. Consequently, as an example, in China and then in Europe, the impetus given by the demands of an increasingly developed society for luxury fabrics woven from silk led to the invention of the drawloom, its mechanization and metamorphosis into the Jacquard loom and, ultimately, into today's industrial shuttleless looms passing the weft through the warp over 300 times every minute.

If for no other reason than that of 'know thine enemy', as handweavers today we need to be aware not only of the historical basis of the craft but also of its modern developments. To my mind, there is no benefit to the craft maker in replicating work that a machine can do faster, and therefore much more cheaply. That way lies frustration at best, and bankruptcy at worst.

But machines cannot do everything and this is where we can find our niche. The human mind guiding the human hand is still more intelligent than the most sophisticated computer guiding the most modern loom. Or perhaps there is an unfilled market for some specialized textile, because the time and trouble it takes to make renders it unsuitable for long factory-production runs. Or a particular technique, or fibre, or loom, or a combination of some or all of these factors, can be built up by careful workmanship and intelligent marketing into a textile which both pleases its creator and finds appreciative buyers.

This happy and satisfying marriage of what William Morris called 'form and function', fostered by the Victorian Arts and Crafts movement in nineteenth-century England, is one which I feel is still a valid aim for today's handweavers – but perhaps without taking too seriously their rather sentimental view of the so-called nobility of labour. So I would always advocate taking advantage of, as well as making the necessary adaptations to, the facts of modern living.

I know I am not alone in feeling that handweaving, like other crafts, still has a valuable part to play in our lives and that, as civilization makes the world a more and more complicated place in which to live, the satisfaction we get from creating something both beautiful and useful is more than ever necessary to us.

2
The Properties of Fibres

The use to which fibres have been put in the making of textiles has been as much dependent on their particular properties as on their availability. People living in cold countries favoured wool and hair fibres for making their textiles, as these gave them warm, absorbent, comfortable and washable clothes, as well as hard-wearing weather- and draught-proof tents, floor and wall coverings and general household furnishings.

The ancient Egyptians prized linen for its great absorbency, its ability to take strong dye colours and to be spun and woven into fabrics so fine as to be almost transparent, yet still retain excellent properties of strength and washability. Wild silk was found in China and wild cotton in the Ganges valley of northern India; they were developed because they were suited both to the climate and to the requirements of their producers.

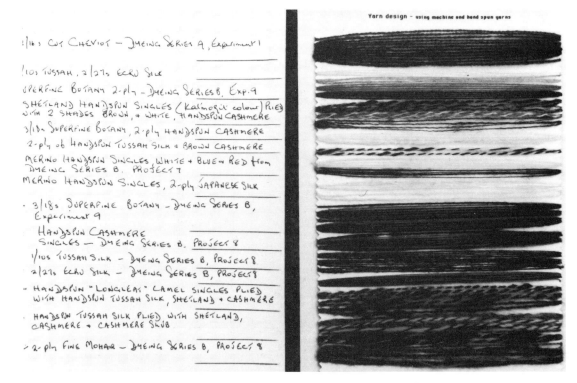

A yarn design using machine and handspun yarns - and keeping a record of yarns used in weave sampling.

Since the introduction of the first man-made fibre (rayon, first manufactured in the period between the two world wars) we have grown to value the strength and durability of the many fibres now manufactured, and to find ways of improving their absorbency and making them more comfortable to wear. Mixtures of natural fibres, or of natural and man-made fibres, can be used to create yarns with the qualities required for particular projects. This combination of fibres in the spinning process, the combining of machine-spun with handspun fibres, and even the re-combining of machine-spun yarns are techniques which can be used by the handspinner and weaver to make versatile yarns to his or her own design.

Mixing fibres can undoubtedly add originality and excitement to yarns, and thus to the work in which they are used. But, if disasters are to be avoided, *sampling* the various processes which the textile is to undergo during the course of its manufacture, and careful thought about the final form which it will take, are essential.

MAN-MADE FIBRES

These fibres fall into two categories. The first are the purely *synthetic* fibres, made from a chemical element (coal tar was used in the past, today's synthetics are a by-product of the petroleum industry). Various methods are used to manufacture fibres from the chemical. One way is to cut a thin film of extruded filament into strips, combine the strips into a sliver-like form, chop to length and spin. Alternatively, the strip can be used as a mono-filament yarn. Another, and the most usual, way is to extrude a liquid solution through holes in a device rather like a watering-can rose. This is called a *spin-naret*, and the holes vary in size and in cross-section, so the 'melt' forced through the holes may be circular, hexagonal or in fact any shape which suits the manufacturer's requirements. On emerging from the spinnaret the filaments are either so-lidified in a chemical bath (wet spinning) or dried in warm air (dry spinning). The threads of solidified solution may be left in monofilament form, or bunches of the

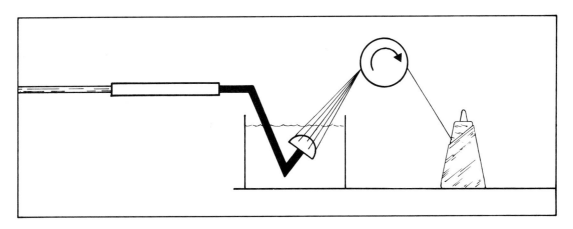

Spinning viscose rayon. The thick solution is passed through an acid bath, filaments are formed in the spinnaret, stretched and spun, and the yarn is then wound on to a cone.

filaments may be combined, cut into suitable lengths and spun by the same method that is used for the naturally produced staple-length fibres such as wool and cotton. Various process of stretching, crimping, bulking, curling, and so on, may be applied to the filament yarns to make them softer and more pleasant to wear, while additives to give, for instance, flame-retardancy, or dyestuffs with a high degree of colour-fastness, can also be put into the chemical solutions at the start of the process.

A secondary category of man-made fibres includes those made from natural fibrous materials such as cotton linters or wood pulp, *regenerated* into fibres and then spun into yarn. First the raw material has to be refined into a cellulose solution. This is then forced through a spinnaret and after that put into an acid bath to re-coagulate the fibres. After this, various manufacturing processes are used to make the yarns, and any required additives can be incorporated at this point, as with the chemically based man-made fibres.

One point is worth remembering if you are creating your own yarns by blending or mixing the natural and man-made varieties. Most synthetic yarns are shrinkproof to abrasion or in water, but may not be if other forms of excessive heat are applied (ironing, for instance.) However, most are pre-treated by heat-setting to stabilize them so, as long as the optimum heat is not exceeded in its after-care, you can improve the shrink- and abrasion-resistance of, say, a wool fabric by adding nylon.

The following is a description of some of the regenerated and synthetic man-made fibres which handweavers may find useful:

Acetate

Acetate is one of the two families of fibres manufactured from regenerated cellulose obtained from wood pulp. The combination of cellulose with sulphuric and other acids produces cellulose acetate, a thick fluid which can then be manufactured into a fibre capable of forming a yarn. 'Triacetate' is a term used, and Celanese is a well-known brand name. Because the cellulose has been altered chemically the properties of the acetate fibres are different from those of the other man-made cellulose derivative, rayon. Its snags are a lack of absorbency and elasticity, and the fact that it is not very hard-wearing. This needs to be borne in mind when deciding where to use it. It has a poor wet strength, and little heat-resistance so must be ironed at low temperatures. In its triacetate form it can be heat-set into pleats. It is probably not as useful to the handweaver as rayon.

Acrylic

This is a large group of varying petroleum-derived fibres, usually spun from staple fibres round a cotton core to give a *lofty* (bulky, soft) yarn. Best-known brand names are Acrilan, Courtelle and Orlon. A low twist in the spinning gives a yarn as soft as lambswool but, like its natural counterpart, it has a tendency to pill. Very useful to the handspinner, it can be bought ready to spin, and it gives a cheaper but good-quality way of increasing the amount of expensive fine wool or hair yarns. Alternatively, it can be plied with stronger linen or cotton yarns to give added softness and drape (and again, cheapness) to the final fabric.

Metallic Fibres

These are manufactured from metal, plastic-coated metal or various core yarns sheathed in metal, giving a non-tarnishing and flexible yarn. Glitter and glitz is not to everyone's taste but, used sparingly to accent and highlight, these yarns give handweavers the opportunity of adding excitement to their fabrics.

Nylon

Nylon is another man-made yarn produced from synthesized polyamides (the basic fibre-forming substances). It is lustrous, strong and resistant to abrasion. But by itself it is non-absorbent and so most uncomfortable to wear in hot weather. Therefore its value to the weaver is probably as a yarn to use with others. In its fine and virtually colourless form, it comes into its own when used to add strength where this is needed – perhaps as an invisible core for the rather weak yarns handspun from short-staple hair fibres such as rabbit, or to add stability to metallic yarns.

Polyester

Polyester is manufactured from various combinations of fibre-forming synthetic substances to give a variety of fibres with slightly different properties. The best-known are probably those found under the brand names of Terylene and Dacron. It is strong, and the fibres do not stretch or sag. Its high moisture-absorption properties plus a resistance to abrasion, with consequent pilling and fluffing, make it an excellent choice for blending with wool, either in the spinning process or by plying. It can also be heat-set, so a crisp pleat can be ironed into garments made from a polyester-mix woven cloth. Conversely, of course, excessively hot washing will give permanent creases and pleats where they are not wanted.

Rayon

Rayon constitutes the second of the two families of regenerated cellulose fibres. The standard variety is known as *viscose*, or *viscose rayon*. It was known originally as 'artificial silk', although it has very different properties. However, this does not mean that it should be despised. Like its relative, linen, it takes strong dye colours beautifully and, like silk, it has an enticing sheen and a silky strength – and all this at a considerably lower price than the natural fibres. The extruded filament can be cut to staple and spun by either the cotton or woollen systems (described in Chapters 3 and 5 respectively). It has the highest absorbency of any man-made fibre and like linen, a natural cellulose fibre, is a good conductor of heat and so makes excellent summer fabrics. It also takes dye colours well. It is, however, weak when wet so care must be taken when washing it. Also it will shrink and mildew if left wet for too long. The high-lustre viscose rayon yarns are very slippery and rather hard to handle (try keeping the ball or cone inside an old piece of nylon stocking to stop it unravelling) but when used with a matt yarn such as wool will add attractive highlights.

TESTING YARNS FOR FIBRE CONTENT

There are two simple tests which can be done at home to determine which fibres have been used in a particular yarn. (We have all been tempted at times by the special-offer-at-an-unrepeatable-price yarn which is distinctly coy about its contents.) Knowing what it is can be particularly useful, and in fact is essential if the yarn is to be dyed successfully. But in any case it is a good idea to know what you are dealing with; shrink- and heat-resistance, for instance, are matters you have to think about.

For the first, the burn test, take particular care. Light the fibre sample, which you should hold with tongs or pliers rather than in your fingers, over a safe fireproof surface – the kitchen sink, for instance. The reaction to fire of various fibres is as follows:

Asbestos and glass   do not burn.
Acetate   burns and melts in flame, and continues to do so after removal from flame; may smell acrid like vinegar; leaves a hard brittle black 'bead'.
Acrylic   burns and melts in flame, continuing after removal from flame; leaves a hard brittle black 'bead'.
Cellulose   burns rapidly with a yellow flame, glows after being removed from the flame; smells like burning paper; leaves a soft grey ash.
Nylon   shrinks away from flame, burns slowly and melts, usually self-extinguishing when removed from flame; smells like celery; leaves a hard grey 'bead'.
Protein   burns slowly, sizzles and curls away from the flame; sometimes self-extinguishes when removed from the flame; smells like burning hair or feathers; leaves a crushable black ash.
Polyester   shrinks away from flame, burns and melts giving off black smoke; usually self-extinguishing when removed

from the flame; smells slightly sweet; leaves a hard black 'bead'.
Viscose rayon burns rapidly with a yellow flame; glows after being removed from the flame; smells like burning paper, leaving a soft, grey ash.

Another test, for acetates only, is done with acetone (nail varnish remover). Place a small piece of yarn, or just a few fibres, in a dish of acetone. They will dissolve, leaving at most only dye pigments.

YARN COUNT

This is a method of notating the thickness of yarn, and it helps handweavers to know exactly what they are buying without necessarily seeing the yarn, or even a sample of it.

Monofilament man-made fibres are measured using the fixed-length *denier* system, as with the natural monofilament fibre, silk. This is based on a fixed yarn length to a variable weight and the unit of measurement used is called the denier. One denier is the weight in grams of 9,000 metres of yarn, so a 10-denier yarn will weigh 10 grams and measure 9,000 metres. The coarser the yarn, the higher the denier number. (Many of us will be familiar with this system through nylon stockings and tights.)

There is another fixed-length system of measuring yarn, called the *Tex* system, which is based on the weight in grams of 1 kilometre (1,000 metres) of yarn, so 1 Tex equals 9 denier and 10 Tex would represent a yarn weighing 10 grams and measuring 1 kilometre. This more modern international labelling code for monofilament yarns also includes the ply (fold) of the yarn, so 20 Tex/2 S means that two 10-Tex yarns have been plied together in an S (anti-clockwise) direction. The resultant yarn will still measure 1 kilometre in length but will weigh 20 grams.

Man-made fibres can also be produced as spun yarns (after the continuous extruded filament has been combined and cut into staple fibres) in order to give them properties that are more allied to natural yarns. When this has been done, the spinning system appropriate to the natural fibres can be used. Information about the most commonly used, the woollen and worsted systems, can be found in Chapter 5.

3
Cellulose Fibres

There are many plants that produce fibres which are potentially suitable for weaving. The fibres are found mostly round the seeds, in the stems or in the leaves. But only a few plants possess fibres which fulfil the prime requirement of a good textile fibre – that it shall be long, strong, fine and flexible – so well that they have become universally used and valued.

Great empires, both political and financial, have been built on the two most famous, cotton and linen; and in spite of the multiplicity of man-made fibres and their lower production costs these classic fibres are still important in textiles today, not only in high fashion but in the mass market and in the craft field.

COTTON

Although the soft, downy fibres which we call cotton (from the Arabic *quoton*) are formed in the ripening seed pods of a large family of trees and bushes, the variety which has proved most useful to man, and which he has consequently developed into the plant we know today, is a small, bushy member of the mallow family (*Gossypium*). It thrives best in the tropical and warm temperate areas of the world. I first saw it growing in Sicily on an early autumn visit and, in my excitement at the sight of fields of little bushes with their burst-open heads of white, silky fluff, I had the tourist coach stopped and went foraging for the cotton bolls,

much to the surprise of the rest of the coach party. (Incidentally, I planted some of the seed in our greenhouse the following year, just to see what would happen. Unfortunately, as I had rather feared, the English summer is just not long enough to allow the plant to achieve its full growth, and although the seeds set they never ripened.)

What I saw in Sicily was Egyptian cotton which, after *Sea Island cotton*, is considered to be the finest quality. Sea Island is a long-stapled, fine and very white cotton which was first grown on the island from which it takes its name, and which lies off the coast of Georgia in the south of the United States of America. It is now also grown on the mainland of the United States, in Mexico and in the West Indies.

Egyptian cotton is particularly lustrous, strong and long-stapled and has a lovely, creamy colour. However, you will also find some very white Egyptian cotton. This is because some varieties, although they are also of good quality, have a seed-head containing brownish fibres, which are therefore heavily bleached. My feeling, which may well be scientifically irrational, is that this bleaching not only weakens the yarn but also affects its softness and shine, particularly when the chemical processes of dyeing are added. So I look for the creamy *slivers* if I am handspinning cotton for accent yarns.

Pima cotton is another long-stapled, lustrous and white fibre from the south of the United States, and from South Amer-

Cotton yarn samples, machine- and handspun.

ica. It was developed from Egyptian cotton seed first grown in Pima, Arizona, and so more resembles Egyptian than Sea Island cotton.

American Upland cotton makes up the bulk of the US cotton production. It is shorter in staple length, less lustrous and not so strong as the varieties grown in the southern states.

Eastern cottons are grown in large amounts in India and China, but their varieties are relatively short-stapled, coarse and dull in appearance.

It is this wide range of quality in the fibre which accounts for the variety of cotton yarns on the market. Prices vary considerably too, as does the strength of the yarn, so it is not safe to assume that all cotton yarns are strong yarns, fit to use as a warp. The colour of undyed cotton yarns varies considerably too, as already mentioned. (By the way, beware of trying to bleach cotton yarns at home using ordinary household bleach. You may end up with an ugly yellow tinge because the yarn has been treated in manufacture and is chlorine-retentive.)

Cotton fibres are reasonably strong because they are constructed of spiralling fibrils (small fibres) which twist into each other and thus form a close bond in the spinning process. This gives a smooth yarn, lustrous, strong and with a good affinity to dye. All these attributes can be increased in the *mercerization* process, during which the yarn is treated with caustic soda. The visual and tactile effects of mercerization on a really good-quality, fine cotton yarn can make you wonder if it is not actually silk.

As with any yarn, the strength is determined by the length of the staple and the amount of *twist* put into the yarn during the spinning process. Cotton has the property of increasing in strength when it is wet, but it also shrinks considerably. It is therefore wise to preshrink handspun cotton yarns before weaving with them, while a very hot laundering will shrink and set the woven cloth. These and other factors to consider when using cotton are discussed at greater length in Chapter 20.

Cotton has very little elasticity, but it is an excellent conductor of heat with a high degree of absorption, and so is ideal for hot-weather wear. Moths don't favour it, but being a plant material it will attract mildew in hot, humid climates. Generally, however, its value to today's handweaver is as great as ever it was – but it has to be said that the way it is grown, and the processes used in its manufacture, are coming under increasing scrutiny as the concept of workers' rights takes hold even in Third World countries. So, inevitably, cotton is likely to continue to get more and more expensive.

LINEN

Linen is produced from the fibres in the stem of the flax plant (*Linum usitatissimum*), an annual plant which man has known and grown since the Stone Age. (Remains of the plant – seeds and stems – and yarn in the various processes of manufacture have been found in neolithic Swiss lake dwellings which date back to about 8000 BC, while the Catal Huyuk textile is either linen or wool. Because it is so old and therefore so carbonized it is impossible to tell which.) The flax plant grows easily in many of the cooler temperate regions of the world, but the process of extracting the fibres from the plant and preparing them for spinning into yarn is a long and complicated one. As a result the finished yarn, like most of those produced from natural sources, is expensive.

Some 8 million hectares of flax is grown world-wide, although not all for the production of linen. Linseed oil is extracted from the seed (most of the United States and Canadian crop goes for this purpose) while the root and tip ends of the fibres are processed into tow, used primarily for rope making. Russia is the world's biggest producer, though mostly of lower-quality fibre for coarse linen fabrics. France follows with a better-quality product, while Belgian fibre and fabric is considered of very high quality. And there has recently been some resurgence of the once world-famous Irish linen industry – not only on the manufacturing side but also in an attempt to revive, if only in a small way, the cultivation and processing of flax.

Varying methods of production, as well as the quality of the fibres themselves, affect the quality of the yarns produced. The basic method is to pull the plant from the ground root and all, to retain fibre length; to strip the seeds and leaves by a process known as *rippling*, which passes the plant through coarse combs; and to steep the stalks in water, usually nowadays with added chemicals to hasten the process, in order to rot away the plant tissue surrounding the fibres. This process is called *retting*. Retting can also be

Linen yarn samples, with woven linen/mohair cloth samples.

speeded up by being done mechanically, but as with the chemically induced process this gives a weaker fibre. The traditional methods of stream-retting (the slower the stream flows, the better the fibre quality), pond-retting (in a stagnant pool) or dew-retting (where the fibres lie out on grass in all weathers) can take some weeks but still give the best results.

After retting the fibres are still not fully cleansed of the surrounding tissues so they are washed by various methods, and finally thoroughly dried to halt the decomposition process. They are then *hackled* by being pulled through iron combs to remove short or broken fibres and to arrange the remainder so that they lie smoothly parallel to each other. The bundles of fibre are then cut into sections and the ends are separated for tow manufacture while the valuable middle section, even in quality and length, goes to make the flax known as *line*. The resulting bundle of fibres varies from around 30cm in length to nearly double that, and is ready to be spun. But if the fibres are really long they are cut yet again into suitable lengths (cut line).

Line fibres are wet-spun. In the mechanized process this means they are soaked in hot water just before being *drafted*, the drawing-out of the bundle of fibres as a preparation for spinning. Handspinners of flax have a small container of water, usually attached to the distaff round which the fibres are wound, and into which they dip their fingers while drafting the fibres from the distaff on to the spindle of the bobbin. Even in mechanically spun yarn there are slubs, naturally thick and thin areas, which give linen yarn an attractive hand-made look, much prized by devotees of ethnic and traditional textiles.

In the grey is the term used for unbleached linen yarns. Irrespective of whether they remain as *singles* or have been folded (plied) they are very strong, since the staple from which they have been spun is so long. But, being made from a natural plant fibre, linen, like cotton, is subject to attack by mildew. It is therefore almost always bleached, so its intrinsic strength is somewhat reduced.

Three types of linen yarns, in three grades of strength, are spun: grey, natural and bleached. I haven't myself come across grey on offer from suppliers of weaving yarns. The term 'natural' covers the pleasant, pale biscuit-coloured yarns which even as a fine singles I find quite as strong as I need. (It is worth remembering that a handloom puts less stress on the yarn than do most mechanical ones, so what a manufacturer would term 'weak' may well suit you perfectly.) Bleached yarns are the right ones for the home dyer who wants the really clear pale colours that would be impossible to get when dyeing the biscuit-tinted natural linen yarn.

Consisting, as they do, of very dense, hard fibres, linen yarns do resist dye take-up, although, once the dye has fully penetrated, the depth of colour which can be achieved is excellent. Therefore, it is wise, particularly with strong hues, to untwist a little section of the yarn to make sure the colour has gone right through to the core.

OTHER PLANT FIBRES

There are a number of other plant-derived cellulose fibres in common use in various parts of the world, either in industrial processes for the manufacture of rope, twine, sacking, upholstery stuffing, nets, felt and many other more specialized uses, or for cloth weaving. Few have much relevance to the handweaver, and the following are the ones most likely to be of interest.

Hemp

Indian hemp (*Cannabis sativa*) is very closely related to the plant from which the drug is extracted, the growing of which is prohibited – so beware. When it is harvested, which is done in much the same way as with flax, the smell given off is powerful and narcotic. Hemp provides a yarn similar to linen, but not so fine. It is used for twine and rope, including rug and carpet warps, nets, tarpaulins, sailcloth and canvas, with the better qualities woven into utilitarian household linens. *Manila hemp*, or *Abaca* (*Musa textilis*) is a quite different plant, being categorized as a grass fibre and actually derived from the banana plant. It gives a fine silky fibre used for cloth weaving.

Jute

Jute (genus *Corchorus*) is another *bast* fibre (strong, woody fibres found in tree and plant leaves or stems). It is very coarse, not very strong and, like tow – the root and tip ends of flax fibres – is used for rope and twine making, matting, upholstery stuffing and sacking.

Raffia

Raffia (sometimes spelt raphia) is a fibre derived from palm leaves, and is perhaps more useful to the handweaver than some of the other bast fibres. Although it has little intrinsic strength it can be used as an accent yarn, and it takes dye well. It has been successfully synthesized and the man-made variety is stronger than the natural one.

Ramie

Ramie, or China grass (genus *Boehmeria*, the nettle family), is a most interesting fibre for the handweaver. I think of it, along with really good-quality mercerized cotton, as poor man's silk – although, like many other vegetable fibres, it is not as cheap, relatively, as artificial silk or rayon. However, it certainly costs less than silk, and has many of that fibre's excellent qualities. It is white, lustrous and absorbent and takes all the colours of the dyer's rainbow well. While there are coarser fibres which are used for canvas, nets and upholstery, the best quality spins into a yarn worthy of consideration by the most exacting handweaver.

Sisal and New Zealand Flax

These, *Agave sisalana* and *Phormium tenax* respectively, are two more coarse bast fibres used mainly in the rope, twine and matting industries. Sisal has the benefit of being a white fibre, and so dyes to good, clear, strong colours – but in fact all the bast fibres take dye well, although perhaps rather unwillingly.

YARN COUNT

There are variations in yarn count systems to allow for different types of yarn. For instance, in the previous chapter I described the denier and tex systems which are used to measure monofilament fibres. These systems are also used for a naturally produced monofilament fibre.

The system used for spun yarns, and therefore the one applicable to the various bast fibres discussed in this chapter, is known as the *fixed weight* system. It is based on the length of spun yarn per pound weight. The finer the yarn is spun, the greater length of yarn there will be per pound weight. The yarn count indicates the number of unit lengths (skeins, hanks, cuts, leas, and so on) per pound. Just to confuse, there is a nasty tendency to call this unit by a different name for every different yarn. Cuts and skeins apply to spun wool, and are discussed in Chapter 5. The unit for linen is the lea, but most of the other fibres, including cotton, are normally classified as hanks.

Obviously, various fibres, and various spinning systems, produce yarns of different weight, and therefore the unit length – that is, one single spun length of yarn (known as singles or 1s) – varies.

For linen, a 1s lea measures 300 yards and weighs 1lb.

For cotton, a 1s hank measures 840 yards and weighs 1lb.

It follows from this that spinning cotton at one-tenth the thickness of the basic method above would give you a 10s cotton hank measuring 8,400 yards and weighing 1lb – that is to say, the higher the count number the thinner the yarn. Note that whatever else changes the weight (1lb) remains the same. Hence the reason why this is called the fixed-weight system – self-evident, maybe, but perhaps worth emphasizing.

When a yarn is plied (when two yarns of identical count are twisted together) the yarn is twice as thick and so the length per pound weight is halved. The numbering system therefore has to record both the count of the yarn and the number of singles that make up the ply. So two units of 10s cotton plied together would be shown as 2/10s and would give you a 2/10s cotton hank measuring 4,200 yards and weighing 1lb.

I am afraid the words 'yarn count' tend to be one of the great turn-offs to many new weavers struggling to come to terms with what sometimes seem to be the endless complications of their new craft. My suggestion is, don't panic. If you look at yarn samples, select those you like the look of, try them out, see what results you get and, next time you want to weave the same or a similar cloth, either go back to the previously successful yarn or use another if you didn't like the first – well, you are actually learning about yarn counts all the time, without really noticing.

So as time passes you will, without thinking about it, learn exactly what a 2/10s cotton looks like because you have used it before and recorded the results. In other words, as with everything, read, mark and learn as you go along, and the 'inwardly digest' bit will happen quite naturally as skill and confidence grow.

4
Silk

Between the vegetable fibres and the animal ones in its molecular structure and its receptivity to dyes lies silk. I think I should declare an interest here because it is quite definitely my favourite yarn, this variously coloured dream coat the silkworm spins around itself to shelter its metamorphosis from plebeian caterpillar to aristocratic and beautiful moth. To my mind it is the most exciting and romantic of all fibres, the desire for which has motivated man the artist-craftsman for centuries.

China is the home of silk, and legend has it that nearly five thousand years ago the Empress Hsi-Ling discovered that the fine thread encasing the silkworm cocoons on her mulberry tree could be unwound and, so strong was it, woven into cloth fit even for an Empress of China. (Apparently she made this discovery when a cocoon dropped accidentally into her bowl of tea, and even today the cocoons are floated in hot water to loosen the *sericin*, the sticky substance the caterpillar exudes as it spins to bind the cocoon more firmly.) So started the development of *sericulture*, the production of silk, and the Chinese so prized their treasured yarn that they ensured that its origin and production remained a closely guarded secret for many centuries.

Although fragments of silk dating back to *circa* 1500 BC have been found in China, the oldest written record of its use is found in the epic Indian poems, the *Ramayana* and the *Mahabharata*. These are the sacred writings of the Aryans who, in the second century BC, conquered India from the north and established a Hindu empire from India across Persia to the Mediterranean. They introduced the horse to Europe, and quite probably silk as well, and this strong Indian connection is probably why there has always been some confusion about where silk first originated.

The journey from China to India of these two most valuable commodities, the horse, which was first domesticated by the Chinese, and silk, is also a matter of legend. There is another delightful tale about a Princess of China being escorted for many months in her palanquin over the mountains of central Asia on her way to be married to a great king of India. As she went she carried, tucked into her elaborate hairstyle, that most valuable of all dowries, a few silkworm cocoons. A good way of ensuring a warm welcome from one's future husband, I imagine. Another version of how the secret of silk was lost to China tells the tale of two Persian monks who, in the sixth century AD, sold some smuggled silkworm eggs to the Emperor Justinian of Constantinople.

Aristotle, writing about 300 BC, is the first western writer to mention silk, accurately reporting it as coming from 'a curious horned worm' and giving it the romantic name of 'woven wind'. But this appears to be an isolated reference and although soon after this silk became a commonplace commodity in China it was

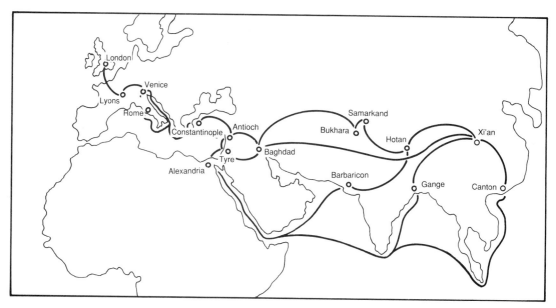

A map of the Silk Road.

not until the first century BC that regular trade routes were established by the Chinese across the central Asian deserts, the Silk Road came into being and the European love-affair with this sumptuous fibre started, and continues to this day.

The Silk Road started from Canton and ran to X'ian in northern China (where the army of terracotta soldiers was found guarding a royal grave which also contained magnificent examples of early brocaded silks). Then, with a branch down to India ending in the Ganges delta region, it continued across the great deserts of central Asia to Samarkand and Bukhara. From there it went to Baghdad and west to Antioch and Tyre, from which eastern Mediterranean ports the precious cargoes continued by ship to Alexandria in Egypt and through the doorway to Europe – Venice, and the Italian ports of Genoa and Rome. There were other routes by sea also: from Canton round the southern tip

of India and thence up the Red Sea; from ports at the end of the Ganges delta spur; and via an overland route which struck due south, down to ports in what is now Pakistan, and then continued by sea.

The value of silk as a trading commodity was almost incalculable. Like gold and precious stones it had a market price, and that price was so high that inevitably it became a focus of all manner of attempts to break the Chinese cartel – the thirteenth-century journeys of Marco Polo of Venice to the court of Kublai Khan, financed by European silk merchants; raids on the silk caravans by the nomadic tribes across whose land the Silk Road cut; the creaming off of profits by the Persians who 'cut' the road in order to gain a monopoly of the trade. All these methods, and more, were tried. But eventually silkworm eggs and the seeds of the white mulberry tree were smuggled to Constantinople and, so valuable was the prize, sericulture was developed by the Turkish sultans themselves in the grounds of the Topkapi Palace.

The cultivation and weaving of silk consolidated round the eastern and southern shores of the Mediterranean, and eventually arrived in Europe with the Arab invasions of Sicily and Spain. The final stage of the establishment of the famous medieval silk-producing and manufacturing centres of northern Italy and France – Venice, Lucca, Florence, Lyons – came as a result of the contact, if you can call it that, between Christian Europeans and Muslim Arabs during the Crusades. Fine silk fabrics were pillaged by noble Christian warriors to deck out members of their families, while both humble soldiers and their captains offered their spoils to the Church to the greater glory of God, thus enriching the ecclesiastical tradition of richly patterned robes and furnishings. And so, some four thousand years after the Empress Hsi-ling floated that first cocoon in her dish of tea, sericulture finally reached Europe. And with the colonization of the Americas by Spain, England and the other European empire-builders, it came to the New World and completed its circumnavigation.

In spite of its travels over the centuries silk is still produced in greater quantities in China than in any other country, with Japan, Russia and India also pre-eminent. India particularly processes large quantities of both cultivated and wild silk, and due to government insistence on the preservation of small-scale rural industries there is still considerable production of patterned silks on handlooms in village workshops.

Silk has many qualities which go to explain its lasting popularity: its visual and tactile appeal, the natural translucent lustre of the fibres, the fact that its smooth reflectivity enhances the depth of any dye colour used on it, its very real strength with apparent delicacy, and, perhaps most important, its sheer wearability – it is warm to the touch in winter, while its silky feel and its high absorbency factor make it comfortable next to the skin in hot summer weather. When you add all this to the romance of its history and the value which we tend to put on things which are not freely available and which require considerable effort to obtain, process and produce, then it is hardly surprising that, even in these mechanized times and in an ever-shrinking world, it is still expensive and much sought after.

For the handweaver it is a wonderful fibre and most of us who use it find it an inspiration in itself. Its colours, both natural and dyed, are positively succulent, and its versatility immense. From fine reeled silk woven into materials for scarves, throws, summer skirts and shirts to chunky spun-silk cloths or layered fine-spun ones for warm winter wear, it can be all things to all men. And, particularly with the thicker spun silks, it need not cost as much as might be expected. Handspinners are lucky as they can create their own yarns – blending silk with fine wools to give the best of both worlds, for instance. The differences in elasticity of the two fibres seem to complement each other, while the effect of the lustrous silk against the matt wool mixes the reflected light and gives movement to the fabric. Or they can try combining a fine, strong and smooth silk warp with a softly handspun and more irregular cotton weft to create another lively fabric. And the occasional glint of fine silk thread lying alongside textured linen doesn't add a great deal to the cost of the cloth, but adds immeasurably to its appeal. Fortunately, however, it is not only handspinners who can create their own yarns; combining machine-spun yarns to get special effects is an interesting and worthwhile field in which handweavers can experiment too.

There are two main types of silk, the almost-white variety produced from various members of the domesticated mulberry silkmoth family, which produces the best silk when fed on the leaves of the white mulberry tree (*Morus alba*); and the variously tinted pale biscuit browns of wild silk, from the many wild types of silkmoth. Probably two of the best-known and easiest to 'farm' are the Indian Moon Moth (*Actias selene*), whose caterpillars feed on hawthorn and rhododendron leaves, and the Indian Tree of Heaven silkmoth (*Philosamia canningi*), whose diet is the leaves of privet and of the Tree of Heaven (*Ailanthus*).

The methods of producing silk have remained relatively unaltered through the ages, and are much the same whether done on a large scale in a factory or by individuals processing just a few cocoons. In fact, with considerable care and attention to detail, silk can be, and is, produced in this country in spite of our cold and distinctly wet climate, by keeping the insects in suitable conditions indoors. The famous silk-weaving centres established in Macclesfield and at Spitalfields in east London during the sixteenth and seventeenth centuries imported their raw material, the colonies as always being expected to do their bit to the greater glory of the home industry. Attempts were made to establish sericulture in North America, for instance, but were never really successful. And of course silk was one of the enticements, along with spices and precious stones, which sent British merchants sailing to establish trading empires in India and China.

About a month passes from the time the eggs of the silkmoth hatch to the time the caterpillar starts to spin its cocoon. During this period it eats enormous quantities of mulberry leaves, which have to be just right – clean, sweet and growing strongly without checks from bad weather or sudden cold snaps. Otherwise the fussy worm will either die or, at best, simply produce silk of poor quality. Nursed lovingly from tiny egg to fat, creamy-white horny insect, it will repay you by spinning its cocoon, about one thousand metres of finest thread. You will then reward it, when it has done the job, by dropping it into a vat of boiling water. This will kill it before it can chew its way out and become a moth, ruining the silk in the process by reducing it to short lengths. But some of the silkworms must be allowed to turn into chrysalises, sleep a while, emerge from the cocoon, fly, mate and start the whole wonderfully productive cycle again.

The boiling water execution also helps to loosen the sericin holding the thread snugly around the cocoon, and allows the silk to be *reeled* off. A minimum of two cocoons are reeled together, but more usually four, going up to as many as are needed to give the thickness of yarn required. (To avoid thick-and-thin bits in the yarn, filaments from extra cocoons are introduced, or dropped, as necessary.). The cocoons are floated in a bowl of warm water, then guided and fed up through a machine which imparts a very light twist to the fibres. One person can, if very skilled (and it is a tricky business), reel about a half a pound of silk a day, roughly the product of 6lb of cocoons.

The fibre at this stage is known as *raw silk* and still has to be de-gummed (there are various methods of doing this) to rid it of the sericin which coats and stiffens it. If some of the sericin is left in, the silk is much stronger but less lustrous. After this the silk then has to be re-reeled, probably the most difficult part of the process as the fibres are now all too easily inclined to tangle, break and snag. Finally, the reeled silk threads can be recombined into yarn of the thickness required, a process known as *throwing*, which produces yarn sold as thrown silk, dyed and woven.

The whole business is of course mechanized now. Cocoons are fed automatically to basins, water temperatures automatically regulated, the thickness of reeled threads automatically controlled and dozens of basinfuls of hundreds of cocoons processed by one machine. But it is not a quick or easy process even then, and reeled silk, although beautiful in its smoothness and apparent simplicity, is nevertheless an expensive yarn.

Reeled silk waste, as well as short lengths from the holed cocoons of moths allowed to develop for breeding, and of course from wild silkmoth cocoons, has always been handspun in small quantities. But traditionally these fibres were used for wadding, having quite exceptional insulating properties, and in small quantities in the rag paper industry. However, the development in the late eighteenth and early nineteenth centuries of cotton- and wool-spinning machinery led to a similar process being adapted to the short staple-lengths of silk fibre.

The cocoons and waste lengths have to be degummed and dried before they can be teased apart and fed through various wire-covered rollers. These are similar to the drum carders used by some wool handspinners, and perform a similar function: to comb out the fibres and lay them parallel to each other. The combed fibres are then cut, combed again and formed into the long, thick ropes of fibre called *tops* or *rovings*. Whether for machine- or handspinning these tops are then drawn out thinner and thinner, between rollers or in the fingers, until the resulting fine sliver, or *pencil roving*, is ready to be twisted into a singles thread. These singles can then be plied together, usually from two to four singles twisted in the opposite direction to the original spin, to give the final yarn. This can then be *gassed* or run through a flame to singe off the fuzzy ends and enhance the smooth lustre of silk.

Silk goes under many names, some applying to the woven fabric as well as the yarn. Here are a few of them:

bourette   short-stapled spun raw silk
duppion   a French term for raw (that is, not degummed) reeled silk
ecru   reeled raw or only slightly degummed, silk
floss   soft silk yarn with very little twist
noil   very short-stapled textured spun silk with little tangled balls (noils) of fibre embedded in the yarn. Not a very strong yarn, black-flecked with bits of the silkworm chrysalis. Tussah noil is stronger than white
raw silk   a term used to describe the fibres after reeling but before degumming. Also used for a fabric woven from cultivated, unbleached silk noil yarn
reprocessed silk   fibres of silk waste from spinning, weaving and garment cutting are torn apart, carded and respun into a somewhat cheaper yarn which is attractively textured

65% VISCOSE / 35% LUREX		
	L1	
Available on 100g Cones	L2	
	L3	
This is a Corded Yarn constructed	L4	
	L5	
by knitting Lurex with Viscose.	L6	
	L7	
resulting in a 'full' round yarn	L8	
perfect for machine and hand	L9	
knitting and weaving.	L10	
	L11	

100% COTTON / SLUB YARNS		
100% COTTON 2/12 WC Ecru	25028	
100% COTTON 3/6 WC Ecru	34046	
Mercerised Cotton 2/9 WC	25118	
100% COTTON 8/12 WC	Ext 1	
100% COTTON CREPE 8/12 WC	Ext 2	
100% COTTON 8/12 WC Bleached & Mercerised	Ext 3	
100% COTTON CREPE 8/12 WC Bleached & Mercerised	Ext 4	

90% SILK / 10% COTTON		
Also available SINGLE approx 320yds per oz. Ref AA / 2 FOLD approx 160yds per oz. Ref Z / 4 FOLD approx 80yds per oz. Ref X	3 FOLD approx 107yds per oz. Ref Y	
Also available SINGLE approx 320yds per oz. Ref H / 2 FOLD approx 160yds per oz. Ref J	3 FOLD approx 107yds per oz. Ref K	
100% SILK MARL 4.7 WC approx 160yds per oz.	SMA47	
100% SILK MARL 2.3 WC approx 80yds per oz.	SMA 23	
100% Superfine Camel Hair 2/9 WC approx 157yds per oz.	RefCM	

SPUN SILK YARNS - 100% SILK		
2/2.2 WC Ecru Super	25095	
2/53 WC Ecru	25127	
2/4.5 WC Ecru Super	25145	
2/36 WC Ecru Extra	24084	
2/7 WC Ecru Extra	25052	
2/60 WC Bleached Tussah	25128	
2/27 WC Ecru Super	25091	
2/14 WC Ecru Super	25188	

BOURETTE SILK YARNS - 100% SILK		
Also available 1/12 WC Ecru Ref 14048 / 2/12 WC Ecru Ref 24048 / 4/12 WC Ecru Ref 44048	3/12WC Ref 34048	
1/27 WC Ecru	15063	
3/5.5 WC Ecru	35122	
1/5.5 WC Ecru	15005	
1/10 WC Bleached Tussah	15133	
Bleached Tussah 1/5 WC Ref 15129	3/5WC 35129	
Also available 1/11 WC Ecru Ref C / 2/11 WC Ecru Ref D / 4/11 WC Ecru Ref A	3/11WC Ecru Ref B	
2 FOLD Brown Mix approx 60yds per oz.	P	
2/3.5 WC Ecru	M	
2/3.5 WC Brown Mix	N	

FANCY SPUN SILK YARNS - 100% SILK		
1/4.5 WC Ecru Fancy Heavy	15125	
2/4.5 WC Ecru Fancy Heavy	25125	
3/9 WC Bleached Fancy Tussah	35085	
1/9 WC Bleached Fancy Tussah	15085	
1/2.5 WC Bleached Fancy Tussah	15134	
2/9 WC Ecru Fancy	24014	
2/36 WC Ecru Fancy	24013	
1/4.5 Ecru Fancy	15246	
2s WC Silk Softspun	S	
Silk Corded approx 106yds per oz.		

A card of samples of silk and cotton yarns from a supplier.

shantung a white, slightly uneven and slubby silk. A term also used for reeled duppion silk

tussah a name generally given to all wild silks. Less lustrous, usually various tints of pale brown, so dye colours are slightly muted, although this is not noticeable in the stronger hues

YARN COUNT

Like other continuous monofilament yarns, silk is graded by the European fixed-length denier system (*see* Chapter 2). A double filament of silk (the result of reeling two cocoons together) is about 2 deniers and the standard for fine silk is 13–15 deniers, the result of reeling together the filaments of six to eight cocoons.

Using the calculation that one denier equals one gram in weight and measures 9,000 metres, then a kilo of a standard fine silk yarn measures about 640,000 metres, and a pound measures 300,000 yards – nearly 200 miles. Seriously, though, these are necessary facts to know when working out the amount of yarn to purchase, and doubly necessary when using expensive yarns such as silk. (More is said about buying yarns by length at the end of the next chapter.)

Just to complicate matters, silk is sold under two different yarn count systems. Because some of it is spun, this type of silk uses the fixed-weight system, the one based on the length of spun yarn per pound weight. The calculation is made in exactly the same way as that used for cotton described in the previous chapter in which one *hank* of spun silk is 840 yards long and weighs 1lb.

To make even more problems for us, it is normal practice when numbering spun silk to reverse the count number, so 2 units of 10s spun silk plied together will be noted as 10/2s and represent a two-ply hank of 8,400 yards of 10s silk weighing 1lb. But this rule is not absolute and some spinners, including the one from which I get most of my supplies, record silk as for other spun fibres and therefore show 2/10s silk in their yarn lists.

However, do not let all this yarn count business worry you. Just carry on and use, and enjoy, one of the most satisfying and beautiful yarns that we have at our disposal – and thank whoever looks after us weavers for the lucky chance of the Empress and the dish of hot tea.

5
Wool

For the past twenty-five years I have lived in an area which, for five hundred years, produced some of the most famous woollen cloths in England. My loom sits in exactly the same position under a main beam of the weaver's loft in the eaves of our cottage as did that of my eighteenth-century predecessors, and it would be surprising if my work were not affected by such a powerful spirit of place. So while silk epitomizes for me the strong colour, heat and romance of my Indian birth and upbringing, fine wools are the cool and misty tints of England, my home for a good part of my adult life. (Cashmere, my third love, takes its name from the mountainous northern Indian state where this superfine goat hair first came to western notice. Processed even today almost entirely in England, it combines those qualities of colourful, silky softness which I look for in a textile.)

Wool was central to the economy of England from the start of the early medieval cloth industry in the twelfth century. It was governed, strictly controlled and made great by the Weavers' Guilds. The lucrative trade with the continent of Europe, first of wool and then of finished cloth, was by the sixteenth century providing almost three-quarters of the export earnings of the realm. Only in the past hundred years have we seen first the contraction and then the virtual collapse of an industry which, based first on wool and then on cotton, has so dominated the history of England. And, since textile manu-

facturing was one of the prime catalysts of the Industrial Revolution, which started in this country, it is surely not too fanciful to say that it has also dominated the modern history of the world.

SHEEP BREEDS

There are many breeds of sheep in Britain. The latest edition I have of *British Sheep and Wool* published by the Wool Marketing Board lists 34 main breeds, 20 minor breeds and rare breeds and 16 hybrids, half-breeds and recent introductions. In the last group come the 'man-made' purpose-bred breeds, these days (as has been the case from the middle of the eighteenth century onwards) entirely given over to those selected for good meat-producing qualities. Wool is of virtually no importance in assessing the value of the animal in monetary terms today, except in some specialized wool breeds such as the native *Shetland* and the foreign *Merino*, so low has the once-great woollen industry slipped in importance to this country's trade. Included in the second group, amongst other so-called primitive breeds, is the little, goat-like *Soay*, which is probably closer than any other breed to the first domesticated sheep.

Tan-coloured animals such as the Soay evolved from wild sheep, the European *Mouflon* and the Asian *Urial* and *Argali*. It has been argued that, after the dog, the sheep was the first animal to be domesti-

Primitive-type sheep and a traditional British breed – Soays, and Dorset Horn ewes and ram at Norwood Farm (the Soay sheds its fleece naturally in summer and needs no shearing).

cated by man. Certainly the relationship goes back to the days of man the hunter-gatherer and herder of flocks, before he settled in one place and started to till the land. Originally valued (before the domestication of the cow) primarily as a meat- and milk-producing animal, whose skin came in handy when it was dead, it was only in neolithic times that the sheep's wool was first spun. But, once started, inevitably the animals were selected for this product as well as the others, and the final result of this process of selection can be seen in the 1,000 million sheep of nearly 500 different breeds which exist today and produce some 55,000 tonnes of wool. Although the British Isles has only about 3 per cent of the sheep, and produces only about 2 per cent of the world's wool clip, the influence of this country on sheep breeding worldwide has been immense. Not for nothing have the British been thought of as 'stockbreeders to the world'.

The process of selection for softer and longer fibres of wool was based on the fact that primitive sheep, like their wild forebears, grow a dense, soft, woolly, wind- and waterproof undercoat covered by long, coarse guard hairs. The undercoat is shed in the spring and no doubt was originally picked off the bushes; this progressed to combing out the dead wool, then to hand-shearing and finally to the ultimate mechanization of Australasia's high-speed shearing gangs, touring round the flocks de-fleecing thousands of sheep a day. Slowly, as selection progressed, the undercoat grew longer, denser and softer while the guard hairs grew fewer and fewer until they disappeared entirely. Only in some primitive and unimproved breeds can vestigial remains of them be found, particularly as a cape over the shoulders of the rams.

So in effect the modern sheep carries just an undercoat, with no guard hairs to protect it from the weather. This explains why sheep can sometimes be seen wearing little plastic raincoats – valuable, fine and easily felted wool cannot be left unprotected from heavy rain. Full circle, some might think, but of course it is far easier to take off their coats than to pick quantities of unwanted coarse hair out of the short fleece. (I do feel that macintoshed wool breeds are a little less silly than meat sheep fitted with a set of false teeth to allow them to go on grazing after their own have worn down to the gum, thus lengthening their breeding life. But perhaps I am a bit partial.)

When the Romans arrived in Britain in 55 BC they brought with them an improved type of white sheep with wool of medium quality. These were crossed with the resident tan-coloured descendants of Nordic sheep which had come over with successive waves of Scandinavian invaders. The cross appears to have been very successful and it resulted, in fact, in the start of the long export trade in wool from these islands to Europe. The Roman nobility prized this soft wool above all others and would have nothing else for their finest togas – and this link has continued through two thousand years with Italy still one of the most important markets for British wool. Certainly as far as the fashion industry is concerned we have the finest wools and they have the technique and know-how to produce from it high-quality cloths. And I believe they take large quantities of coarse wool, such as that from the *Rough Fell* sheep, to stuff their mattresses. Nothing like British wool for a good night's sleep, it appears.

The process of selection continued throughout the ages, culminating as far as wool breeds were concerned with the work of the great Robert Bakewell, a farmer of Dishley in the county of Leicestershire, in the English Midlands. He epitomized the early eighteenth-century spirit of enlightenment, and set a pattern for pedigree livestock selection and development which is followed to

this day. Though primarily interested in meat production, he kept records of wool quality too, and to him can be directly or indirectly attributed the development of many modern longwool breeds, not only the *Leicester* and the *Border Leicester*, but the *Lincoln, Wensleydale, Devon Longwool* and others.

Towards the end of the eighteenth century John Ellman of Glynde in Sussex set about the improvement of the shortwool sheep native to the downlands of that area. By selection for meat and wool-producing qualities he evolved the *Southdown* breed which is behind all today's shortwool sheep breeds. This process of experimental and selective breeding continued throughout the nineteenth century, consolidating and finally slowing down into the multiplicity of local variants on main breeds which were found all over the British Isles until up to the beginning of the Second World War.

Since then things have changed enormously and, many would say, not for the better. Improved communications and more intensive agricultural practices have sounded the death-knell of many of our native breeds of farm animals, including sheep, and the Rare Breeds Survival Trust was formed in the early 1970s to save some breeds from total extinction. They were no longer seen as being of any value by the modern farmer. Not that the industry was averse to experimental breeding, but unfortunately fashion decreed that better crosses were to be obtained from expensive imports from the continent. So the valuable gene bank of qualities, bred carefully and specifically for our conditions over centuries, was ignored in the rush to Europe. And of course joining the Common Market was seen as somehow legitimizing the practice.

A Shetland ewe with her cross-bred lamb (by a Dorset ram) at Norwood Farm.

A Shetland ewe with her lamb at Norwood Farm.

However, thank goodness, there is new thinking abroad at last. Societies to preserve native domestic livestock have sprung up in Europe and America alongside the encompassing international moves towards conservation of the natural world itself. Scientifically controlled tests are now regularly carried out to discover and record what those old breeds saved by the RBST can still offer. So now we occasionally come across pigs hardy enough to graze outside, pigs giving much tastier meat on less food and cheaper housing; and small, easy-lambing ewes producing 'their-size' lambs which grow quickly and cheaply on the dam's rich milk alone (and that from relatively poor pasture land) to rival their large improved sire in size. In fact, the once-scorned traditionals are beginning to fight back. And long may it continue, say I.

WOOL TYPES

The Wool Marketing Boards method of classifying wool into various types is based on their length and lustre. The following is a list of some of the best-known British wool breeds in each classification, together with the uses to which their wool is put.

Longwool and Lustre

Border Leicester dress fabric, hand-knitting yarn
Cotswold fine tweeds, handspinning/knitting/weaving yarn
Dartmoor carpet or, as lambswool, suitings
Leicester and Lincoln Longwools dress fabrics, upholstery and carpets, handspinning/weaving yarn
Romney hosiery, hand-knitting yarn, worsted and woollen cloth
Wensleydale fine tweeds and suitings

Medium

Jacob speciality, naturally coloured handspinning/knitting/weaving yarn
Lleyn hosiery, dress fabric, hand-knitting yarn

Shortwool and Down

Clun Forest woven cloth, hand-knitting yarn

Dorset Down hosiery and hand-knitting yarn, flannel suitings

Dorset Horn hosiery, flannel and fine tweed suitings

Hampshire Down hand-knitting yarn, flannel and felt

Kerry Hill knitwear, fine tweed, flannel, furnishing fabric

Oxford Down hosiery and hand-knitting yarn

Ryeland hosiery, hand-knitting yarn, fine tweed

Shetland fine tweed, machine- and hand-knitwear, hand-knitting yarn

Southdown hosiery, hand-knitting yarn, flannel and fine tweed

Suffolk hosiery, hand-knitting yarn, flannel, fine tweed and dress fabric

Mountain and Hill

Scottish Blackface carpet wool

Cheviot woven suitings

North Country Cheviot tweeds, heavy suitings

Exmoor Horn regimental cloths and doeskins, hand-knitting yarn, tweed and felt

Herdwick carpet and coarse hand-knitting/weaving yarn

Manx Loghtan hosiery and knitwear

Soay speciality hand-knitting yarn

Swaledale carpet and coarse hand-knitting/weaving yarn

Welsh Mountain rough tweeds, furnishing fabrics

Of the above list, the Cotswold, Leicester and Lincoln Longwools, Manx Loghtan, Oxford Down, Ryeland, Soay and Wensleydale are classified as rare breeds, while although the Wool Marketing Board includes the Shetland under main breeds it is in fact still under the protection of the Rare Breeds Survival Trust. This is largely because it is an important breed to this country for two reasons – its wool is the finest of any native breed, and it comes in a vary large range of natural colours. Both these valuable attributes (and, in fact, the breed's very existence) are threatened by uncontrolled cross-breeding for commercial reasons (to get a larger meat carcass – the Shetland is one of the easy-lambing breeds mentioned above) and to increase the weight of the wool clip. Unfortunately, the first aim has reduced the numbers of pure-bred Shetlands, even in their own Islands, to alarmingly few, while the latter has certainly produced more so-called Shetland wool, but at the expense of the special qualities, the soft, short fineness of the fleece of the pure-bred Shetland.

Among recent importations probably the only one of real value to the hand-weaver is the Texel from Holland and France, now well anglicized as the British Texel. It carries a medium fleece classification, and handspinners find the white wool worth seeking out.

The Merino

Even though there are only a very few of them in this country, being essentially a breed of warmer climates, it would be impossible to close a section on wool breeds of sheep without mentioning the Merino, and its two best-known crosses (primarily with the Lincoln Longwool), which are the Corriedale and the Polwarth.

The Merino originated in North Africa and went from there to Spain. Its long,

Shetland fleece and wool in the shop at Norwood Farm.

fine wool fleece became justly famous, and was imported from there in the eighteenth century to become the raw material of the superfine lightweight 'Spanish cloths' which ousted the old, heavy medieval broadcloths manufactured in my part of the west of England. Broadcloths – 60 inches (1.5 metres) wide – took their name from the broadloom which, until the advent of the flying shuttle, required two weavers to operate it.

Production of fine wool from English breeds had all but ceased with the sixteenth-century Enclosure Acts, when sheep were brought down from the high ground into lush lowland meadows. These medieval sheep were probably very like the Ryeland, which originated on the rye-growing uplands around Leominster in Herefordshire, its highly prized wool being known as Lemster Ore. Today's Ryeland has not changed a great deal; an infusion of Southdown blood has made it a little 'meatier', it is true, and the fleece is certainly not as fine as in its medieval heyday, but it is still well worth seeking out.

It had been assumed that improved grassland would result in improved wool, but actually enclosure turned out to be the death-knell of English fine-wool production. Confining sheep on lush pasture may fatten them but it coarsens the fleece; sheep need to be lean, and to have to walk for their sparse forage, to carry a fine fleece. Which is, of course, exactly what the Merino did and does in North Africa, in Spain, in South Africa and, most famously, in Australia.

It arrived in Australia, probably from the Cape, to feed the almost starving convicts who from 1784 on were shipped there by the British government in a desperate attempt to empty goals overcrowded by the severity of our penal system. It was a futile idea, too. Merino sheep are hopeless meat producers, skinny and stringy. However, I always think this is one of those classic tales of good arising out of old evils. Undoubtedly the prosperous growth of the young Australia was intimately bound up with this 'golden fleece', which they exported in great quantities to the mills of nineteenth-century England. Even today Merino wool, Botany wool, Superfine Australian Lambswool – call it by any name, these highly desirable yarns all owe their existence to the one and only peripatetic Merino.

YARN COUNT

And the Merino gives us an excellent lead-in to the subject of wool classification, a system of measuring the fineness of wool, usually called *wool quality*. This method is used in America, Australasia, Britain and Europe to denote the thickness of yarn that could be spun from a particular wool fibre. The unit of measurement is the *micron*, which equals one-thousandth of a millimetre. Merino wool measures 24 microns and is classified as 60's; that is to say, wool this fine can be spun to give 60 hanks of a fixed length in every pound weight, whereas fibres from a coarser fleece, say a Romney at around

24–26 microns, would be classified as 50's–54's and give from 50 to 54 hanks per pound.

In other words, we are back to the system we have seen before in Chapter 3 – the fixed-weight system of recording the yarn count. But in the case of wool there is one more thing we need to know before being able to make final calculations as to the yarn needed, and that is the method used to process and then spin the wool fibres into yarn. There are two of these, carded or *woollen-spun* yarn and combed or *worsted-spun* yarn.

Briefly, the differences between the two methods are that in woollen-spun the fibres used are generally shorter, 2.5–10cm, sheared from short- and medium-wool breeds of sheep) and so have to be *carded*, a process familiar to handspinners. The short fibres are teased out between two surfaces set with short wire teeth until most of the broken ends, noils and unwanted bits are eliminated and the *web* is a thin 'sheet' of more or less parallel fibres (the *batt* of handspinners). This is then rolled into a *rolag*, a small sausage of fibres which lie more or less at right angles to the length of the roll. Another way is to pile two or three webs on top of each other, roll them up and then draw them out into a sliver or roving. These are then drawn out more – that is to say, they are drafted until they are fine enough to be spun, to have the twist inserted into them. Because the yarn is spun from rovings in which the individual fibres are lying across as well as parallel to the roving, woollen yarn has both bulk and loftiness, terms used to describe a soft, warm yarn with good insulating properties.

Longer fibres, those up to 25cm in length, come from the longwool sheep breeds and cannot be processed in this way. They are formed into a fine, smooth, strong yarn which, after an initial carding is combed, (the same process as hackling, used to make flax fibres lie straight and parallel in linen manufacture). These combing processes give a smooth, strong web without any short ends or noils which, when rolled into tops ready for spinning, will produce a smooth, strong, high-twist yarn from which to weave worsted suitings and cloths.

The main differences between the properties of the two types of yarn are that woollen-spun yarns are weaker, softer, warmer, thicker and more subject to shrinking, felting and pilling. Worsted yarns are often more expensive, as more processes are needed to finish the yarn; they are lustrous (due to the quality of the fibres in the fleeces used), smooth, strong, and hard-wearing. Their 'crisp' quality shows up the patterning of intricate weaves, whereas woollen-spun yarns are best used in soft, tweedy or brushed fabrics, where the visual and tactile emphasis is on the yarn rather than the weave.

Due to all these variations in fibre length and quality, and consequently in spinning systems, the unit length of spun 1s, or singles, yarn to the pound weight varies a good deal. Some of the more generally used classifications for yarns, which often take their name from famous wool-producing areas, are:

Worsted-spun: a 1s hank measures 560 yards and weighs 1lb.
  Woollen-spun:
Galashiels: a 1s cut measures 200 yards and weighs 1lb.
Yorkshire: a 1s skein measures 256 yards and weighs 1lb.
West of England: a 1s hank measures 320 yards and weighs 1lb.

To end this first chapter on the animal fibres, just a brief mention why newcomers to weaving, who may up to now have been used to buying wool for a project by weight – in 50-gram balls from the wool shop, for instance – will find it so much easier from now on to calculate how much they need to buy in order to finish a piece. Handweavers in fact are lucky compared with those working in other textile crafts – the nature of the woven construction makes it easy to calculate the length of yarn required, and this is why weaving yarn is sold by length. More about this when we get on to designing and weaving in later chapters.

6
Hair

The animal fibres capable of being used as the raw material of yarn fall into two categories – wool and hair. The two main differences between them are the quality and the actual construction of the fibres. In the case of the sheep's coat the guard hairs have been eliminated while the soft insulating undercoat has been developed into longer but slightly coarser fibres (the undercoat of the Mouflon, the wild-sheep ancestor of our domestic breeds, averages about 15 microns, whereas the finest Merino fibre is 24 microns). This modification has not, however, taken place with the various hair-fibre species such as goats, camels and rabbits, whose double coat remains the same. Consequently all these animals produce relatively small amounts of very fine fibre. For instance, cashmere ranges from about 12 to 20 microns and a good yield is only around 250g per year from each animal, though exceptional amounts up to 500g have been recorded from carefully selected animals in China, the world's biggest producer of cashmere.

The other major difference between wool and the hair fibres is worth noting. Wool has – to a greater or lesser degree, depending on the breed of sheep – a curl or wave in it known as *crimp*. This, together with the fact that the individual fibres have scales on the outside, gives it its characteristic easy-handling qualities – when spun, its crimp and roughness prevent the fibres from slipping uncontrollably against each other. And the

production of highly felted cloths, such as the old West of England broadcloth, or indeed felt itself, is made easier by the fact that if you move wool around in very hot water all the scales open up, interlock with each other and quite swiftly felt the fibres together – as anyone who has put a pair of socks or a precious sweater into the hot cycle of the washing machine by mistake can confirm. (This quality of wool fibres will be mentioned again in the chapter on finishing woven textiles.) Hair fibres, however, have neither crimp nor scales. As a result, they slide against each other and so are more difficult to spin, and they felt together far less readily.

GOATS

From the point of view of the textile industry, the winner of the title of 'volume producer of fibres in the animal kingdom' is undoubtedly the sheep. But the goat's history of fibre production in appreciable quantities down the ages, added to its ability to produce milk and meat on the sparse vegetation of some of the world's driest and most arid areas (in fact, those where man originated), seems to challenge the position of the sheep as man's first domesticated animal. So it is probable that the various wild species of the goat family (*Capra*), the *bezoar* of Turkey and Iran, the *markhor* of Afghanistan and the European *ibex* are all ancestors of the many varieties of domestic goats, and that mixed flocks of goats and sheep followed man in the neolithic period, just as they still do in the Middle East and the countries bordering the Mediterranean.

When you add to this the fact that the fibres they produce – cashmere and mohair – are considerably more valuable than the finest quality sheep's wool, then the important place in textile manufacture of the hair-producing goat breeds has to be acknowledged.

Cashmere Goats

This is a generic name used for various types of domestic goats native to Asia. In the late eighteenth and early nineteenth centuries Kashmir, a Himalayan mountain state in the north of India, was a centre for the spinning and weaving of the fibre combed from the soft, fine undercoat of these animals. Consequently the British, who introduced it to Europe, gave it the name of the place where they first saw it – Kashmir was spelt with a C in those days. The undercoat from this particular species of mountain goat (*Capra lincus*) moulted naturally in the spring, and was then collected and brought to Kashmir. Using this *pashmina* (derived from the Persian word for wool, *pashm*), the craftsmen of Kashmir and other centres in northern India created the famous Cashmere shawls. These were skilfully and intricately woven by a method similar to tapestry weaving, a method which was so time-consuming that one shawl could take over a year to weave. So it is not surprising that the shawls, and the fibre from which they were woven, signified the very epitome of high-priced luxury from the moment they were first seen in Europe.

As explained, the term 'cashmere goat'

Focusing on the fine fleece of a young British Cashmere nanny goat (Norwood Farm).

is used to describe a type of goat, rather than a particular breed. They originated in central Asia and from there spread east into Tibet, Mongolia and China, south into Afghanistan and India, west into Persia (as it then was) and north into Turkmenistan, Uzbekistan, Tajikistan and the other central Asian tribal areas swallowed up by the Soviet Union.

These goats come in many colours and one of the main uses of their hair since ancient times has been in the felting of both the topcoat and the undercoat together into a thick, weatherproof material from which nomadic tents, or yurts, were made – black being the favoured colour. And the use of goat hair continues to this day. Michael Ryder, renowned authority on animal fibres, says in his booklet. *Cashmere, Mohair and Other Luxury Animal Fibres for the Breeder and Spinner* that some

43

1,000 tons are imported annually into Britain, and used for the manufacture of brushes, felt and cloth for suit interlinings, and as a binder for plaster.

Where selection has been carried out in order to improve the quality and yield of the fibre – primarily in China, and in Australasia – the cashmere goat (which in its 'unimproved' state comes in all colours) is usually white, this being the colour favoured by the processors and spinners. Again quoting Michael Ryder (to whose booklet I am indebted as the source of a lot of my information on cashmere production), grey cashmere fetches only 80 per cent of the price of white, while brown (tan) fetches only 66 per cent.

Britain has always been the centre of cashmere processing, but over the past few years supplies from China, the main producer, have slowly dwindled. New sources are being looked for, and both Australia and New Zealand are developing their herds, with animals averaging about 250g of fibre a year. This selection and improvement in Australasia has been based on their herds of feral goats (goats once domesticated, now gone wild).

Cashmere fibre has always commanded a high price and seems to keep that price, whatever the vagaries of fashion (or politics) may be. So, although figures change rapidly and are therefore rather meaningless in a book, it may help to illustrate the place of cashmere in the context of world textile fibre prices if perhaps I use some figures I collected in the middle of the 1980s. Then, the British Wool Marketing Board paid £1.40 per kilo (their top price that year) for the finest quality white Shetland fleece, while cashmere was purchased by the British processors at between £50 and £70 a kilo. And this difference in price is not that much affected by differences in yield – the Shetland does not carry a heavy fleece and a really good-quality one will seldom weigh much over a kilo, and so only four to five times heavier than an average year's combings of down from a goat. (Incidentally, while on the subject of prices, that same year British processors, who have also been pre-eminent in the mohair market, paid around £10 a kilo for top-quality mohair imported from South Africa.)

To return to the breeding of cashmere goats: the work being done in Australasia was watched with interest by the Hill Farming Research Association in Britain. Feeling that a similar selection project was feasible here, and that grazing of improved hill pastures by mixed flocks of sheep and goats would be of benefit too, plans were laid for some experimental work. This has been under way for a few years now in Scotland, using the feral goats which have roamed there since their ancestors were let loose by dispossessed crofters leaving their little farms for America and Canada in the last century.

These feral goats carry very fine undercoats, with fibres measuring less than 15 microns, but in tiny quantities. So goat size and thus fibre quantity is being increased by crossing with bucks of breeds which carry the double coat, mainly the Toggenburg, the British Alpine and the British Saanen; while fibre length and quality is being improved by the use of imported semen from white cashmere bucks. Although the imported cashmere bucks and the British Saanen are white animals, inevitably – because the feral does and the Alpines and Toggenburgs are coloured – a high proportion of the British cashmere production will be coloured, at least for some time to come.

However, a start has been made on the establishment of a white 'British Cashmere' goat, and in the meantime the small quantities produced, and the fact that much of it is coloured, mean that handspinners and handweavers are likely to benefit by finding this locally produced cashmere offered to them, rather than to the big processors.

The processors of cashmere's grading of the fibre is based on the amount of hair remaining in the downy undercoat after it has been combed off the goat (the mechanical processes necessary to remove these hairs are complicated and expensive), the colour of the down and, most important, its fineness. After the wild goat, Chinese cashmere is the finest, averaging 15 microns, while Iranian and Russian average around 19 microns. British and New Zealand feral goats average 12–13 microns, and the Australian variety 16 microns. So with the breeds being used on the British feral goats to upgrade the product being between 13.5 and 15.5 microns, it would seem that eventually British cashmere fibre should be able to rival the Chinese product in quality, even if it never can in quantity.

The high cost of cashmere yarns makes the use of them a matter for the most careful consideration – though it is worth reminding handspinners that they can lessen the shock of the bill by buying combed tops of cashmere and spinning their own yarns, a slightly cheaper process. But looked at any way cashmere is expensive, so the yarn tends to be used in blends, particularly with lambswool. But, even if the cost of the materials is high, so too is the price that can be asked, and which will happily be paid in the right market, for the finished product.

Angora Goats

This is the other famous fibre-producing goat breed and, just to confuse, the yarn spun from their hair is not known as angora (that comes from the angora rabbit) but as *mohair*. Again, they originated in central Asia, but moved west into Turkey where they were developed in the province of Ankara, which is in the high, mountain-rimmed Anatolian plain. (The modern capital of Turkey is the city of Ankara, which has an excellent ethnographic museum which holds the famous Catal Huyuk woven textile.)

When we were in Turkey a few years back on what turned into a most wonderful 'textile' holiday, what with the carpets, the woven fabrics, the felts, silk production and the goats, we saw large mixed flocks of sheep and goats grazing on the Anatolian plain. Each flock had a couple of shepherds mounted on small ponies, and was accompanied by the most fearsome-looking Anatolian Sheepdogs – and they were fierce, too; the shepherds would not let us come anywhere near to take our photographs – with huge, spiked collars round their necks to protect them while guarding the flock against wolves. Apparently there are still plenty of these in the mountains around. Altogether, it was quite a sight, even without the wolves.

The Turkish government has now realized the value of these goats, and state stud farms have been set up to control the breeding of them – just as a 'College of the woven rug' was being planned when we were there, to ensure that the skills necessary for making the famous Turkish knotted rugs are not lost. Like every other developing country Turkey finds it difficult to stem the flight from the land; the

A British angora buck (Norwood Farm).

pull of the towns and the seaside holiday resorts draws the country folk in, and old farming ways and the ancillary crafts are lost. So, for all our sakes, I hope these and similar schemes to preserve their heritage are successful; because to see textiles being made in their homeland as they have been for hundreds if not thousands of years was, to my mind, worth any number of dimly lit museum exhibitions, however beautifully staged.

The fleece of the angora goat differs in one unique way from that of all other goats. It completely lacks hair and is made up only of long, lustrous, curly ringlets of 'mohair' – in effect the fibre is, like the sheep's fleece, a development of the undercoat. The animals are almost all white, and though there is a superficial resemblance to the cashmere-type goat – they both have long, low-set and sideways-growing spiral horns, with the does being horned too, though not so spectacularly – the cashmere has a pricked ear and the angora a lop ear. The angora is a small, stocky goat, very evidently not a milk breed, which are generally leggy, rangy and skinny. I think it can best be described by the phrase we used for our red North Devon beef cattle in our

farming days: 'tight to ground', meaning square, short-legged and beefy-looking. In fact angoras are a good meat-producing goat and so serve a dual purpose, which is always a useful attribute and one that is pretty well essential for a domestic animal in peasant or subsistence farming conditions.

Angoras were not seen outside Turkey until about 150 years ago, being exported first to South Africa and then to the United States. These countries are still the main producers of mohair fibre as they have the dry, high upland pastures on which the goats thrive. More recently they have become established in Australasia and in Europe – in France, Spain and the United Kingdom. In spite of the apparently unsuitable climatic conditions (past attempts to breed them here have failed), a determined effort in the beginning of the 1980s established them on a Devonshire farm. Although a county not exactly famous for its high, dry uplands would seem the last place in which to succeed with angoras, determination and good stockmanship triumphed. The original imports, some twenty in all, were housed indoors with infra-red lamps at the ready, but in a couple of seasons their progeny were sufficiently acclimatized to be kept in huge plastic-covered open-sided poly-tunnels, and a year or two later there was a herd of some 250 pure- and cross-bred (with British Saanens) angoras grazing the North Devon fields. What a triumph for famed British stockmanship – though I had better add here that the originator of this finally successful adaptation of the breed to English conditions is in fact American.

For the past few years the angoras-in-England tale has had its ups and downs. Scarcity value originally meant that stock was extremely expensive so, sensibly, a five-generation grading-up process was started using British Saanen nanny goats and putting back the best (the most 'angora-looking') females in each generation to pure-bred bucks. One interesting sideline from this project arose in the first- and second-generation crosses; goats were produced carrying a short, fine 'undercoat' with just a sparse topcoat of hairs. This new fibre was called *cashgora* and there were great hopes that it might prove to be a new and worthwhile addition to fibres for textile manufacture, since although it was not as fine as cashmere it was longer. Unfortunately, processing difficulties, largely the problem of separating the fibre from the hairs, have made it less useful than was originally hoped. However, imported tops, processed in Australasia, can sometimes be found, and it is a lovely fibre for handspinners, giving a soft and lustrous yarn at rather less than cashmere prices.

The grading-up scheme provided the market with its first chance to buy into the new breed and selling started, mostly of grading register animals but also of a few pure-breds. These latter fetched enormous prices, and consequently great efforts were made to import more pure-bred stock to satisfy the market. Embryo transplant proved to be the answer, but the market was then flooded with large numbers of pure-bred animals, leading to an inevitable collapse in prices. Things now seem to be levelling out, and whatever else happens at least the angora goat now seems to be firmly established in Europe.

Mohair yarn is well worth the attention of handweavers. Personally I particularly like the fine worsted-spun yarns rather than the more usual fluffy 'brushed'

mohair, but there is a sufficient variety of lustrous, strong yarns, very ready to take dye colours, to please most tastes.

OTHER HAIR ANIMALS

There are various other hair-producing animals whose fibre is soft, often attractively coloured, and well worth seeking out. None of it is produced in volume, so it is inevitably expensive but, as with cashmere, it can be combined with other yarns and is certainly worth using where special projects suggest that its soft, light warmth is desirable.

Angora Rabbits

Angora rabbits give one of the best known luxury fibres, having been farmed in the United Kingdom, in France and in the United States since the nineteenth century. Like the goats, the breed also comes from Turkey, but unlike them the fibre is actually called 'angora' too. There are thriving angora-rabbit clubs, which promote the spinning and use of the fibre, which comes in an excellent range of colours. The animals can be seen at most rabbit shows and the spun yarn, or fibres for handspinning, are readily available through contacts made at these shows.

South American Camelids

The *vicuña* and *guanaco* are wild members of the South American camel family, while the *alpaca* and *llama* have been domesticated. The vicuña provides the highest-quality fibres from its downy undercoat, measuring only 15 microns with a harvest of only about 500g from each animal. Unfortunately they are desperately nervous and attempts to do-mesticate them have always failed. They were once hunted and killed for their coats, but are now protected, and so are rounded up (not necessarily annually, as the coat does not moult) for the down to be col-lected, although even this proves too stress-ful for some animals. Consequently it is not only the finest but also the most valuable of the llama family's fibres – the ultimate in expensive classical style for the man-about-town is surely a vicuña overcoat.

The two domesticated varieties are the smaller alpaca and the llama, which was traditionally used as a pack animal. In these llamoids the difference in fibre quality between the down and the top-coat is not so marked as in other double-coated animals, so the whole coat is shorn when the fibres have grown to 20–30cm in length, usually every two years. Again quoting Michael Ryder, the alpaca fibre has a mean diameter of under 27 microns, with that of the llama ranging from 27 to 30. Alpacas give about 2.5 kilograms per shearing; llamas rather more. They have been farmed in this country for some years now, and the soft and colourful wool, in a range from black through browns to white, is a valuable addition to the yarn cupboard of the handweaver.

Camel Hair

Imported camel-hair wool from the un-dercoat of the *Bactrian camel* can be bought, either as a spun yarn or in tops for handspinners, from some specialist suppliers. Particularly in the case of the baby camel down, it can rival cashmere for softness, and is usually an attractive deep honey colour. Worth looking out for – or, if you live near a zoo, try talking nicely to the camel keeper and you may be able to acquire a sack of moulted under-coat in the spring. Dehairing by hand is tedious, but the resulting yarn is worth it.

Other Speciality Hairs

Two unusual speciality fibres which can sometimes be found are *quiviut*, the grey-brown downy undercoat shed by the North American musk ox, and the grey, fawn and chestnut-brown fibres from farmed *mink*. Both these fibres are short and very soft and, although inevitably they are expensive due to being in short supply, it is worth knowing of their exis-tence, I think. Finally, to end this list of fine-quality animal fibres I must mention dog and cat fur. Some breeds of both spe-cies have the double coat, with a resulting soft, downy undercoat which, although very short, can and often has been most successfully spun. It is not generally com-mercially available, but dog-breeder friends, or a glance at the weekly dog papers, may lead interested handspinners to a source of supply.

YARN COUNT

Commercially spun hair fibres are mea-sured and sold by the usual woollen or worsted systems. These fibres are also spun into hand-knitting yarns (2-ply, 4-ply, chunky knit, etc.) which, although they may not be strong enough to use as warp threads unless re-spun, can cer-tainly be used as weft yarns./These soft knitting yarns, or perhaps handspun yarns, combined with a fine wool warp, and maybe with the same warp yarn woven pick-and-pick with the expensive speciality yarn, would give a luxurious fabric at a lower cost.

7
Why Design?

Design, designer, designed – all words which most people will agree have been much overused and abused in the past few years. So what does 'designing' really mean and, more importantly, what does it mean to us as handweavers?

Philip Rawson, in his most interesting and valuable book *Creative Design: a New Look at Design Principles*, starts with the heading 'Design defined' and goes on: 'Design is the means by which we order our surroundings, reshaping natural materials to suit our needs and purposes . . . [it] expresses human intentions, desires and hopes.'

For me, this says it all. Design is not just a meaningless word, part of the sales packaging of some fashionable article; part of its marketing; another way of tempting the money out of our pocket. It is something we all do, all of the time, every day. In other words, to reduce it to its bare bones, designing is problem solving.

Saying that a matt-black object (yesterday's fashion now, but never mind, it will do as an example) is not necessarily good design just because it is called a 'designer

watch', or whatever, is not to say that there are no well-designed matt-black objects. And the teapot from whose spout the liquid trickles down on to the table instead of pouring into the cup is undoubtedly bad design – even if it is a quirky handmade object modelled and decorated to look like the whole tea table rather than just part of it. William Morris's call for 'fitness for purpose' comes in here – with most craft work we are making something which has a function, and therefore its 'rightness' can be measured against that. In other words, we are not asked to make a subjective judgement as to whether the teapot is a good or a bad teapot because it is unconventionally shaped, but merely whether it is good or bad at doing the job teapots are designed to do – pouring out tea.

When, as textile workers, we stray into the 'decorative arts' or even the 'fine art' area – textile collages or textile sculptures, for instance – it is then that we enter the real minefield. The argument about 'art' versus 'craft' has raged, I suspect, since those neolithic wall painters tried to make out that their art, intended as it was to

49

placate the gods and give better hunting, was on an altogether more elevated plane than their wives' craft, the woven, decorative and celebratory garments for the same gods' feast days.

And it will continue to rage while artists, like all professionals worth their salt, jealously guard their corner, and while craftsmen push the boundaries of their work into constantly new and experimental directions, some perilously close to fine art. Not to mention the artists who push the boundaries of their work towards the crafts. Think of the *papiers collés* done in his old age by Matisse, or of the recent photographic collages of David Hockney. (Admittedly, he now denies that these had any artistic integrity to them in comparison with his paintings, but nevertheless photographers will undoubtedly disagree with him in order to maintain the status of their craft, while collectors will continue to buy them at fine art prices simply because they are Hockneys.) And of course in this century of artistic experimentation there are many other artists who work in materials once quite unthought of in the art world – scrap iron, old electrical equipment, found objects of all sorts. The list is endless.

Is there so much difference between their work and that of, say, contemporary basket makers who make their 'art baskets' from the same found objects of the city streets or country lanes? I think it is only a matter of the way we see these things. By this I mean that if a gallery owner is prepared to exhibit those baskets in a fine art gallery, and a collector is prepared to buy them as fine art – that is to say as purely decorative objects to grace his home – then, for that moment at least, they are fine art.

Perhaps because of the essential difficulty (perhaps the impossibility) of defining exactly what is 'good' fine art, many artists have an arrogance, if I may call it that, which enables them to work just for the sake of the work itself. They do not really think about selling their work, or gaining recognition, or whatever. The actual act of making is all that matters; once that is done, the work is dismissed from their mind and they go on to the next one.

Most craftsmen do not, I believe, think like this. Their attitude is unlike that of the fine artist in a way which underlines the essential difference between the two art forms. The creative urge is no less strong in the craftsman, but the need to have the work recognized is also strong – perhaps because there is an objective standard against which the worth of the craft object can be assessed.

To me this recognition of my work means having it first admired by people whose judgement I value, and possibly then having it bought by someone who likes it enough to lay out good money on it. Which is why I for one am happy to have an objective 'marker' against which to measure craft work: does the teapot pour properly, or is the weaving technically good for the purpose for which the textile is intended?

While this objective assessment is a strength for us, it can also be a great weakness, which both diminishes the quality of our work and the pleasure we get from it. By this I mean that if we think of nothing but the objective, the technical, qualities of the work then doing it becomes a mere mechanical repetition of skills learned, and ultimately a burden if not a complete turn-off. Think of the incredibly skilled tapestry weavers of seventeenth-century Brussels weaving from the cartoons of Raphael and Rubens, and the English weavers of the Mortlake workshops whose work was based on the cartoons of Rubens under orders from his patron, Charles I. These men were skilled weavers, but nevertheless were required simply to copy exactly the designs of fine artists. Their day was long, their pay poor, and by the seventeenth century they did not even have that self-regard, the sense of master-craftsmanship, given by membership of their guild, with all that implied in status and position amongst their peers. The close and creatively satisfying interaction between the designer and the master weaver (often one and the same person in medieval times) had gone, and the distinction between the fine artist who walked with kings and the mere artisan craftsman who reproduced his work had started.

So I believe there are lessons for us here, not the least of which is that if we do not look at, and use, the history of our craft we will not only diminish our own satisfaction in our work but we will also diminish the craft itself. And I also firmly believe that, given the commitment and the necessary visual and tactile skills, 'any fool can weave' – or knit, or pot, or do woodwork or whatever. Technical expertise can be learned by those who are fired by the need to express themselves through their hands, but this is not in itself enough; the objective, technically led approach alone leads to dull work and duller weavers; a cultivation of, and an appreciation of, artistic matters – line, shape, form, proportion, scale, colour – is not only necessary to give a subjective, artistic dimension to our work but to our own personal satisfaction as creative craftsmen.

Some people might think that these are rather serious considerations for weavers at so early a stage in their work. But I make no apology for raising them because I do feel very strongly that, if we are to get a real and lasting pleasure from our weaving, we should from the word go aim to do work which asks to be judged not simply on an objective, technically competent, fit-for-the-purpose basis, but which also evokes an emotional response, both from the maker and the viewer. For instance, craft objects should not just make us wonder: 'Has it been properly knitted? Have all the ends been neatly darned in or do they all hang out at the back?' Our first and immediate reaction should be 'What a stunning use of colour!' or 'Oh, I just love that patterning.' After that, we can start thinking about technical matters – but simply as part of the design, not its whole, and most certainly not as its *raison d'être*.

HEAD, HAND AND HEART

Any piece of craft work, if it is to be something more than a handicraft object, must contain all these three elements. (Handicrafts are absolutely right in their place, and many of us learned manual dexterity by making small decorative things, often to traditional patterns, to brighten up our surroundings.) And the difference between craft and handicraft? Well, this we all in fact recognize quite instinctively. For instance, we see something; we feel it 'looks right', we 'like its proportions'; we decide the 'lines are good'; we think the colours are 'exciting'; or maybe we even say, 'Oh, no, that's all wrong, its hideous.' All these are serious and subjective judgements which it would be ridiculously pretentious to apply to, say, a furry toy for Christmas or a crochet egg-cosy, however well made. These objects simply do not, to our mind have the 'importance' to warrant such strong feelings.

So it seems to come down to the fact that craft, like art, is in the eye of the beholder, because our reaction to it comes from the heart – and it follows that if the craftsman has not exercised those disciplines of head and heart, as well as hand, the object will not evoke the response. 'You gets what you pays for', as it were – or perhaps that ought to be 'You get out of things only what you put into them.'

From my own experience over the past few years I find that handweavers, including those coming new to the craft, tend to fall into three categories: those who feel the urge to create but, perhaps because of other commitments, don't feel they can take their work further than making things for the house, for family and friends; those who would like to turn their craft into an income-generating activity, a small business, working probably from home, maybe with one or two in- or outworkers; and finally the full-time professionals, either designing freelance on their own loom and selling their designs for quantity production and/or designing and marketing lengths woven for them by one of the smaller mills, or designing in-house for one of the big cloth manufacturers. (Weavers starting in the first category quite often find changing circumstances lead them into the second or even the third. So I believe that we can all save ourselves a lot of time if we start our weaving in such a way that, however our lives change, our work will still be satisfying and useful to us.)

I was lucky enough to be taught, for the last two years of my training at least, on a very professional basis and I try to pass on the benefits I have gained from this approach whenever I can. By a professional basis I really only mean encouraging the instinct which is there in all of us – the one which says that if a job is worth doing, its worth doing properly, and well. (Subjective judgements again, I know, but in craft work you really cannot avoid them.) To put it another way, it takes just as long to knit up somebody else's pattern as to knit up your own, and what have you got at the end? Even at best, if it has come out of one of the many books by a top designer, just something every other fashion-minded knitter will be wearing. Whereas knit and wear your own and not only will nobody else be wearing it but it may well be admired and bring in orders for more of the same thing. So, you stop wearing it, because others will now be doing so, and design yourself another. And – well, you are in business.

Before I go any further, I would like to apologize for constantly quoting knitting as an example to illustrate my arguments. The fact is that weaving is very much the Cinderella of the two main constructed textile crafts in this country. The same does not apply in some parts of the Continent, or in America, where the virtues of handweaving have been vigorously marketed and are much more generally appreciated.

There are historical reasons for this, of course, not the least of which is the legacy of the Industrial Revolution. This major upheaval, sparked off by the threat (as it was seen by the workers) of the mechanization of the various processes in textile manufacture, ended the appalling sweated labour of handweavers and substituted the equally appalling 'dark, satanic mills'. And, more recently (and this certainly did not apply in the craft revival of the 1920s and 1930s, where weaving was pre-eminent and knitting seen simply as a suitable handicraft for housewives), it has been the sheer cost of the tools – the loom and its accessories – which has turned would-be makers to the cheaper knitting needles and knitting machines.

But there are some signs of change, and a few of the young professionals mentioned in my third category of weavers are beginning to make their mark. However, there is a long way to go if handweaving is to be restored to its position as the first and richest of the textile crafts, and, though I'd like to think that if I were asked to revise this book in ten years time I would be able to find lots of weaverly quotes by then, I do rather wonder.

Craft, like art, is a creative discipline in which there are no real absolutes, no right or wrong, because every individual has his own way of interpreting his work – in our case, interpreting the techniques of weaving. There are certain methods of, say, threading up a loom which have been tried and tested through the ages, and it is always worth finding out if they work for you too. Why bother to reinvent the wheel? But these are not rules as such, and you may find that they do not suit you and that you have to work out your own solution to the problem, a solution with which you feel comfortable.

This freedom to make our own choices means that there are great challenges, and also great problems, for the creative craftsman. And our solutions to these designing and making problems will need to be original and imaginative if we are to succeed. Success, I believe, means producing an object which will not only fulfil the criterion of fitness for purpose, but will also satisfy both our own creative urge and the market for which it is designed (be it family, commissioning client or employer).

In fact, this creative freedom with its lack of rules is one of our greatest difficulties, because most people tend to work better within a framework, to order, to a deadline. When we are told 'You decide, I really don't know what I want' that is when our problems start. And that is why so many of us fall back on the disciplines of the craft itself to give us the framework we want; that is to say, we allow the actual techniques and structures of weaving to dictate to us what we are going to do, rather than designing the project and then deciding how it would be best to weave it.

We have all heard someone say, 'I design on my loom. I never worry beforehand about how I'm going to do it.' Don't believe it. No weaver, however skilled, can work this way. If you inquire you will find that, however unstructured and uncontrolled the weaving appears to be, there is a theme. Maybe it is a colour scheme, or ideas and feelings inspired by the actual yarns, or perhaps by the memory of shapes and patterns admired and recorded in a holiday snapshot. There is always something there, even if it is not on paper but simply in the mind. It is just a different approach to designing and making which happens to suit the personality of that particular weaver.

Though as designer-craftsmen we are working in a discipline without any clear rules as such, there are certain aids to creative designing and making which can help us, certain guidelines to point the way towards the making of a harmonious and pleasing whole. And these guidelines do not apply only to the weaving of art objects, things that have no other purpose but to be decorative. (We can easily appreciate that this sort of work aims to be exciting, imaginative and original, that it tries to evoke subjective feelings.) They also apply to things which are designed to be useful – just because something is to be worn, or hung at the window, or eaten off, does not mean it should not also aim for excellence. We must make sure that these things too will be visually pleasing and carefully and thoughtfully designed, as well as being technically correct and suitable for the purpose for which they are made.

I believe it was a growing awareness of these necessary self-applied disciplines which moved me from sheep-owner to textile worker some years ago, although what actually started me off in textiles was our Shetland sheep. As someone who had knitted all my life (it was something that was learned at mother's knee in my day) I was fascinated with their fleece, the way it could be spun up into fine, soft yarn in a range of natural colours – blacks, browns, greys, and white shaded with all of these. With care, because it felts readily, being so fine, I dyed it, using plant dyes which I felt were as near as I could get, in the south of England, to the traditional dyes used by the Shetland islanders. I read up all I could find about the woollen industry on the Shetlands, and started to knit Fair Isle and fisherman's jerseys, and fine lace shawls, from my handspun, hand-dyed wool. Very satisfying, almost something from nothing, as it were, although of course it took a long time and consequently, when I started selling, my prices were rather high. And I wasn't

always happy with the results, because the strong chemicals used to fix the plant dyes tended to turn my bouncy, soft handspun into a hard, dry and lifeless yarn just like the so-called Shetland wool bought in the shops.

However, because I felt strongly about the need to preserve traditional textile crafts, and had pushed this aspect of my work as my main sales pitch, I did my best to overcome the problems. I made some modest sales, and then started weaving, as I felt this was a logical extension to my work (Shetland tweeds, to mix and match with the jerseys, were my aim), when suddenly I realized that I was . . . bored. I also realized that I really had no answer to the person who asked why my Fair Isle pullover was four times the price of the one in Marks & Spencers, the one which looked just the same to her. Mine was handmade throughout, yes – but did that make it any 'better'?

So it had taken me about three years to learn one of the hard facts of life: that just because you are labouring long hours over a hot loom, so to speak, nobody owes you a living; and that a craft article is not worth the extra money it will inevitably cost just simply because it is handmade. It is only worth extra if the market is prepared, or able, to pay extra. And to gain that sort of recognition of its worth it has to have that difficult-to-define something, that touch of individuality which will distinguish it from all the other hand-crafted articles at the hundreds of craft shows all over the country. The indefinable something – the style, the flair, the excitement, the quality, the originality, the . . . yes, well, the design.

All this is why, in my middle age, I went back to school. I wanted to do work which would be taken seriously, and not just thought of as a nice little hobby; and I realized that if this was what I really wanted then I needed some serious training.

So I started along the route so many have followed, through part-time classes in what were known as Creative Studies and which led eventually to an examination by the City & Guilds of London Institute. And again, like so many others have done, I literally found myself in a new world.

If I am to be quite honest it was not so much the actual techniques learned which helped me, because I already had some experience in quite a few of the disciplines which then made up the City & Guilds

textiles syllabus – although, of course, anybody who thinks they know it all is a fool; we never stop learning. But at that stage in the development of my work what I needed, and what I got, was a push towards that cultivation and appreciation of things artistic which I spoke of earlier. And that push started me down the path of using my own likes and dislikes, my own way of seeing things, as the source of ideas for my work rather than, as before, the ideas of Shetland islanders long dead. So, whatever going back to school may have done for the quality of my work, one fact is unarguable: I may well at times consider myself to be overworked and underpaid, but I am never, never bored.

8
Setting up the Framework

Eventually, as with the weaver who designs on the loom, some weavers may find it more comfortable to work in a less structured way. But certainly to start with (and I for one still find it essential) setting up a programme of work to help in the planning of each project is a good idea. These basic self-made rules are a guide through the process of translating inspiring source material into the actual craft object, giving us a disciplined framework within which it is easier to work.

Each weaver will need to think out his or her own working method, a personal checklist, but sometimes it can be helpful to use someone else's format as a starting point, so perhaps my own pro forma reproduced here might serve the purpose.

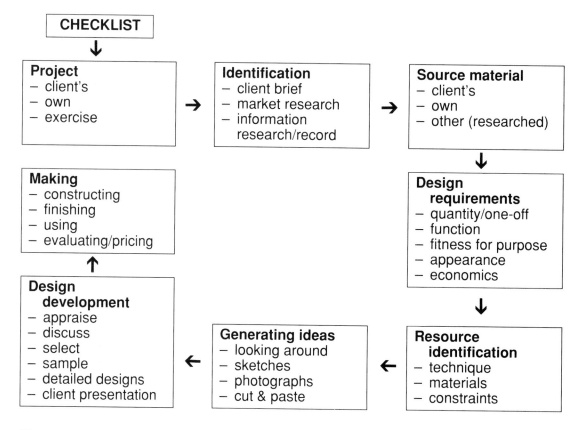

CHECKLIST
↓

Project
- client's
- own
- exercise

→

Identification
- client brief
- market research
- information research/record

→

Source material
- client's
- own
- other (researched)

↓

Design requirements
- quantity/one-off
- function
- fitness for purpose
- appearance
- economics

↓

Making
- constructing
- finishing
- using
- evaluating/pricing

↑

Design development
- appraise
- discuss
- select
- sample
- detailed designs
- client presentation

←

Generating ideas
- looking around
- sketches
- photographs
- cut & paste

←

Resource identification
- technique
- materials
- constraints

As each project progresses, test it against the checklist, step by step. In this way you will slowly evolve your own personal method of working, one which will help you to think ahead, to foresee possible problems and to solve them before they become disasters, and finally to achieve the satisfying end result you have planned for. (I know we are never entirely satisfied with what we make; if we were, creativity would come to a full stop because we would have done it all. But a structured and carefully thought out method of working can help to avoid some of the pitfalls – or, if the worst does happen, at least we can see where things went wrong so as to avoid similar horrors in future projects.)

Of course what your checklist cannot do is actually create the original ideas for you. But this creative process can be learned too. It is a state of mind, a way of looking at things, at the sights, shapes and colours of the world around, and is something we can all practise to make perfect. And in a surprisingly short time, and quite subconsciously, this looking for ideas becomes a continuous process and the recording of them, in whatever way is best for each individual, becomes second nature.

DESIGNING THE PROJECT – FROM THE BEGINNING

In the beginning there was the source material. And this first stage in any project comes in various ways. Let us use a tapestry-weaving project in this chapter. It is a nice, user-friendly technique which allows the weaver to incorporate a greater degree of figurative imagery, all the things around us to which we can relate

directly and easily, than with some other forms of weaving.

There are many reasons for starting work, but they all tend to come under one of three categories. The first is a commission from a client; the second is making something to your own design which you hope to sell through a third party – a shop, a craft stall or an exhibition, for instance; and finally there is the project you do as an exercise to test out a new idea you have, and which needs to be worked right through from original design source to finished artefact before you can reasonably hope to market it. To illustrate these three starting points, let's use the following examples.

A   Friends have asked you to make them a wall hanging picturing the old seventeenth-century cottage which they have just bought.

B   Your county weavers' guild is putting on its annual exhibition, for which you like to enter work. The chosen theme this year is 'water gardens'.

C   It occurs to you that, knowing the English passion for their homes, a series of tapestries based on houses and gardens might well attract orders from clients. You decide to start with your own, to try out the idea.

Perhaps it might be a good idea to have a quick word here about the exercises in this book. Take, for instance, C above – marketing tapestries of clients' own houses and gardens, or for that matter the whole general theme of 'houses and gardens' in A, B and C. It is such an obvious idea that it has been done many times, in various ways and with various techniques, by various craftspeople. So for this very reason, because it is an obvious idea, I am using it as an illustration of the design process. Likewise the exercises. They all have familiar, unoriginal themes because they are not meant to be woven for their own sake, like patterns in a knitting book, but are simply meant to illustrate certain generally used designing and making ideas and techniques which can, later on, be applied to your own projects.

Right, back to work. As a start, what is needed now is to identify exactly what is to be made; how, and from where, the design idea, the source material, is to come; the techniques to be used; and the way the source material is to be recorded. Following the stages through on the checklist will help to organize these first steps in designing a project.

In the case of A, it is all pretty straightforward. You are working to a commission, so the client (your friends) will brief you as to what is wanted. The source of the design is their cottage; they have asked you to do a one-off wall hanging in tapestry technique, because they have seen your work before, and know and like your style. And, hesitatingly, because it is always more difficult with friends, you have negotiated and fixed a price. Because they are friends, it has been based on the rock-bottom cost price of the materials together with a minimum fee for the time it will take you to make it – all amounts being rather less than you would aim to get for a purely commercial project. (Do beware here. Selling your work at an unrealistic price because it is to friends is something we all do, but the friends should always be aware that this is a price to them, and not one which you would generally quote. If you do not make this

clear, then word will go round that your work is very cheap, and the connection between 'cheap' and 'nasty' may well be made. Nor is it easy to raise your prices once you have set them too low. Besides all this, you will infuriate fellow weavers whose realistic prices you are so drastically undercutting.) Finally, you must start the process of actually designing the hanging, so you go along and take some photographs of your friends' new house.

For B, the project still originates with a client because your work must keep within the 'water gardens' theme set for the exhibition. However, this is a pretty wide brief and one which you can interpret in a number of ways, so you will need to do some research before you finally decide on the source material you will use. Let us say that you have recently visited the National Trust property at Stourhead in Wiltshire, and quite fallen in love with the setting, the lake, the scatter of eighteenth-century follies and the many exotic trees and shrubs. So you collect up the photographs you took, the postcards and the guidebook you bought. All these go up on your *ideas board*.

At this point let me say that I can't stress too strongly that this ideas board, this display area which is yours and yours alone, will be one of your main aids to design. Ideally we all need a workroom so that we don't have to clear everything away every time we want to lay the table for the next meal. But if this just isn't possible then at least we need a corner of a room, a bit of wall space, which is our private domain. Here we can pin up images which are important to us, found objects that have attracted us, work in progress – almost everything to do with the process of designing and making goes up on it at one time or another. Then,

Preparatory work for tapestry A – a montage of photographs of the cottage.

Preparatory work for tapestry B – a montage of photographs of Stourhead gardens.

Preparatory work for tapestry C – a montage of photographs of house, garden and animals.

every time we pass, we look at it. We *see* it, both consciously and subconsciously, and in this way the ideas begin to flow, the problems are spotted, the mistakes noticed, and the final project is assessed before it goes out into the world. This process of seeing, of really looking at things, is the very essence, the core, of all craft work and it is something which we can and must develop in ourselves.

So your source material – the photographs, postcards and anything else that evokes the place – plus some samples of possible yarns go up on the ideas board, and both in your head and on paper the design starts to take shape. You have decided upon the design requirements: that this will be a series of three tapestries (you have nine months to do them in before the exhibition, so plenty of time) linked together as a triptych. And while you are doing this you start to make notes of how much time you spend on the project. This information, together with the price of the materials you buy, or take from your yarn store, will give you an idea of how much the tapestries have cost you. On this you will base the final price to be put on them in the exhibition – remember, you hope to sell them there.

The tapestries are to be based on images of what you think are the most interestingly shaped of the various stone and marble classically styled follies at Stourhead. Glancing at your checklist to see where you have got to, you start to identify your resources, and you decide that the technique of tapestry weaving will give you the greatest scope for getting the effect you want. To make the process of recording design ideas easier, you use a photocopier to enlarge arrangements and combinations of the photographs until you have them the way, and

the size, you want them. This gives you the basis for the shapes of your three-part tapestry. You then darken in the main lines with pencil or pen, and you are ready to pin up the first cartoon behind your loom.

The final way of approaching the designing and making process, as suggested in C above, is rather different from both the other methods. This is because, unlike the other two designs which are either entirely or at least partially determined by the wishes of the client for whom you are making the piece, this project is entirely yours. It is an experiment, an exercise, to enable you to decide whether the idea you have – that of promoting your work as a way of recording clients' houses and gardens in the form of decorative, tapestry-woven wall hangings – is worth doing. And, apart from the consideration of whether this is work you are going to enjoy doing (and, since you are a tapestry weaver and you have had the idea, we will assume you do), the other main criterion by which you will have to judge the idea is the financial one. In other words, you will have to make at least one tapestry from start to finish in order to decide what it has cost you, and whether the market at which you are aiming will be prepared to pay the sort of prices you will have to charge.

So, to return to the checklist, the project is not only your own, something for you personally; it is also an exercise to determine whether this particular idea has marketing possibilities. You will therefore have to identify and research the market you are aiming at. Let us say that you feel that this is what the market-research professionals call the AB sector: professional people on good incomes, those likely to be living in a house of some character, and with an attractive garden, quite possibly in the country – in other words, people who are willing and able to pay realistic sums of money for art and craft objects with which to embellish their homes. You must also consider here such matters as advertising. To start with at least, until word-of-mouth recommendations establish your work, will you take a stall at country events such as horse trials, places where you might expect to meet the clients you are looking for, and/or will you advertise in the glossy country journals? Both are expensive ways of promoting work, but probably necessary if you hope to reach your market.

The design requirements are fairly straightforward, since it is to be a one-off, as will all future work in the series if you do decide to go into business with the idea. As such questions as size and finish will tend to vary from piece to piece, base costings on a consideration of the materials needed and the time taken to do a specific amount of weaving – say, 90 square centimetres of tapestry. In this way your price can easily be adjusted to the different requirements of future projects.

Your source material is fortunately conveniently to hand as, for the purposes of this exercise, you are going to do a tapestry of your own house and garden. So you sort through photographs you have taken in the past, trying to decide on the pictorial style you will adopt and also the season of the year you will use. The overall colour scheme of the work could depend on this. The tapestry technique you are using allows you a great deal of freedom in this, so you consider the possibilities that attract you, arrange the photographs you have taken and either do some preliminary sketches or use a photocopier to help you again.

You finally consider three possibilities. The first is a straightforward, representational interpretation, with the house, trees, garden features and so on all in proportion and accurately positioned. This is rather limiting. Just as you can only get a part of the house and garden into the viewfinder of your camera, so too you are limiting yourself in your tapestry. Looking around galleries and museums at pictures and textiles depicting houses, gardens and country scenes you find yourself attracted to the *naif* style of art. In this, colour is used somewhat abitrarily, perspective is non-existent, and the true proportions between various images in the picture are ignored in favour of the composition of a visually pleasing and decoratively coloured design, a 'pattern' of shapes. This, you feel, is definitely a possibility, and shares with your final idea the benefit of being in an old and traditional style – and may therefore well be a selling point in the market at which you are aiming. This final idea of yours is to adapt the simple horizontal lines of an old embroidery sampler in order to arrive at a tapestry which, while containing all the elements of the house and garden, will have been rearranged and developed so as to become a patterned and decorative abstraction of them, rather than just a 'woven photograph'.

With a thought for the marketability of traditional textile forms which have stood the test of time, plus the fact that you do not like the idea of simply copying (even the seventeenth-century artisan weavers had a Reubens cartoon to copy, not just a photograph), you decide that an adaptation of the sampler idea will give you the freedom to evolve your own style. And you also feel that you would like to incorporate some of the conventions of *naif* art – to ignore perspective and proportion and realistic coloration where this will help in composing a pleasing overall design. Quite excited by now, you start to sketch out the main elements of your house and garden, arranging and re-arranging, changing scale and adapting and simplifying shapes, in a search for a patterned whole which pleases you.

Going back to your checklist again, the final development of the design up to the point where you can start the actual making of the tapestry is not dissimilar, whichever project you are doing. In all three of the tapestries at A, B and C you will continue to work on the design, sketching, selecting elements which please you, discussing ideas with your client or with friends and family, starting perhaps to make small yarn wrapping and card-woven samples to help in the selection of the right yarns and, if you are a dyer, doing some colour-extraction work and dyeing samples of yarn from this.

The last stages of the design process will depend on how you work, but may consist of making a full-size detailed cartoon of the whole picture, as with the 'water gardens' triptych. This will be attached to the back of your loom and will guide you step by step as you weave. With this cartoon might go samples of the various colours and textures of yarn you will use or, alternatively, the textural effects you intend to incorporate by way of particular tapestry techniques. Or, as with the tapestry of your friends' cottage, you may feel the way the design has developed as a floor plan, an almost abstract pattern of geometrical shapes, gives you inspiration for a very free approach to tapestry techniques, laying in texture and colour as you work to enhance the basic

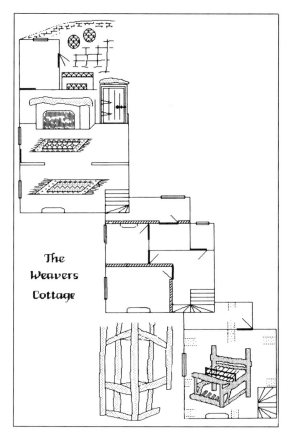

A floor plan of the cottage in tapestry A.

simplicity of line – designing on the loom, in fact. Or you may want a very controlled style such as the sampler idea for your house and garden, sketching out on graph paper the stylized elements which combine to make the whole pattern.

Neither of these methods is right or wrong; it is just a matter of the maker's choice. Nor in fact are things usually quite as absolute as this. Each project is different. Some may prove easier than others; some, even though they seem to start well, may become rather a bore and you have to force yourself to finish them. And you must always be prepared to adapt and even alter your working

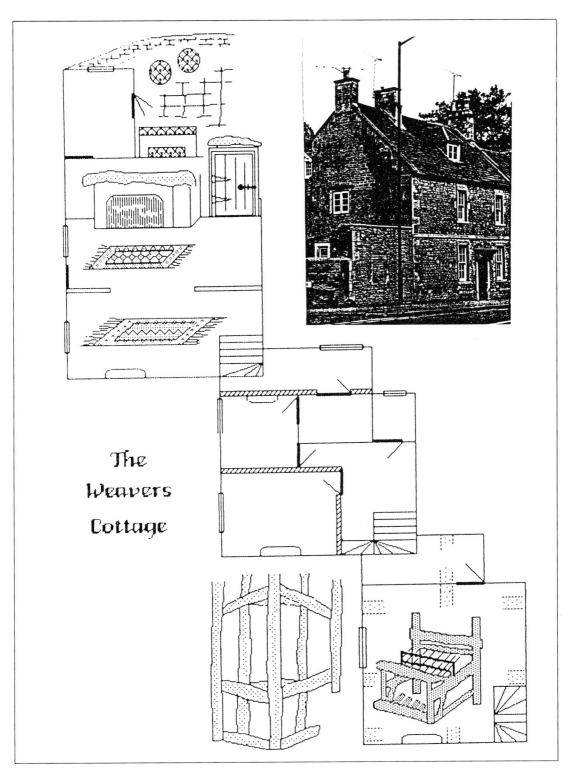

The

Weavers

Cottage

A photocopy of the cottage design ready for enlargement to its final size, and use as a cartoon.

methods. For instance, you should always be ready to take advantage of the happy accidents (say, a mistake you made in executing a particular technique, which in fact expresses much more exactly the effect you wanted); or the sudden changes of design idea you may have; or even – and unfortunately this does happen – the changes in the client's requirements.

Another point: I have used computer graphics to draw the cottage design because my computer does this type of stylized, abstract drawing for me a lot better than I can do it with my pen. I hope this illustrates the point that it does not matter at all what tools you use to record your ideas – pen, pencil, paint, camera, computer – just that you are comfortable with them, and they work for you.

Craft work should always seek to have the appearance of freshness, of spontaneous creativity, however hard the maker has actually worked in refining the original ideas. One way of ensuring this is not to let yourself get into a rut, to think that just because something you are doing is admired, and sells well, that this will go on happening for ever. It will not I am afraid. It is a hard fact of life that not only do fashions change but so too do you, and that something which satisfies you and your market now is most unlikely to do so for years to come. Therefore, you must always be open to new ideas and new influences. In other words, as I said at the beginning of this chapter, all craftsmen need to be constantly looking and learning, and be receptive to new ideas.

9
Looking and Learning

The idea for a design, the source material, can come from the most obvious places, but also from the most unlikely ones. For most of us, I suppose, it is the world we live in that offers the richest and most stimulating variety of shapes, colours and textures; and in fact many craftsmen find that one small aspect of their world, something like the seashore or the river bank nearby, is an endless source of inspiration and provides them with all they need.

Other people tend to need to renew the source of their ideas periodically, and sometimes this will mean that there are visible changes, perhaps even marked alterations, in their style of work. We can see this demonstrated by the fashion designer, who has no choice but to design a new collection each season. Even then it is interesting to note that sometimes a theme, or maybe a shape or a colourway, will not have been fully worked through and will crop up, subtly altered but still recognizable for those with eyes to see, in the new season's work.

In other words, a good idea can not only come from many different sources but it can also be developed into a number of sometimes quite different designs.

In practising this art of looking and learning, what should you look at and learn from? The sources of design ideas are as many or as few as you yourself care to make them. Working with nature as source material suits many of us, and you may well be creatively satisfied with some

small aspect of the world around your home. Or you may decide to vary your designs by taking as your theme for the year the place you visit each summer when you go on holiday. A lot of people find that a combination of sources such as these is right for them. This gives them the pleasures of working from nature, but with two completely different colour palettes – the soft, neutral, rather understated colours of the northern hemisphere contrasting with the clear, primary, sunlit hues of the south.

Counterbalancing the natural world is the other main source of design ideas, the man-made world we have all around us and, most particularly, the world of art. In the man-made environment we might look at the shapes of buildings, the contrasting textures of brick and metal, the colours and reflections on wet, oily tarmac. Everyone will have his or her own ideas. In the world of art we could include fine art works, the ethnic crafts seen on holiday, the rich collections of museums and galleries, things seen and admired in other people's homes, and of course contemporary craft work. Suggesting this last may well seem to be an invitation to copying, to pastiche or even to plagiarism, but I don't think so and in fact I find that as an exercise it can be quite useful. Many art students are set to copying the works of some old master, or they may decide to do so themselves in order to improve their painting techniques or their colour sense. I believe that similar exercises can

A montage of natural shapes and textures to use as design references.

A montage of man-made shapes and textures.

help some student weavers – hence the reason why I, who have a positive horror of anything that smacks of just making up someone else's design, include some designing and weaving exercises in this book. They are here simply to offer suggestions on technical matters. I hope some people will find them useful, but inevitably some will not – probably because they just do not think or work the way I do.

These different ways of working are the reason why two weavers, or even a whole class of textile students, can be asked to photograph the same design source – colourful tropical birds, for instance – to use as a colour extraction exercise and yet will end up by developing this into quite different work. From the initial way we 'see' the source material through to the actual techniques of designing and making that each of us uses, we all work individually and personally. This is good not only because it means that, as we gain in expertise, our work develops that personal touch, the style which sets it apart from others, makes it recognizably ours; it is also good because, let's face it, there are a finite number of major sources of inspiration in this world and if we all made the same thing from the same source material life would be very dull. Fortunately we are not robots and this is not likely to happen.

We should never be frightened of looking for ideas from those whose work we admire. We will often be working in another field anyway, so the link will be obvious only to us – using the colours from a postcard reproduction of an old master painting, for instance, to give a colour palette from which to dye yarns. Even if the source material is woven – for example, some ikat-dyed silk scarves seen at an exhibition, the chances are that they will give you quite a different idea, maybe for a range of mercerized cotton furnishing fabrics based on some photographs of patterns and reflections in water which you have been wondering how to use. So the scale, the colourway and the final use to which the weaving is put will be very different and only you will know where the first germ of the idea came from.

COMPOSING THE PICTURE

Although decisions on what is 'right' and 'wrong' in art and craft objects are very subjective ones and there are really no rules as such, there are certain guidelines which will help in the process of developing the original source material into the woven textile. Do not believe anyone who says you cannot learn to record your ideas – or, to put it more specifically, to draw and paint. You can. I did. Thousands of others have done so. It is certainly no more difficult than learning any other technical skill – weaving, for instance. Obviously, you may never rival the masters, but you will be able to do what you need to do, which is to get down on paper a representation of the way you work, in a form which you (and your clients, or your outworkers, or people buying your patterns) can understand.

Before we start on particular ways of recording designs, let us look at some general ideas which have been tried, tested and found helpful through the ages. This is not to say that you should never do otherwise, never break the rules. Of course you can, and it is a most effective way of approaching design, but it does help to know the rules before you decide when, where and if to break them.

One more important thing to remember

is to trust and follow your judgement. This is because in the art world rules should be made to work for you rather than be followed slavishly. These days we are bombarded with images of works of art and craft of the highest quality – in books, in magazines, and on the television. We are all a great deal more visually literate than we realize, or give ourselves credit for, and this is a valuable back-up to that instinctive sense of what looks right which is within us all.

Harmony

An aspect of design which you will often hear referred to is harmony. This means that if a design is to be successful it must look as if it belongs together, as if the shapes, colours and textures have a common purpose – have in fact been 'designed' to go together, not just thrown together by random chance. Visual similarities in shape – the stylized trees, say, in 'An Illusion of Depth' – can be blended together to give the unified, organized concept which we all unconsciously tend to look for. This organization pleases our eyes much more than a chaos that we cannot understand.

Harmony by proximity is one method of unifying the elements of a design. The random shapes appear at first to have no connection with each other, but rearranged they begin to look like the basis for a related pattern. If you then *repeat* this pattern (another device for achieving visual harmony) you are on the way to creating a satisfyingly unified design. Another element in this whole is the fact that you have *variety*, in that the elements of the pattern are shaped differently. But beware; some designs are so orderly, so unified, that they are positively dull, and the result is visual boredom instead of excitement and inspiration. So introduce vari-

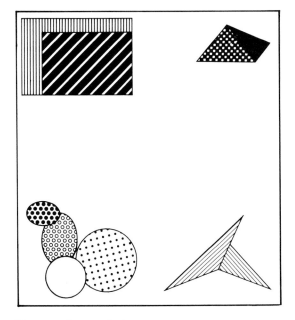

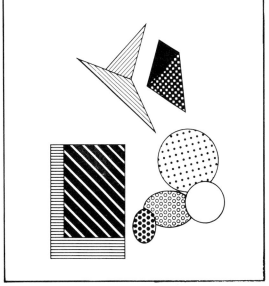

Harmony by proximity.

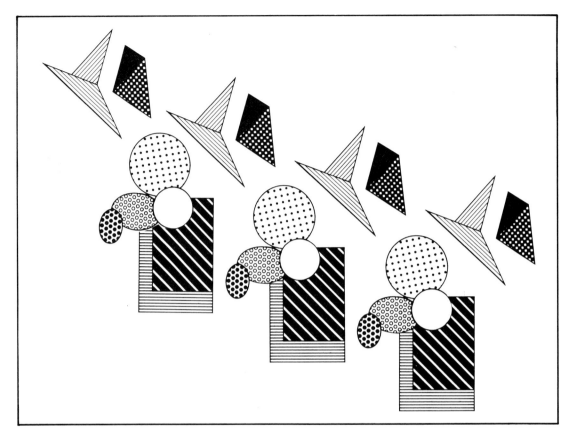

A repeating pattern.

ety by differences in colour, tone, texture, shape, or size.

Emphasis

Since one of the problems in composing a design is that it can all too easily become very dull, another way of adding a bit of spice, of livening things up, of making it visually exciting, is to introduce a focal point, a *point of emphasis*. In a pictorial design this can be done by placing the most important element – the centre of action, as it were – in a prominent position. This might be just off centre vertically and slightly below centre horizontally (*see* the *Golden Section* mentioned in 'Mathematical Formulae in Design' at the end of the chapter). In abstract or non-objective patterns emphasis can come from the use of colour and shape, and by the use of *contrast, isolation* and *placement*. There can be more than one focal point, but they should not be of equal importance; one should be the primary point of emphasis, the other or others merely backing up and emphasizing the emphasis, as it were. But again beware. Total confusion reigns if there is too much emphasis; if everything is emphasized, then nothing ends up emphasized.

Something else to bear in mind is the

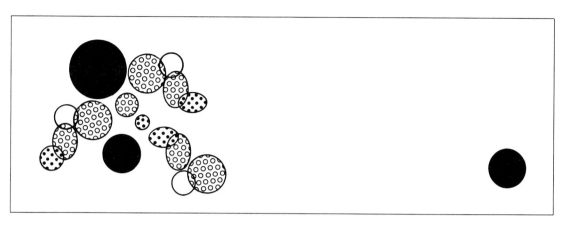

Emphasis by isolation.

importance of the *degree of emphasis*. If a focal point of contrast is too big, too dark, too brightly coloured, it will destroy the unity of the design. Although this is one of the cases where breaking the rules often operates – for instance, in a design for an advertisement, where the designer is commissioned to create an overwhelming, dominating focal point – it can actu-

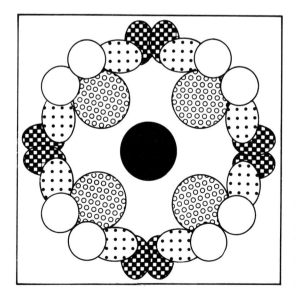

Emphasis by contrast and placement.

ally fail to get its message across. This is because we sense that the design is 'wrong' and therefore, subconsciously, we refuse to accept the message it is trying to give us.

Before worrying too much about emphasis and contrast remember that you can, particularly in textiles, create very successful patterns which have no point of emphasis. Repeated patterns (geometrical and abstract), weaves and stitches with colour or textural variations will have sufficient contrasting values to give plenty of surface interest but not so much that the cloth cannot be used in such a way that the real design emphasis comes from its cut and shape. Another point relates directly to the 'too much emphasis' syndrome: never get so carried away that you find you are using colour and pattern and texture all at once. The net result may well be way over the top – unless, of course, you are designing for something like the teenage market, or for visually spectacular opera or theatre productions, in which case you can and probably will throw away the 'good taste' rule book and mind only the particular disciplines of that market.

73

Balance

We all have a sense of balance; we avoid ladders with paint pots perched precariously on them, and we straighten crooked pictures on our walls. We feel happier and less threatened if things around us seem to be well balanced, well ordered, what might be called normal. So, in design, we unconsciously look for and expect to see balance. The way we express this in our mind's eye is by putting in a central vertical axis and distributing what we see as the weight of the design equally on either side of it (*symmetrical, or formal, balance*); or by putting in a horizontal line which acts like a see-saw and in this way balances the visual weight of the components of the design (*asymmetrical, or infor-*

mal, balance). To illustrate symmetrical balance, draw a line from top to bottom through the middle of the illustration 'Emphasis by Contrast and Placement'. The two sides balance each other perfectly as they are mirror images. (This is a classic formula used in designing both repeating and all-over patterns.) Another type of formal balance is provided by *radial balance*, where the elements of the design radiate outwards from the centre of a circle, like a clock face or the spokes of a wheel.

These symmetrical designs can seem rather static, with little movement. An asymmetrical design can be very dynamic and exciting, with a sense of visual movement created by the flowing lines of the image leading the eye in a particular dir-

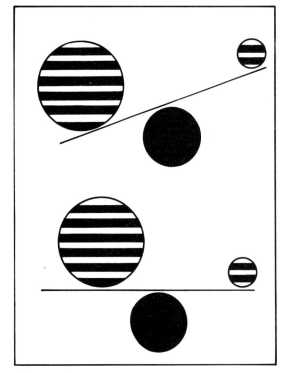 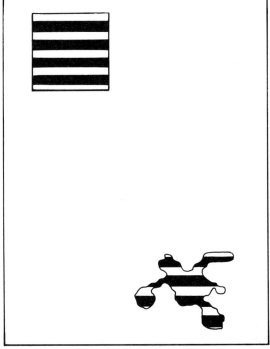

Asymmetrical balance.

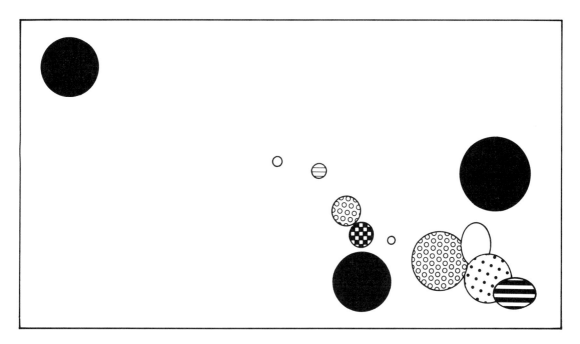

Emphasis by imbalance.

ection, perhaps towards a point of contrast. Think of the image of speedy beauty conjured up by the lines of the supersonic aircraft Concorde. For an instance of asymmetrical balance, look at the see-saw design. In order to balance the large and the small circle, it is necessary to place the larger one near the middle of the design. In the other illustration, the small but complicated shape balances the larger, more simple shape even if they both have the same *tonal value* (the degree of luminosity of a colour).

Vertical balance, above and below the horizontal axis, is important in design composition. Our sense of the force of gravity attracts us to a design with the weight, or with the visual interest, the point of contrast, towards the bottom. But as with all these 'rules' there is a reverse side to this one: placing the point of contrast above the balanced position gives

emphasis and excitement to the design. Compare this with the somewhat similar 'Emphasis by Isolation' diagram. The effect of instability in a design can be used to attract attention, which it will certainly do if only because it is unexpected. But, as with any decision to 'break the rules', a great deal of care and consideration must be given, and the decision must be capable of justification if the finished design is to work, rather than just appear arbitrary, self-indulgent, or even downright silly.

Colour and/or texture can also assist in balancing shapes. As an example of *value difference* (value here means lightness or darkness) the small dark (or it could be textured) shape in the illustration appears equal in weight to the larger, lighter or smoother ones. Similarly, a textile woven with textured yarns, or in a looped or pile technique, will appear darker than one

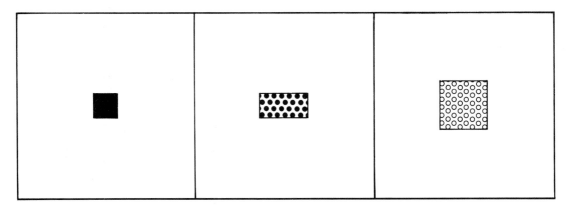

Value difference.

without texture in the weave or one with a smooth yarn, even if all the yarns have come from the same dye batch. This is simply because a smooth surface reflects more of the light falling on it.

Scale

Scale and proportion are also important conventions in the decorative arts. A tapestry suitable to cover the stone walls of a

Scale and proportion. (a) (b)

draughty medieval castle would be somewhat overpowering in the living-room of the average modern house. Similarly, the proportions of the individual elements of a design must be kept in mind. A particularly large, or bright, or dark, or textured shape could totally overwhelm the whole effect you are trying to achieve. Using the same design elements, but shrinking or stretching them, can also radically alter the emphasis of the design. The version you choose depends on what effect you are seeking.

Perspective

Finally, we must give some thought to that dreaded word 'perspective' – another of the great turn-offs, I find. Fortunately,

(c)

An illusion of depth, by variation in size.

we are not architects, who obviously need to take it very seriously. But, as with most of these working rules, it does help to know at least the basic facts before deciding how much, or how little, of them you want to incorporate into your work. We tend to think of textiles as being essentially two-dimensional: they have width and height or length, but no depth. Of course this is seldom entirely true, and even the minor variations achieved by the use of a textured yarn in the weave will give depth.

Other ways of achieving an illusion of depth, and this applies to work with either objective or abstract images, is by the use of *variation in size, overlapping* and

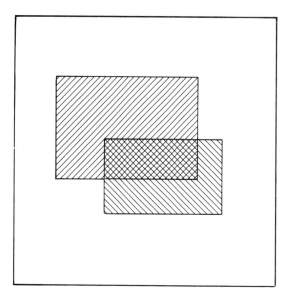

An illusion of depth, by variation in size.

transparency. With the first, big to the front, small to the back is the rule and gives the effect of elements disappearing into the distance. Overlapping also gives the same illusion, as does transparency – in the latter the fact that you appear to be seeing through the small image fools your eye into believing that the larger one is at the back.

Overlapping larger motifs to the front, smaller to the back heightens the effect, although images of the same size will still appear to recede given a combination of overlapping, vertical location, depth of tone and colour. So colour can also be used to give an illusion of depth. If you look at a picture of a landscape it will probably have large, dark and tonally strong elements in the foreground, fading

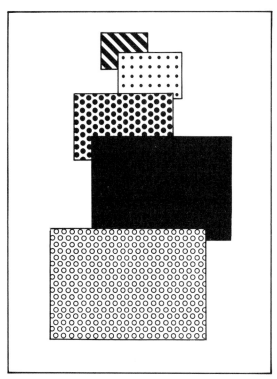

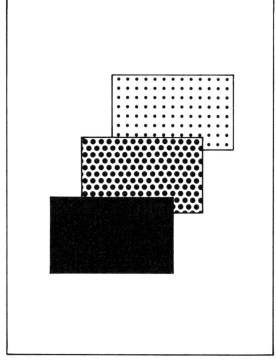

An illusion of depth, by overlapping.

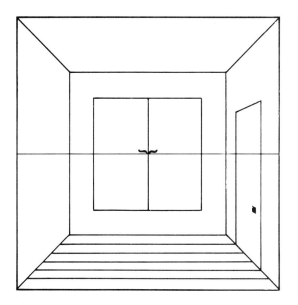
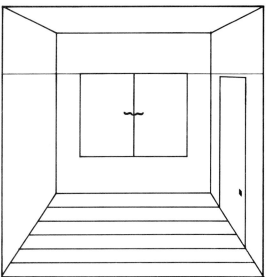

One-point linear perspective (a room seen from central, high and low viewing positions).

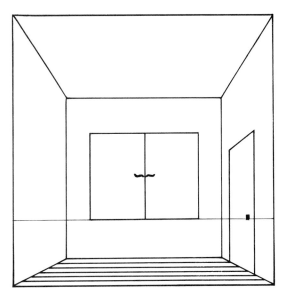

away to misty distances, the paler blue of sky and the grey of cloud.

Finally, the fine-art device of *linear perspective* can be used in design. Briefly and simply, this means that all lines from points on a three-dimensional object converge in a single *vanishing-point* on the *horizon line*. Two or more vanishing points will be needed in more complicated designs. Whether the horizon line is in the lower half of the composition (a low viewing position), in the centre, or in the upper half (a high viewing position) depends on what is known as the eye level, or viewpoint – the height of your eye from the ground, looking straight ahead.

MATHEMATICAL FORMULAE IN DESIGN

From the builders of the pyramids of Egypt and the architects and scholars of ancient Greece, from the artists of Renaissance Italy and the masters of fine art in this century, man has been fascinated by the harmonies of the natural world and their apparent order and precision. Many attempts have been made to express these

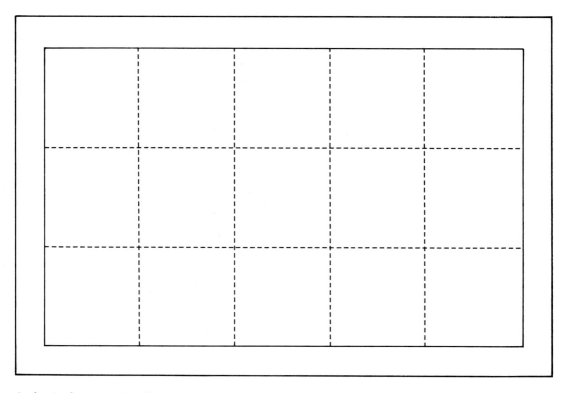

A pleasingly proportioned rectangle constructed according to the rules of the Golden Section. Possible high and low horizon lines on the horizontals. Important elements of a design can be placed on the grid intersections.

ideas in mathematical terms, so they can be used to order art and craft work.

The ancient Greeks developed what is known variously as the *Golden Section, Golden Formula* or *Golden Mean*. This is a way of expressing what is considered to be the perfectly proportioned rectangle, constructed in the proportions of 1 : 1.618. To put it briefly and simply, if you divide a rectangle whose sides are in the ratio of 3 : 5 into 15 equal sections, horizon lines, vanishing points, points of contrast and other elements of your design will appear to be positioned correctly if placed according to this division. Another formula for perfect harmony, suggested by the Italian Renaissance mathematician Leonardo Fibonacci, is 0; 1; 2; 3; 5; 8; 13; 21 and so to infinity, arrived at thus: 0+1=1; 1+1=2; 1+2=3; 2+3=5; 3+5=8; 5+8=13; 8+13=21 and so on to infinity, with each group formed by adding the last two figures of the previous group of three figures together. Interestingly, if you divide one of the higher numbers in the series by the number below it you arrive at almost the same figure as the golden section number, 1.618 (21 ÷ 13=1.61538). This becomes more and more accurate as the series proceeds and the numbers get bigger.

Taking a last brief look at mathematics in craft, three geometrical forms play an important part in design. These are the circle, the rectangle and the triangle.

Philip Rawson, in his book *Creative Design: a New Look at Design Principles*, tells us that these 'geometrical concepts classify a host of direct human experiences . . . the circle standing for the unified whole, the rectangle for the static pairing and symmetrical balance of elements, and the triangle for dynamic movement based on developing asymmetry'.

The *circle*, because it stands for completeness, has both a soothing and a powerful effect in the imagery of design. Concentric circles, spirals, the segments of circles – all these are important in art. They have strong mathematical, religious, metaphysical and even cosmic connotations, which many people will often subconsciously read into designs incorporating them.

The *rectangle* (which includes the square) gives the impression of permanence, solidity, safety. Sides can easily be shortened or lengthened; it gives us a framework upon which to base our designs (grids, the golden section), thus allowing us easy control over our work. It stacks well, and combines in various sizes and shapes without losing cohesion. Finally, it provides a frame for our work, a window into or out of it.

The *triangle* is another very powerful form, with the capacity for infinite variation by the simple device of altering the length of its sides. It is also very stable, since however much you may vary the relative lengths of its sides it cannot be 'tipped over'. The right-angled triangle (in which the square on the hypoteneuse – the side opposite the right angle – is equal to the sum of the squares on the other two sides) in particular has been used through the ages as an important element in design. In the proportions 3:4:5 it is, like Fibonacci's sequence, much used in architecture since it is said to give perfect proportions – something which also makes it of interest to us as designer-craftsmen. Finally, the triangle can give the excitement, dynamism and sense of movement which some circular or rectangular designs may lack.

10
Filling in the Colours

As designer-craftsmen, of all the methods we can use to express ourselves in our work to my mind the most powerful and satisfying is colour. There is hardly a civilization in which either the philosophers or the artists have not tried to explain colour, to pin it down in terms of their world. It has played a part in mysticism and religion, in science and mathematics, in medicine and alchemy, in psychology and the arts. It can excite and soothe, dazzle and dim, confuse and explain. Religions have used it to underline the glory of their gods and the pre-eminence of their priests over common men. Science has explained the rainbow, and looked for the reasons for the vivid display colours of animals, birds, insects and plants. Medicine, from earliest times, has held to a belief in the healing power of colour: gemstones, seen as capturing within their depths the very essence of colour and light, were ground up into nostrums for all manner of diseases, while even today analysis of the colours of the skin, the tongue and the whites of our eyes is a basis for medical diagnosis, while psychologists have argued that the key to the human personality lies in the ways we respond to colour, the way it influences our moods and feelings.

As for artists, it has been central to their work. Leonardo da Vinci related colours to the elements: yellow for earth, green for water, blue for air, red for fire. The Impressionists, in the last quarter of the nineteenth century, used colour to break free from what they saw as the stultifying effects of the institutionalized, dead art of the traditionalists.

In the decorative arts, too, colour has been central. As with fine art, we tend to think of 'traditional' colours as being muted, soft, even rather muddy. But a drastic revision of ideas has come about relatively recently, due simply to the fact that improved restoration techniques have allowed the stripping off of layers of dirt from pictures, walls, and textiles without stripping off the colours themselves, thus revealing the fact that our predecessors rejoiced in strong hues, bold contrasts, harmony and luminosity of colour. In fine art this has led many to believe that artists had some special secret of mixing pigments which has been lost to us. Certainly some ancient skills have vanished on the road to mechanization – Roman glass, for instance, has not yielded up all its technical secrets. But the skill of the Renaissance colourists, artists such as Titian, was no magic. Titian above all was just the right man living at the right time. What he and his fellows did was there for all to do: their exploitation of the new medium of oil-based paints; their skill in the mixing and blending of colour; and their use of the effects they achieved, such as the transmission of light through thin layers of paint, and the reflections off its softly sparkling surface.

In the eighteenth century there was a new renaissance, an Age of Enlightenment. It was genuinely believed that mankind had emerged from the Dark Ages and that social upheavals such as the French Revolution, although cruel, were necessary to bring about the final, Utopian age, and that alongside man's newly achieved enlightenment in things social and political would come an artistic age of elegance. Architects, artists and craftsmen went back for their source material to Greece and Rome, and Palladio's villas for rich Venetians became the ideal for the British neo-classicist designers such as Adam, 'Capability' Brown, Chippendale, Sheraton, Wedgwood and many others. All these men drew inspiration not only from classical shape and form but from the hot, strong blues, greens, reds and golds of the Mediterranean. And, with large windows and great masses of light from candelabra, they contrived for their rich patrons a style which united colour and form, and enriched it with light.

It is hardly surprising that the sudden revelation of such powerful colour comes as a shock, when you consider that we have lived so long with our soft northern light and dirty Old Masters. The cleaning of the Michelangelo ceiling in the Sistine Chapel in Rome has led to furious argument about whether he really painted in such vivid hues or whether the restorers have merely reached a later layer of overpainting and touching up. With the experts differing in the very place where it all started, perhaps the reactions of the owner of a recently restored Irish stately home are more understandable. His bitter complaint that the walls of the drawing room were now an awful 'Germolene pink' suggests that the appreciation of such strong colours takes time, and that not everyone is used to the idea yet.

My personal search for fine-art inspiration in the construction of my textiles really began with my discovery of Turner. He worked from 1790 (when he exhibited his first watercolours in the Royal Academy at the incredible age of fifteen) until not so long before his death in 1851, and to my mind he forged the link between the Renaissance, the Age of Enlightenment and the twentieth century. As a painter of colour and light he is often thought of as the first of the Impressionists. His oils, particularly the early ones, although sombre, have that Renaissance quality of luminosity which I see in my silks, and the layering of colour on colour directly suggests the effects seen in textile pieces, where fine nets or muslins are laid one on the other, building up a richness and depth of hue difficult to get in any other way.

By the end of the second decade of the nineteenth century, Turner, with his oils as well as his watercolours, had given up the honey-coloured ground on which artists had traditionally painted in favour of a white one. As a result, 'the brilliance of his pictures was such that it was said of one "it almost puts your eyes out" '. Thus he initiated a working method taken up half a century later by the Impressionists, and used by most artists painting today. According to David Thomas's monograph on Turner, his first visit to Italy in 1819, and its coincidence with the accession of the Prince Regent as King George IV, and with a period of 'brilliant, rather theatrical taste in English art', meant that Turner was well placed to play an important part in this movement. Discussing 'Sunset, Rouen', a drawing for one of Turner's series of engravings of the French rivers Loire and Seine, Thomas says that 'they are in bodycolour on blue paper, and some important elements in the colour harmony are predetermined *without reference to what Turner actually saw.* Colour instead of being used as a support for the total structure of the work, now replaces it as a means of establishing space and form, and so can be applied in a pure state: here the primary colours red, yellow and blue are predominant and *mutually intensifying'* – (the italics are all mine). And 'Turner's use of colour unsupported by tone to construct his pictures continues and is a key to the revolutionary nature of his late works'. These explanations seem to encapsulate the value of Turner's work to me, particularly in his use of colour to establish space and form, rather than just to decorate it, and in his use also of the effects of *colour harmony* and *colour contrast.*

The methods of the Impressionists later in the century run in a direct line back to Turner, and through him to the beginnings of the colour revolution in Renaissance Italy. The group of late nineteenth-century French painters known as the Impressionists, and led by Monet, Renoir and Degas, felt that the newly discovered and rapidly developing art of photography should be allowed to take over the recording of absolute happenings. As a result, painting need no longer be a precise record of line, form and colour and could now interpret the artist's fleeting impression of that moment, of the mood awakened by the image. And, most important, their work would reflect an innocent and childlike way of seeing things, a true clarity of vision, of how the play of light broke up all the different hues, tints and shades contained in the image. In this way, as with Turner, colour actually constructed the space in their paintings, and gave form to the images.

With the evolution of Impressionism into neo-Impressionism, the work done by Gauguin, Van Gogh, Robert Delaunay and Seurat, and their use of the colour theories developed by Eugène Chevreul (who started working in the dyeshops of the Gobelins tapestry works and ended his immensely long working life as their director), were combined ideas which underpin the seminal importance of the Impressionist movement. And particularly, from the point of view of the textile worker, the relevance of all this body of fine-art source material is underlined by its connection with Chevreul, the dyemaster of the Gobelins tapestry works.

USING SOME OF THE THEORIES

Chevreul's work on colour theory, and the painting techniques used by these late nineteenth-century artists, hold most useful lessons for us. As a Gobelins man, Chevreul knew of tapestry-weaving techniques such as *hatching*, where contrasting colours – say, yellow and blue – are alternated to give the visual effect of green. This is known as *visual colour mixing* (as opposed to *atomic colour mixing*, where dye or paint pigments are mixed together in the dye bath or on the palette before being used). Possibly as a result of this connection, the Impressionists' methods were strikingly similar to tapestry techniques. They dotted, striped, and dappled contrasting colours on to the canvas, so that it was the eye of the beholder rather than the brush of the painter which mixed them together into the required hue.

In order to understand the basics of colour mixing it is a good idea, as always, to learn a few of the rules. The major problem posed by mixing colours atomically is that there is really no such thing as an absolutely pure pigment. To quote Faber Birren, the American translator of Chevreul's work and an extensive modern writer on colour theory in his own right, 'as far back as 1766 Moses Harris, who developed the first wheel ever to be exhibited in full colour, remarked that while the three principal colours would make fair intermediates, the results were likely to be "dirty and unmeaning". He wrote "Suppose an orange colour was wanted, red and yellow will effect it . . . but red-orange and yellow-orange mixed will do much better" .' To overcome this problem the Impressionists used visual rather than atomic colour mixing, setting pure, unmixed pigments side by side on their white canvas so that they altered each other by contrast and, when viewed from the right distance (and this was important), gave the desired effect. Whether selecting the colours before weaving a tweed (visual colour mixing) or sampling with various dyebaths for a colour scheme (atomic colour mixing), weavers use both these methods.

My reason for suggesting that putting paint to paper is the way to start the process of colour selection is quite simply because it is easier, cheaper and quicker than searching out large quantities of yarn from which to choose, or calculating a number of mixtures for a range of sample dyebaths. The best way to explain the principles, which are the same whether one is colouring work with paint, dye, fabric paints or using already-dyed materials, is by using Michael Wilcox's *colour bias wheel*, an extension and simplification of the colour wheels of Moses Harris and others. In his book *Blue and Yellow Don't Make Green* – yes, the 'don't' is right, as you will see – Wilcox gives a masterfully

simple explanation of matters which, I have to admit, many other colour theorists have in the past made so complicated as to be just about unintelligible. I know this follows in a long and dishonourable tradition of technical works which add nothing at all to their subject, and simply appear to be trying to blind with science; but I feel that this is both extremely irritating and makes for books which are seldom worth struggling through.

GETTING DOWN TO MIXING AND MATCHING

We are usually taught that the *primary colours* are red, yellow and blue, and they are defined as those colours which are not made up of any others, and from which all other colours are mixed. If you look at the diagram of the colour bias wheel you will immediately spot one strange thing about it – no primaries are shown. This is because there is no such thing as a really pure true pigment.

Briefly, the three-primary system tells us that we can mix, say, a good clear orange by putting red with yellow. Anyone who has tried to do so, either with paints or dyes, will know that this is by no means always the case. So, as a start to finding out why the mix doesn't always work, let us look at the two sorts of primary colours.

The first sort of primaries are called the *additive primaries* (orange-red, green and blue-violet), from which white light is formed. These are known as additive primaries because when they are mixed together they become lighter – that is, light is added to them. Thus mixing red with green gives yellow, and mixing blue with green gives a blue-green; and these two, yellow and blue-green, are paler than the colours from which they were mixed.

Red, yellow and blue are known as the *subtractive primaries* and as weavers these are the colours which really concern us because pigments, the name given to tiny particles of colouring matter, are what we shall use in paints and in dyes. The reason these primaries are called subtractive is that colours mixed from them become darker than at least one of the colours in the mix – that is, light is subtracted from them. To illustrate, red and yellow produce orange, which is darker than yellow; blue and yellow produce green, which is darker than yellow; red and blue produce violet, which is darker than both.

The actual process by which we *see* all the different colours is this. The colours (what we call the spectrum) which are in all white light become visible when the light strikes a surface. If that surface is covered with, for instance, a red paint or dye pigment, all the other coloured light waves are absorbed and only the red is left – so we see the surface as red. In the same way, if we mix the three primaries together in equal strengths we will get a very dark grey-black shade. This is because, with all three pigments present on the painted or dyed surface, all but a very minute proportion of the coloured light waves striking that surface is absorbed, leaving us with a nothingness, a blackness. Additionally, if a colour is mixed with its complementary, the colour opposite it on the colour wheel, it will produce grey/brown neutral colours. The reason is the same: the two colours being mixed still have as their basis the three primaries and, although in different proportions, most colour is absorbed and little remains of the coloured light waves which strike the surface. It is these phenomena that make atomic colour mixing so difficult – the more you mix up your primaries by mixing paints or dyes of the colours derived from them, the muddier your colours become. Hence the Impressionists' use of visual colour mixing, their juxtaposing of pigments of colour as pure as they could obtain.

Colouring in the Wheel

Let us return to the colour wheel and to the fact that no primaries are illustrated and that each of the pair of primaries always veers towards one of the two other primaries. Using blue as the first example, you can see that you actually have two blues, a green-blue veering towards the yellow and a violet-blue veering towards the red. The same applies to the other two primaries, yellow and red. They give you a green-yellow and an orange-yellow, and an orange-red and a violet-red, to complete what has now become a six-colour circle.

If you then add in the three colours which come in between each pair of primaries – that is to say, green, orange and violet – you have the *complementary* or *secondary colours*. These complementary colours, the colours opposite the primaries on the colour wheel, are most important in colour designing. They give dynamic colour mixes and provide visual colour contrast, as opposed to the more harmonious and restful colour schemes provided by combining colours close to each other on the colour wheel.

(The names I have used for these six colours are those under which you can be sure that you are buying good-quality paints. Unfortunately, dyes and fabric paints are not as well organized and, like the cheaper boxes of children's paints, are given some very fancy names. All the dyer can do is ask the supplier for a 'green-blue' or a 'blue-red', and hope for the best. Alternatively, get the whole range and then do a series of test samples so that the palette of dyes can be arranged in the best possible way to allow successful mixing and matching.)

To sum up, then, the central fact of successful colour mixing and matching is that, in order to get the clearest colour mix with, say, Cerulean Blue you follow the direction of the bias. So if you mix Cerulean Blue with Lemon Yellow you will get the clearest possible greens. Conversely, if you want dull, muddy, sort-of oranges, mix Cadmium Yellow with the red that lies against the bias (Alizarin Crimson).

This brings us back to where we started – blue and yellow don't make green. Of course not, if you use Cadmium Yellow with Cerulean Blue, or Lemon Yellow with Ultramarine. And even less so if – ultimate horror – you mix Cadmium Yellow with Ultramarine. The reason for that is that Cadmium Yellow has got a lot of orange in it and Ultramarine has got a lot of violet in it, and orange and violet most certainly don't make green.

FROM PAINTS TO DYES

Not every weaver will want to dye his or her own yarns, in which case knowledge of colour mixing and matching will be all that is needed in making a choice from the offerings of the commercial yarn spinners, some of whom, at least, carry a good range of colours.

However, these are not always sufficient, especially if the precise matching of colours is critical to your work, so I am including some information on two classes of synthetic dyes which are readily available from suppliers and easily used in the home. (I am not including plant dyes here, simply because I do not use them myself, partly because I find the strong chemicals necessary to fix them harmful to delicate fibres, and also because they are not consistent in their effects – a colour obtained from a particular plant cannot be relied on to repeat itself exactly the next week, let alone the next year. For weavers who are interested in them, books on the subject are listed in the 'Further Reading' list.)

The two classes of synthetic dyes I would recommend are fast-to-milling (super milling) acid dyes and fibre-reactive (cold-water) dyes.

Fast-to-Milling (Super Milling) Acid Dyes

These dyes are sometimes referred to as hot-water dyes and are used for wool and other protein fibres. Silk, which has properties akin to both protein and cellulose fibres, can be most successfully coloured with these dyes too. The name fast-to-milling comes from their use in the woollen industry, for goods which require severe hot-water treatment to full or mill (shrink) the fabric during the finishing process. They have very good wash-fast properties due to the fact that their large dye molecules are slowly attracted to the yarn during a gradual heating-up process, which lasts about 30–45 minutes, and are further fixed by the acid dye-bath. The dye-bath is made even more acid by the addition of vinegar to it during the process, while Glauber's salts can also be added to ensure an even colour. It is not necessary to actually boil these dyes;

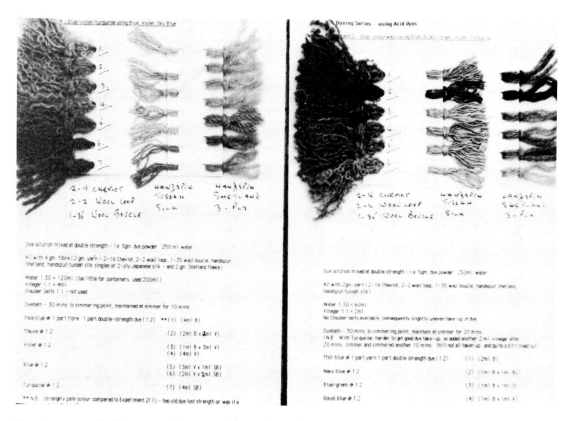

Keeping a record of dye sampling - pages from the author's dye book.

maintaining the temperature at just under boiling-point is quite sufficient. Therefore, they can safely be used with very fine wool and hair fibres.

Fibre-Reactive (Cold-Water) Dyes

This family of dyes is used on yarns made from cellulose fibres, and also on silk. Very fine wools can also be dyed by the cold-water method, but they will only have a pale tint compared with the colours silk and the cellulose fibre yarns will take up from the same dye bath. These colours are particularly wash-fast, and also light-fast.

Both families of dyes are bought in powder form and must be mixed into a solution with measured amounts of water. The whole dyeing process is carefully measured and controlled, so that once the particular proportions used to obtain a certain colour are known the process can be repeated and exactly the same colour obtained time after time. As with any other technique, it is a good idea to build up a collection of samples (tiny amounts of yarn, a few grams only, can easily be dyed) in order to give a quick and easy reference for colour matching and mixing.

Most suppliers give full instructions for using the dyes they sell, but I would like

---

The Dyeway Code
1. Wear rubber gloves and an impervious apron.
2. Wear a face mask to protect against chemical fumes and powder dyes.
3. Ventilate dye room adequately.
4. Keep separate utensils etc. for dyeing, *never* use cooking pots.
5. Label and date dyes and mordants; store them in a cool place, out of reach of children.
6. Wash your hands and all working surfaces carefully after dyeing.

Two safety points to remember

1. Make sure fire-fighting equipment is in place and in working order, and that you know how to use it.
2. Make sure that you have a properly filled first-aid box.

---

to recommend Frances and Tony Thompson's book *Synthetic Dyeing* to any weaver intending to colour his own yarns. It gives information on every type of dye and the many and various ways they can be used, and is quite invaluable.

Finally, no mention of dyeing in the home should be made without pointing out that chemicals (including all types of dye) are potentially dangerous and should be handled, stored and used with care. This is particularly important when there are children and pets around.

I do hope that this rather fast trot through the fascinating but complex subject of colour has been enough not only to give you a basis from which to start to develop your own colour palette but also to whet your appetite for more. If what you have read here, together with the suggestions for further reading, are of help in developing the creative satisfaction you get out of your weaving – well, what more could any author ask for?

DESIGN EXERCISE 1

A colour extraction exercise to obtain a colour scheme for a project.

You need:

• the six basic colours of gouache paints: Cadmium OR Spectrum Yellow, Lemon Yellow, Cerulean Blue, Ultramarine Blue, Alizarin Crimson, Cadmium OR Spectrum Red together with Black and White
• a medium paint brush (sizes 5–7)
• a fine paint brush (around sizes 0–2)
• watercolour paper
• a postcard reproduction of a fine-art painting (pick one that you really like, with large, definite shapes and strong colours in a good number of hues – nineteenth-century artists such as Matisse, maybe, or van Gogh would be good for this first exercise).

Using as a guide the colour extraction exercise in this book, based on the plumage of tropical birds, paint the various colours you see there round the edge of the card, getting as near as you can to a good colour match by mixing your eight paints.

Follow the same proportions as the artist has used (in the parrot card, there are large areas of various greens, then pale and mid-blues, reds and yellows). It is easiest to do this *all round* the card; in the example in the book this has not been done, for reasons of space.

Rearrange the colours into a strip of patches in an order that pleases you (perhaps from light to dark, or primaries with complementaries between), while still keeping to the proportions used in the original painting. Try to find at least five different colours. If you have more, discard those you do not like; if fewer try the exercise again, finding yourself another painting with more colours in it.

DESIGN EXERCISE 2

Creating harmonious and contrasting coloured stripes.

You need:

- paints, brushes and paper as in Design Exercise 1
- 2B and HB pencils
- stout card – mounting board, black one side, white the other, is perfect
- double-sided sticky tape

Draw two strips with either three or five patches in each (about 20cm² per patch gives a good idea of the colour).

Referring to the colour harmony and colour contrast arcs illustrated in the colour pages of this book, paint in one strip with harmonious colours that you like (those near to each other on the colour wheel) and the other with contrasting colours (those opposite each other on the colour wheel).

Match your choice of colours as closely as you can with short ends of yarn. (It is a good idea to start building up a 'yarn store' – buy up cheap end-of-range balls of yarn from shops and markets whenever you see them; embroidery shops provide small skeins of tapestry wools in a wonderful range of colours too.) If you can't find yarns in all the colours, cut out – or tear out, which gives an interestingly

textured edge – suitably coloured strips of paper from magazines and the like and use these to provide the colour for a cut-and-stick collage of your designs.

Now choose a short sequence of numbers – say, Fibonacci's (1, 3, 5), or the proportions of the Pythagoras theorem (3, 4, 5), or your house and postcode numbers (3, 1, 3, 9) – any combination you like, in fact, and make a series of stripes in each of the two colourways (say, 3, then 4, then 5 and then reverse 4, then 3 in five different red-oranges from Cadmium Red to Lemon Yellow; or the 3, 4, 5, 4, 3 in turquoise and green-blue mixes of Cerulean Blue and Lemon Yellow, contrasted with orange from Cadmium Red and Cadmium Yellow. Either stick the stripes down, if using paper, or 'wrap' the yarns, in the same way as described on page 96, using card about 10cm square with double-sided sticky tape at the back to anchor the yarns.

You can use each number in your series to indicate the number of stripes of a certain width (3 Cadmium Red, 4 red-orange, 5 Lemon Yellow, then reverse) or indicate the width of each stripe in wraps, pairs of wraps, or in, say, millimetres. It is your decision.

Try different combinations of colours and figures to give a whole series of stripes. The same sequence and colourway, done twice, once on to the white side of the mounting board, the other on to the black side, will demonstrate the effect these background colours have. The black will intensify the hues of the stripes, the white will make them appear more muted. Later, using the same stripe and colour combinations as a basis, you could try out some card weaving (see Chapter 12) to design some quick and easy checks.

DESIGN EXERCISE 3

A geometric design of stepped blocks.

You need:

- paints, brushes and pencils as in Design Exercise 1
- ruler, scissors, paper glue
- A4 cartridge paper pad, for paper on which to mount your design
- a picture of a cityscape of tall buildings (your photograph, or cut out a suitable one from a magazine. It is well worth while starting to build up a scrapbook of magazine pictures, to serve as both colour and pattern references – and as sources of tricky shapes to trace, too. Why do the work when a much better artist has already done it for you?)

The picture should be about 10 × 15cm. (Cut it down if necessary, by selecting just that part of it you like. Use a cut-out frame – like a card weaving frame – the size you need, and move it over the picture until you like what you see in your frame. This is a useful trick, and a series of different-sized frames is a handy thing to have in your collection. Even cut them out sweater-shaped, or whatever, to use in the same way.) Draw parallel lines lengthways on it, 20cm apart, and cut the picture into five strips. Stick the strips on to the bottom left-hand quarter of an A4 sheet of cartridge paper, with each strip parallel but stuck down 2cm higher than the previous one.

Use tracing paper to draw the vertical lines between each strip, and *every* horizontal line in each strip. Join these verticals and horizontals into a series of blocks (squares or rectangles) to form what you think is an interestingly random chequerboard pattern. Rub out lines which do not seem to be in the right place, 'cheat' and put in others if you feel they are needed, even if they are not in the original cityscape. ('Cheating' just does not exist in designing – after all, *you* are the designer, *you* are setting the rules, it is *your* checklist you are working to and you can change it as you please.)

When you are reasonably happy with the outlines of the shapes in your block design, rub the front of it with the HB pencil, turn it over and transfer the design to the other half of the paper; in other words, make a mirror image of it which will fill the bottom half of the A4 paper. By repeating the tracing and transferring, fill the top half of the paper, so you have a design of stepped blocks covering the entire A4 sheet. (If you are not keen on tracing, the mirror imaging can be done easily on a photocopier.)

Finally, using whichever series of strips of colour from Design Exercise 2 you like best, and working block by block from the bottom left-hand corner of the paper to the top left-hand corner (or in any other direction you prefer – working from the centre out would be another possibility, for example), paint in the colours according to the strip, repeating the sequence as many times as is necessary to cover the whole page.

11
Completing the Picture

In Chapter 1 we looked briefly at the probable origins of weaving, and at some of the tensioning devices, that is to say the looms, which have been and still are used to construct woven textiles. We then went on, in later chapters, to look in some detail at the various fibres used in weaving and finally to consider some of the ways we might use to take control of our work, to stamp it as our own personal creation.

So now, to complete the picture I have tried to draw, which so far consists of the actual tools of our trade and suggestions on how to use them to express our ideas, we need to look at some of the techniques of weaving. This means learning how to use a loom in the way that suits each individual best, using methods with which we feel comfortable, in order to achieve the work we want to do. I hope that this will then complete the picture by giving enough information on the basic techniques needed in order to make a start with weaving. Later you can select and discard from these basics; you can experiment and develop your work with them; you can add to them as and when you require.

GETTING STARTED

From my own experience the easiest way to learn the various weaving techniques is by actually doing them yourself – the 'take the frame in one hand and the cotton cord in another, and start warping' method. I know it seems to be stating the obvious, but in fact no amount of demonstration, or book learning for that matter, however expertly and clearly done, seems to work as well as doing it yourself, and making your own mistakes. For instance, you can be told a hundred times, 'Don't forget to secure the cross when you've finished winding your warp.' But you won't really appreciate the importance of the cross in a warp until you have taken your warp off the frame, having forgotten to tie it up, and realized to your horror that the whole thing is useless and that the last hour's work has been entirely wasted. The only good thing about such a disaster is that you will not make the same mistake again.

Another thing I have learned, often to my cost, is to make sure that you really know what you want to do before you start to spend your money. Weaving can be a very expensive craft to finance, but it can also be relatively cheap, providing you know what you are doing. It really is not a good idea (even if you have got the money) to spend large sums on a loom and then decide to try and learn to weave. Much better to start by making your own – yes, this is perfectly feasible, as you will see – collecting up some yarns, and then trying out some basic weaving steps at home. (Personally, I have always preferred to make a fool of myself in private and we all make some pretty silly mistakes when starting to learn a quite complex new technique.)

Then, a bit later, or at the same time – it just depends on how quickly you pick things up, and how well served your area is – look for a beginners' weaving course to join. You may find one run by your local college amongst its part-time adult and further education classes. Or there may be a weaver not too far away who gives private lessons – as I've said before, few weavers can entirely feed and clothe themselves by weaving alone. It is also certainly worth contacting your county weavers' guild for help and information. Finally, you may have a friend who weaves; in fact, I think many of us, those who are known in the trade as 'mature students', come into craft work for this reason. In that case, and if you don't think it will be the end of a beautiful friendship (and this can happen, so be careful – think of the sometimes dire results of husbands trying to teach their wives to drive), then negotiate a 'fee' and ask him or her to guide you through the first steps.

What all this boils down to is that, although it is by no means impossible (I know, because I did it myself) it is really not very easy learning even the basics of weaving just by teaching yourself. Apart from the fact that some of us find diagrams hard to figure out, books are only as good as the writer succeeds in making them, primarily to my mind by trying to anticipate all the questions and to answer them clearly and simply. So, in teaching yourself, you are constantly having to re-invent the wheel because there is no one there to show you the easy way, the short cut, the obvious solution to the problem – obvious, that is, once you have been told.

As well all this, there are two more considerations which I think are rather crucial. The first is the question of self-discipline: it is much easier to go to a class for a set number of hours each week, at a predetermined time and for a predetermined number of weeks, than it is to discipline yourself to spend a regular number of hours a day teaching yourself to weave. The second point is the question of human interactions. Most of us are naturally gregarious. We get on well with those of our fellow humans with whom we have interests in common, and we work and learn better in a group. Problems are not so awful when there are friends there to help solve them; and, conversely, there is a certain sort of horrible satisfaction in seeing others making even more of a mess of things than you are.

So, to anyone who wants to start weaving, my suggestion would be to try it out both by yourself and in company. That way you will soon, and relatively cheaply, find out if weaving really is for you. And if it is? Why, then you have the best of both worlds; you can make your worst mistakes in private and keep quiet about them if you want to; or you can take your problems to the class for solution. And all the while you are sharing ideas, tools and techniques with like-minded friends.

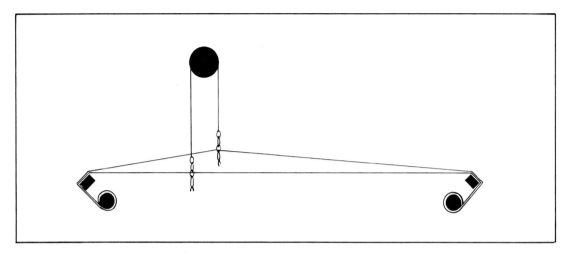

Two shafts – one harness lifting half the warps above the level of the other half to form a shed.

CONSTRUCTING WOVEN FABRICS

The main moving part of a loom is the *shaft* – hence *two-shaft* loom, *four-shaft* loom, *multi-shaft* loom, and so forth. The lifting of the shafts can be done in many ways: from simple manipulation by the fingers alone, through various combinations of fingers, sticks and string *heddles*, by *rigid heddles* and by wire heddles set in a frame – the usual method with four-shaft looms.

The purpose of the heddles is to lift the warp threads in each shaft so that a *shed* is formed. The weft is passed through this shed in the warp, and the action of passing the weft through different sheds on each pick (that is, with certain predetermined warp ends lifted and others not lifted) is how cloth is constructed.

In order to achieve a stable construction pairs of alternating picks of weft have to be taken through the warp, so that any warp ends left uncovered by the first pick will be covered by the second, returning pick. As an example, to form one shed the first shaft lifts all the even-numbered warp ends, and leaves the odd-numbered ends unmoved; so the first pick of weft goes over warp ends, 1, 3, 5, 7 and so on, and under warp ends 2, 4, 6, 8 and so on. To form the alternate shed, the second shaft lifts all the odd-numbered warp ends, and leaves the even-numbered ends unmoved; so the second pick of weft returns under warp ends 1, 3, 5, 7 and so on, and over warp ends 2, 4, 6, 8 and so on. For an illustration of this in simple, diagrammatical form, see the section on the basic weaves later in this chapter.

From the above it becomes obvious that a minimum of two shafts are required to weave. In fact many fabrics, particularly tapestry, do not need any more than these two alternating shafts. Any manipulation of the warp threads over and above this can easily be done with the fingers, as we shall see in the chapters on tapestry weaving. Additionally, stick manipulation of warp ends to form extra sheds can be used with any two-shaft loom to allow a great variety of complex weave techniques to be done. The only drawback is the slowness of hand-controlled weaving, as opposed to loom-controlled.

As a result, most cloth weaving is done on at least four shafts. But the fact that variations in the weave, requiring a greater variety of sheds, can be loom-controlled simply means that the work goes rather quicker – not that it is intrinsically any better. For these reasons weaving can be said to fall into two main categories: on two shafts, or on four or more shafts. The following chapters on the technique of weaving are divided accordingly – two-shaft weaving, including tapestry weaving is described first, followed by four-shaft weaving.

THE STRUCTURE OF WOVEN FABRICS

Before we get down to looking in detail at two- and four-shaft looms, and what kind of fabrics you can weave on them, there are factors which are common to all woven fabrics. The most obvious one of these is their actual structure, the interlacing of two sets of threads at right angles to each other. This makes them what is known as *double-element* fabrics (unlike knitting, crochet, lace, sprang, knotting and netting, for instance, in which one single element of yarn is manipulated around and with itself to form the fabric).

These two sets of threads are known as the warp and the weft. The warp threads are the first to be put in, the foundation upon which the weaving is constructed, as it were. They run along the length of the fabric, parallel to the selvedges. In a vertical loom they run from the bottom, where the weaver starts working, to the

top; in a horizontal loom they run from the front towards the back.

Warp yarns must be held under tension. This varies with the type of loom, with the kind of yarns being used and with the fabric being woven, but generally they need to be strong. They also need to be as smooth as possible in order that they can withstand the friction caused by the movements of the parts of the loom, and by the passage of the weft threads through them, without pilling or fluffing. Usually you will find the warp threads referred to as *ends* and their *sett* (the distance they are spaced apart) as *ends per centimetre (e.p.cm)*.

The weft threads are those which are passed from side to side at right angles through the shed made in the warp threads. (When I started out I helped myself to remember which was which by a simple trick: the warp threads, which have to be threaded first, have an *a* in them whereas the weft threads, which are put in second, have an *e* in them – and *a* comes before *e* in the alphabet. I rather fear that you can now see only too well the simple level on which my mind works.)

Yarns used for the weft, because there is little or no real strain on them, do not need to be as strong as those used as warps. Also, *fancy* or *novelty yarns*, such as *bouclé, slub, chenille* and *loop yarns* can be used to give textured effects. In fact, strips of cloth, most knitting and other types of yarn – not to mention a wide range of materials from plastic to metal, from beads to braids, from fur to feathers – can go into the weft if they will give the effect required. The only real limit is your imagination and the requirements of your design. Each side-to-side movement of the weft yarn through the shed in the warp is

95

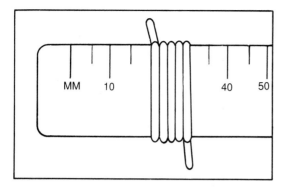

Yarn wrapped round a ruler.

usually known as a *pick* or, rather more archaically, a *shot*. Hence you will see the sett of a cloth calculated not only by the e.p.cm but also by the *picks per centimetre (p.p.cm)*.

The number of ends per centimetre needed for a warp is calculated in this way. Take a ruler, and a length of the yarn you intend to use for the warp. Wrap the yarn round the ruler, keeping each turn butted comfortably up against the previous one; the turns should not be pushed together too tightly, but neither should there be gaps between them so that you can see the ruler. When you have covered a full centimetre, count how many turns of yarn there are and note it down. (The written records of the various calculations you make when starting a new project – in a special notebook, perhaps – are always worth having for later reference. In the chapters on four-shaft weaving I will give a suggested weaving record sheet, but a general notebook is an additional useful tool of the trade.)

For a balanced tabby weave (see below) where the weft yarn is the same, or very similar, to the warp, then the necessary e.p.cm for the weaving project will be half the number of wrappings on your ruler.

Therefore, if you have wrapped 8 turns of yarn, a balanced weave using the same yarn in both warp and weft would need 4 e.p.cm and should be woven at 4 p.p.cm. Obviously, if you are going to use a thicker or a thinner weft yarn adjustments will need to be made, but this method gives you a starting-point from which to work out your calculations.

THE THREE BASIC WEAVE STRUCTURES

These three weaves can be done equally well on two shafts or on four or more shafts. Endless variations are made by manipulating sheds, either manually or with the loom, but they still all come back to one of these three main structures.

1   Plain Weave

As in darning, in this construction the weft thread is passed over and under alternate warp ends in the first pick; on the return pick, the weft thread passes over the ends passed under in the previous pick, and under the ends passed over in the previous pick. These two picks are then repeated until the required length has been woven. This is the simplest weave structure, and can be embellished by the use of yarns with a variety of texture and colour. Since the weave structure is classically simple, very fancy yarns and strong colour combinations can be introduced without overdoing the effect.

Because this is the simplest weave structure it is a good point to introduce the concept of *drafting* a weaving design in order to produce a *weave plan*. This is a way of expressing a woven structure, and the way the yarns interlace within it, in a

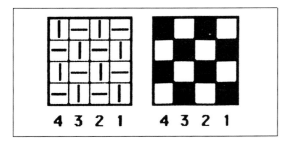

Weave plans (plain weave).

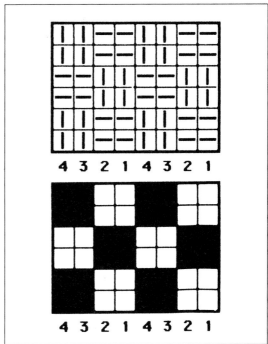

Weave plans (hopsack).

simple diagrammatical form so that it can be understood by any weaver. It is done on graph paper, which weavers call *point paper*, and the main thing to remember is that it is the gaps between the lines on the point paper that represent the warp and the weft threads. These threads can be drawn as horizontal and vertical lines in each square, and this method gives a very good visual impression of the actual structure of the cloth. However, it can be rather fiddly to draw, especially with more complex structures, so it is more usual to see the chequerboard method. In this, whenever a warp thread goes over a weft thread, the square is blacked in. So, in the diagram, the first shed has the odd-numbered ends raised, the second has the even-numbered ends raised.

Plain weave, when the sett is *balanced*, is often known as *tabby weave*. This is a construction in which the warp and the weft are equally spaced. For instance, the picks are beaten down on to the *fell* (the edge of the cloth at the front or bottom of the loom, at the point where the weaving is taking place) with a regular pressure, so that every centimetre of cloth lengthwise will contain the same number of picks as there are ends widthwise.

Hopsack or *basket weave* is another plain weave variation. In this, two or more warp ends are crossed by an equal num-

ber of weft picks. As an example, the first pick passes alternately over two ends and under two ends. The second returns over and under the same two ends as in the previous pick. The third pick then passes alternately over the two ends passed under in the previous two picks, and under the two ends passed over in the previous two picks. And the fourth pick is laid exactly in position over the third, thus completing one full hopsack repeat – in this case, what is known as a 2/2 hopsack. As you will see, it is much easier to demonstrate this in a weave plan than it is to try to explain it in words. The plan shows clearly that in the first two picks shafts 3 and 4 are raised, and in the third and fourth pick shafts 1 and 2 are raised.

By virtue of the fact that each pick and end in plain weave passes over and under each other pick and end, giving the closest possible interlacing of the threads, plain weave is the most stable of all fabrics. And given a sett which takes proper account of the thickness of the yarn or yarns used, and takes into consideration how much the finishing process will affect the yarns, and thus the cloth, plain weave can be used to make many types of cloth. At one end of the scale you might choose fine, smooth cotton yarn at a count of 2/18s, sett at a balanced weave of 16 e.p.cm and 16 p.p.cm. This would give you, after a really hot-water finishing to shrink and set it (as we discussed in the Chapter 3 section on cotton), a cloth as strong, smooth and stable as cotton sheeting. At the other end of the scale you can weave in a double hopsack – a 2/2 hopsack – using a 2/8s oiled Shetland wool. Loosely sett at 4 e.p.cm, lightly beaten down at 4 p.p.cm and, when the cloth comes off the loom, carefully hand-fulled in hot water and pure soap flakes, the yarn will fluff up and shrink on to itself. So, by careful control of the fulling process, you can give sufficient stability to a loosely woven fabric to create a light, soft Shetland shawl.

This property of fibres to shrink in the finishing process is a valuable tool in fabric design, and by deciding whether to shrink your yarn before or after you weave with it you are making a most important design decision. All machine-spun woollen weaving yarns are *scoured* (to remove dirt, grass seeds and the like). This process also removes most of the natural oil in the wool, lanolin, so this is put back into the yarn before it is offered for sale as oiled wool. This is because the oiled wool passes more easily through the parts of an industrial loom, and fluffs less; the same, but to a lesser degree, applies

with a hand loom. However, scouring does not greatly shrink the wool, so you can use it in the knowledge that it will still shrink appreciably in the finishing process.

Because a balanced tabby weave, woven at the correct set for that yarn, holds every pick and end of the yarn firmly in the tightest possible interlacing there is a minimum of shrinkage. But if you weave exactly the same yarn, at the same sett, in a 2/2 hopsack, individual picks and ends interlace with each other over two ends or picks instead of over every one. It is obvious that, held more loosely, the yarn will shrink more, depending on how long the individual *floats* are. (Floats or skips are the name given to either warp or weft yarns when they pass over more than one pick or end.) The longer the float, the greater the shrinkage, and you can use this fact to create interesting fabrics by combining, say, stripes of plain weave alternately with stripes of hopsack weave into a seersucker type of fabric. And with more complex multi-shaft looms you can weave alternating blocks of hopsack and plain weave to give fascinating bubble effects. All this in plain and simply tabby weave, just by exploiting the properties of the yarn you are using.

I hope these few examples will convey the versatility of plain weave, particularly when allied to the variety of design effects inherent in the properties of fibres, and that they will also show how even the simplest techniques can be used to express intricate design ideas.

2 Weft-Faced Plain Weave

In this variation the warp ends are spaced much further apart (usually at anything up to half the number of ends per cm required for a balanced weave using the same weft yarn). So, using the wrapped-ruler method of calculation, 8 turns of yarn round the ruler would necessitate warping up at about 2 e.p.cm). This is so that each pick of weft can be beaten right down on to the fell of the cloth, so that the warp threads are completely hidden – hence, of course, the name weft-faced. And hence also the fact that in the calculations for the sett of the yarn consideration of the type of weft yarn being used is, if anything, even more critical than for a balanced weave.

Because of the structure of this weave, it is usual to have different yarns in the warp and weft: the coloured and/or novelty yarn which will give the pattern to the fabric goes into the weft and an undyed cheaper yarn is used for the warp, normally cotton or linen. However, in the finest-quality flat-woven wool tribal rugs and furnishings it is traditional to use a thin, highly twisted and tightly spun wool warp to give greater flexibility to the fabric.

So the normal requirement for a warp, that it should be strong and smooth, is even more important in this technique. In every civilization, and in all parts of the world, this weave has been used for textiles which are required to be strong and hard-wearing – textiles such as floor cushions and rugs, tent hangings and dividers, wall hangings and bed covers, and carrying bags of all sorts from the once again fashionable carpet bag to Middle Eastern shoulder bags and Greek farmers' 'back-pack' sacks, not forgetting the multiplicity of bags required by nomadic tribes in which to pack and transport all their goods. Weft-faced textiles need to be woven on strong looms, with the warp

A Turkish shoulder bag made from an old, worn piece of flat-woven carpet, trimmed with an inkle band woven by the author.

yarns held under high tension, and are densely woven, thick fabrics. A good hard beat against each weft pick is needed in order to force it down on to the previous picks; therefore, if breakages are to be avoided, a strong, tightly spun warp yarn is essential.

Tapestry, Navajo wedge-weaving, and *Kelim,* (a flat-weave rug variation in which the different elements in the pattern are not interlocked, and therefore show the typical Kelim 'slit'), *skip-plain weave, pick-and-pick colour weave* – all these are

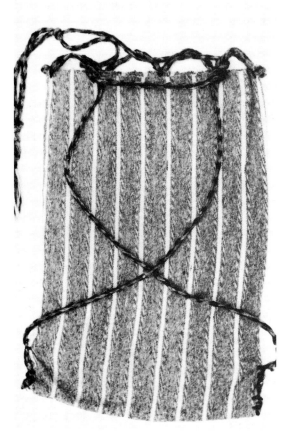

different techniques used in weft-face weaving. Textural interest may be introduced by the incorporation of fancy yarns and materials of almost any kind – providing, of course, the piece is a decorative one, and not functional; or by the use of various knotting and looping techniques – *Rya* (Swedish), *Ghiordes* (Turkish) and *Sehna* (Persian) knots or, when uncut, loops; or by textured weaves such as *twining, chaining*, and the various types of weft-twining weaves, including *soumak*; or by weaving, or *wrapping*, extra warps on the surface of the work.

3 Warp-Faced Plain Weave

This is the precise opposite of a weft-faced structure. Here the warp ends are placed very close together and are the visible part of the fabric – the weft is entirely covered by them and only shows at the selvages. Having wrapped the warp yarn round a ruler, about two-thirds of the number of yarn wraps are needed to give you the necessary ends per centimetre for the correct sett; as an example, 9 turns

A Greek farmer's 'backpack' sack woven in tabby weave with a cotton warp and wool weft.

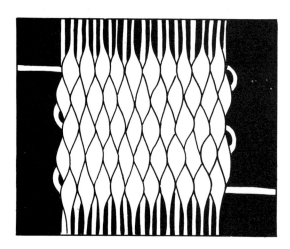

Warp-faced plain weave (left) and weft-faced plain weave (right).

round the ruler would suggest a warp of 6 e.p.cm. As with any weaving, the sett depends very much on the type of yarn being used for the face of the weave being seen – in this case the warps. The ruler-wrapping calculation can only be a starting-point; sample weaving is always essential when you are embarking on a new project if you are not to waste time, and valuable yarn, on hopelessly mis-sett fabrics which are likely to be useless.

Warp-faced fabrics, depending of course on the yarn used, can be very strong also. Since the pattern and colour in this fabric comes entirely from the warp yarns, dyed-warp techniques such as *ikat* come into their own here. Ikat is a technique in which the yarn hanks are tied to give resist patterns, and then dyed, before weaving – either the warp yarns only (single ikat) or both warp and weft (double ikat). Traditionally, narrow bands woven on primitive-type looms such as the backstrap, or small band-weaving looms like the *inkle loom*, are used to make straps, braids and bands for many tying purposes, or narrow woven strips are joined together to make bags and other household fabrics. Woven in heavy yarns on large looms, the warp-faced weave makes excellent rugs, while using a fine warp yarn with a thicker weft yarn beaten down hard into the close-set warps gives an interesting ridged effect, as seen in the strong furnishing fabric called *repp*.

One small final point about weave plans. Although tabby weave, weft-faced weave and warp-faced weave fabrics all look different, they are in fact all variations of plain weave and woven in exactly the same way; they all have exactly the same weave plan. In other words, it is only the sett of the cloth that is different, not the weaving technique.

SAMPLING

To conclude this brief run through some of the factors common to weaving on all types of looms, I would like to emphasize one most important point – sampling. In order to evaluate the quality and behaviour of the yarns, and the sett of the fabric in relation to the purpose for which it is required, sampling is as important a part of the design process as is the selection and development of source material. This is best done with sample weaves, which are finished in exactly the same way as the completed textile will be. Remember too that any sample smaller than about 25cm square is not going to give you a sufficiently accurate idea of the way the fabric will behave. Finally, I assure you that this sampling is *not* a waste of precious yarn – quite the contrary, it saves a great deal of time and money, not to mention dashed hopes, in the long run.

12
Simple Two-Shaft Frame Looms

The word 'simple' in this context can be a bit misleading, unless it is taken quite literally. By this I mean that since all a loom really has to do is to keep the warp threads in tension it can indeed be a 'simple frame' – but this does not in any way mean that the weaving done on it has to be simple. On the contrary, the most complex work can be made on a loom which is no more than a couple of bits of wood for front and back bars, and a few shed sticks (the backstrap loom). It is entirely possible to find that all that distinguishes the hand-controlled work made by an expert weaver on this two-shaft loom from a highly patterned cloth made on today's state-of-the-art shuttleless Jacquard loom is the time taken to do it. But time taken to weave, of course, is an important consideration, one has to take into account when choosing a loom. Since time is money, so they say, we have to consider how much of this valuable commodity we can afford to spend on our work.

There are a couple of other factors to think about too. Some people actually like the feeling of being absolutely in control, the tactile pleasure of being literally in touch with their materials. What is more, they just may not like machines. In fact, many people are downright bad with them. The moment they go anywhere near one, the wretched contrivance falls to pieces. And I can assure you that there is plenty of potential for falling to pieces

with a complex multi-shaft loom. Finally, even production weavers can find a use for a simple frame loom. For instance, I was once shown commercial samples produced by a freelance designer of superfine shirting fabrics for the top end of the men's market. With the yarns, colours and designs intended for the final fabrics, these complex little works of art were literally 'darned in' on a small card frame – the whole thing, frame and all, then being mounted for presentation to the potential manufacturer. This approach was chosen for its speed – it takes a very long time to thread up a large loom – and proves that even when time is money simple tools can be money-savers. And perhaps, to someone who spends most of his or her time working on a large loom, making samples this way gives the satisfaction of getting really close to the work every so often.

CARD LOOMS

I suppose the simplest weaving frame is a piece of card, stout enough not to buckle when the warp is wound firmly round it. If you haven't got any really thick card, glue together several layers of a thinner one until you are satisfied that it is strong enough. If you like, the top layer could be an attractive colour or texture – then you can leave the weaving on the card, which becomes its frame. Cut the card loom out square, oblong or circular in shape, or even cut it to the shape you want the finished piece to be. (I wove an owl once for a friend who collected owls of all sorts. It was one of those experiments which came off, and I thoroughly enjoyed doing it.) Small nicks in the edge of the card spaced at whatever ends per centimetre your warps will be will hold them in place. Then wind on your warp at an even and firm but not too tight tension. Finally, with a square or oblong loom, tuck a couple of strips of card – or more, if needed – in front, at the top and bottom, between the threads and the card. This tightens up the warp threads and makes them easier to weave on. You must tie the strips in position at each end to stop them from slipping out.

The reason why I suggest doing it this way, rather than winding the warp on really tightly, is that the weaving itself as it grows will tighten up the warp and, unless it is very strong, will bend the card as well as making it more and more difficult to weave. But if you have two or three strips of cardboard doing the tensioning job they can be taken out, one by one if necessary, to slacken off the tension as you weave. I find that this is a good tip for any kind of simple frame loom where you are winding the warp on to the loom itself. It also has the additional benefit of raising the top and bottom of the frame, and hence the warps, a little above the back. This bit of clearance makes it easier to insert the weft threads.

Do not forget also that if your piece of card is, say, 25cm square you can actually make a woven strip double that – 20cm wide (you need to keep in a little from the sides for ease of weaving, and the work tends to 'pull in' as it grows) and nearly 50cm long. All you have to do as your

weaving progresses is take out your card-tensioning strips, slide the work round the card until it is in position for comfortable weaving again, and then replace the tensioning strips. Continue this way until you join up with your first pick of weft, take your work off the card and you have a circle of cloth. Gather up the top, add a pompom and you have a woolly winter hat – or even a tea-cosy, if you prefer. Or stop a reasonable distance from the beginning of your weaving, cut through the warps, knot and trim the fringes and you have the first of a set of table mats. Alternatively, you could even make your card frame 25cm wide and 60cm long and, by weaving the double length of the frame, you can produce a scarf to go with your pompom hat.

These useful, versatile and, above all, cheap card looms can be made in a more conventional way too – with their centres cut out so that they are truly a 'frame' loom. The reason for doing it this way is that it is in fact easier to weave with a clear space in the centre rather than

Card frames and the tools for cutting them out of layers of thin card. One frame is warped up for use as a simple loom.

against the solid card back. I have made a series of card frames. They each have three layers, made from the large sheets of comparatively cheap card (not mounting board, which is much more expensive) that you can buy at any good art shop. (Mounting board does make a good, decorative final top layer if you intend to leave the work on the frame as part of the mounting process.)

A series might consist of three card frames, the largest 30×35cm, with a 4cm edge; the next, cut from the centre piece, 22×28cm; and the third 15×20cm, with a 2.5cm edge round it.

When I have stuck the three layers together I sandpaper down any uneven edges – I never find it easy to cut them absolutely accurately, even when using a sharp blade and a steel ruler in the proper fashion. Finally, I give the whole thing a couple of coats of clear wood varnish, just to give a bit of added strength. One more point: you can mark off the top and bottom of the loom in centimetres (before you varnish it) as a guide to spacing the ends when warping up. If you are marking a card frame which you intend to leave as part of the finished piece then do it on the back where it won't be seen. Equally, of course, you can notch the frame to hold your ends steady, but this does mean that you are tied to using that fixed number of ends per centimetre. I don't usually find that I have slippage problems with square or rectangular card frames, but if I do it is a simple matter to anchor the warp threads in place by sticking them down with some masking tape, back and front. Where notches really come into their own, however, is if you are weaving on an irregular shape – like my owl weave, for instance.

Having a measured guide on your frame is a good idea, though, so what I have done is to make myself a series of marked 'rulers' from thin wooden lath. These are stronger than card and so are useful with either the card looms or with the small wooden frame looms which we will discuss later. When warping is finished, the ties securing the rulers are loosened, and any card strips needed to give the warp its final tensioning are slipped under them and the whole bundle tied in place again. If you want to stick to card, just mark a couple of your strips in centimetres and tie them on before warping in place of the wooden lath, then carry on as above.

RINGS AND CYLINDERS AS FRAMES

There are other possibilities for small tensioning devices which can be useful for making one-off objects or small decorative pieces. Card frames can be cut in a circular shape but it is really easier to weave on a wire ring. Various sizes of ring can usually be found in craft shops or in shops selling lampshade-making materials. If the ring is covered with flat knots, perhaps in the yarn used for the warp, then the knots can be spaced out so that when the warp is threaded through – either every loop or every other loop – it is at the correct number of ends per centimetre. Alternatively, cover the ring closely with buttonhole stitch, and thread the warp through the stitches at the spacing you require.

Ready-made wire lampshade frames can be used as weaving frames. Obviously, you leave the weaving in place if it is a lampshade you are making, but suitably sized cylindrical ones can also be

A decorative tapestry calendar woven on a ring (Jo Tether).

lished and finished as you wish. Equally, I have seen most unusual soft toys made by the same methods. They really were little art objects, too, because the method of construction was so unexpected, the design ideas so original and the technical expertise so great that they lifted them out of the realm of children's toys into the area we discussed in Chapter 7 – where beauty (or, in this case, art) is in the eye of the beholder.

What all this means is that the sole basic requirement of a loom – tensioning the warp threads – allows almost anything which will perform this function to be used, and in fact one-off art objects often suggest the right tensioning device. For instance, a memento of a holiday might be woven on a V-shaped piece of driftwood, and incorporate found objects such as shells and pebbles picked up on the shoreline. (Be sure to clean and dry the seaweed and starfish before you use them or the resulting smells may bring back holiday memories rather too forcibly.)

SMALL WOODEN-FRAME LOOMS

These can come in many shapes and sizes, and at all prices but the ready-made version of even a small frame loom, together with all the ancillary tools, is expensive and so, since they are by no means difficult to make, it does seem to me to be sensible to do this (at least to begin with) and save one's money for buying beautiful fibres and yarns. As expertise grows, so comes the knowledge of one's weaving likes and dislikes; this is the point at which to go out and buy the loom that is just right, and will remain so for the rest of one's working life.

used as the frame for making a circular piece of cloth, which can then be cut off and made into a bag or purse. You can also bend the ever-useful strong card into cylinders of whatever size your project decrees. If the join is taped up it is not too difficult to slit the tape on the inside when the weaving is finished and remove the weaving without having to cut it – and the card cylinder only needs to be re-taped before being used again.

These simple cylindrical looms can be used as the tensioning device to make the basic structure for a three-dimensional woven soft sculpture. Taken off the frame, it is ready to be formed, stuffed, embel-

Canvas stretcher frames make suitable
tapestry looms.

Second-hand picture frames are often
suggested as suitable, but I think that
artist's canvas-stretcher frames, bought
from any good art suppliers, are better.
Not only are they stronger and smoother but their size can be tailored precisely
to your needs since the sides can be
bought unassembled in many lengths.
So, to make a small frame 40 × 50cm, you
get two 40cm lengths and two 50cm
lengths. Assembled, with the corner
wedges sold with them in place to give
added stability, this gives you a quickly
made strong frame. And, being equally
quickly taken to pieces, the two 50cm
sides can be reassembled with two 65cm
ones, to give you a larger 50 × 65cm
frame. Finally, by getting two 75cm
lengths you can increase your frame size
to 65 × 75cm – which is probably as big
as can be comfortably hand-held. So for
the very reasonable cost of eight lengths
of canvas stretcher frame you have
made yourself three different sizes of
frame loom.

Since the face of the frame is all in the
same plane, as with the card frames it
does help when putting in the weft

threads if you raise the top and bottom
above the level of the side pieces before
starting to warp up. I do this with a combination of the marked wooden rulers
mentioned above plus thin strips of lath
tied or taped on to the frame at each end.
If the warp ends start to tighten up too
much, a strip of lath can be taken out to
slacken them off.

Warped directly on to the frame in the
usual figure-of-eight method which is discussed fully in Chapter 15, the length of
weaving is restricted to, at most, four-
fifths of the length of the frame. Even if
you use a large sail needle to darn in the
wefts as you get near the top, the warp
will tighten up too much to allow you to
get any closer to the frame. This restric-
tion on the length may not cause a problem in many projects, but, if it does, there
is a way to get round it. By winding the
warp off the frame to the measured length
you require (an explanation of the method
also comes in Chapter 15) you can then
weave a piece that is almost double the
length of the frame.

This is done by laying the wound warp
out flat and slipping two pieces of dowelling rod into the loops at each end, and
then spreading the warp ends out to the
required width over the rods. After this,
lay the frame face down in the centre of
the warp, bring the rods as close together
as they will go (this, of course, depends
on the length of the warp) and tie them
together at the back of the frame. Turn the
frame round and, using the marked ruler
as a guide, spread the warp ends evenly
over the top and bottom of the frame at
the predetermined ends per centimetre.
Give a final tighten to the cords that are
securing the rods together and you are
ready to weave.

As you get uncomfortably near the top

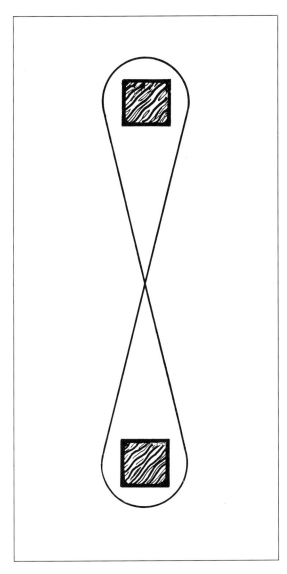

Winding a figure-of-eight warp on the top and bottom bars of a simple frame loom.

weaving has come through a full circle and has reached the rod at the other end of the warp.

This method is actually an adaptation of the way large vertical rug looms, of the type used particularly by American Indian tribes such as the Navajo, are warped up. It is also very similar to the working method used with the more primitive of the central Asian, Turkish and North African looms, which are used to weave both flat-woven and knotted rugs – though some do have a cloth roller on which to wind the finished work. More modern looms have both warp and cloth rollers, respectively at the top and bottom of the loom.

These big looms are discussed in detail in the next chapter, but are mentioned here briefly to emphasize the two benefits of warping off the loom. Making the warp separately and putting it on the loom in such a way that it can be moved allows you not only to have a warp longer than the frame of the loom but also to place the work at a comfortable weaving position. This latter point is quite a consideration, even with a small hand-held loom. With these I find that about one-third of the way up is the best position at which to get the biggest possible shed opening, but with a large loom it is obviously much more critical. You have to be able to position the fell of the cloth (the point at which you are actually weaving) at a comfortable height in front of you as you sit before the loom.

I think this connection between the two types of frame loom also illustrates rather nicely something I have mentioned before – that small tensioning devices should not be despised. They can be incredibly versatile and useful in many of the same ways as their larger counterparts.

of the frame, you should loosen the rod ties, slide the warp round the frame (just as with the small card frame), tighten the ties again and respread the warp ends. Continue weaving in this way, moving your work every so often to a more comfortable weaving position, until your

HOME-MADE WOODEN-FRAME LOOMS

Finally, I'd like to suggest just one more variation on the theme of small hand-held weaving frames, and that is the completely home-made one. Let me say here first that I am no carpenter, except in so far as I suppose people who are reasonably good with their hands one way can often use other simple hand tools too, and that, although some of my friends are blessed with husbands who are brilliant workers in wood, I'm afraid that this is not so in my case. I have just had to 'do it myself' and I can assure you that it is very easy.

The wood I use for small frames is easily found in any timber merchant or do-it-yourself store. It is a softwood, cut and planed, giving a finished size of 2.5 × 1.5cm. For a larger size of hand-held frame, the one which I felt is as big as can comfortably be held (65cm × 75cm), I have used the same type of planed softwood in a size which used to be known as '2 by 1' (inches) and which now seems to be around 4.5 × 2cm. This thicker, stronger wood also allows me to make a collapsible loom which can be broken down into its component parts and carried around with the work in progress rolled up on it. And buying the wood ready planed means that there is the minimum of sandpapering to be done to get it smooth enough to weave on.

Two versions of small home-made tapestry frames. The larger collapsible frame has a tensioning device.

A detail of the tensioning device. In these frames, two screws are necessary to keep a corner at right angles.

The benefits of actually making the frame rather than buying the canvas stretchers and assembling it are not really financially significant, since wood is not very cheap anyway – unless you happen to have a length of the right size lying around at home. The reason I do it is really because I find the finished frame easier to work on. This is simply because the top and bottom rails, instead of being flush with the sides, are set above them and therefore I have more room to pass the weft through the warp without hav-

ing to bother about strips of card or lath to raise the level of the ends. Of course this means of construction is nice and easy for the untutored carpenter – compared, that is, with making dovetailed or mitred corners.

Even with the small frames it is necessary to put in two screws to hold each corner, or at least in two diagonally opposite ones, otherwise the structure will not remain rigidly rectangular but will slide all over the place. (Screw them in one from each side, if that is easier.) With the big collapsible frame I use nuts and bolts rather than screws, as they are easier to remove – particularly if you put on a butterfly nut. (Put the nut on the back of the frame and the rounded, smooth end of the bolt on the front, otherwise you will keep getting your yarns snagged up.)

On the bigger frame I have added a refinement by way of a tensioning device. This can be used both if the work to be made on the loom is within the size of the frame and if it is to be longer. It is a piece of fairly thick dowelling (mine is 1cm in diameter) fastened to the top of the frame with long bolts. The top of each bolt has a sleeve slipped over it in the form of a wire coil or spring. Direct warping on to the loom is over the bottom bar of the frame and over the dowel. When warping is finished, the nuts on the bottom of the long bolts are tightened up against the spring until the required tension is reached. With a warp made off the loom, the warp ends go over the bottom bar and the dowel, not the top bar as with the smaller frame.

One final, quick point about small frame looms. You may sometimes see them with a staggered line of small headless nails set into the front face of the top and bottom bars. These nails in fact serve the same purpose as the notches in a card loom. The warp is wound round them, and consequently is held securely at the ends per centimetre at which the nails are spaced. But, as with the notched card frames, this means that weaving on that loom can only be done at the pre-set e.p.cm, or at the variations which using every other nail, every third nail, and so on, will give you. I feel that this limitation on the sett of the work restricts the value of the nail frame, but that is just my personal preference; other weavers might not agree with me.

Another version of the nail-frame loom that I have seen mentioned (although I have never tried the method myself so cannot really comment on its value) is similar to the notched-card frame which I shaped for my owl project. In this a piece of hardboard or plywood is cut to, say, a simple T-shaped garment shape. Wooden battens, set with nails placed at the e.p.cm required, are fitted top and bottom to hold the warp ends in the correct position to enable the weaver to weave the actual garment shape.

Garment shaping on the loom is popular with some weavers who find the trauma of cutting into their precious handwoven cloth for cut-and-sew garments just too much to bear. There are two ways in which it can be done: either by means of a purpose-shaped frame loom like the one described here, or on a multi-shaft floor or table loom. With the latter, by using a discontinuous weft technique similar to tapestry technique and weaving according to the outline of a garment-shaped *cartoon*, the actual garment shape can be woven. (A cartoon is a drawing of the design or, in this case, shape.) Whether either of these methods is adopted is again very much a question of the individual choice of the weaver. In other words, if you like the sound of the idea then try it out and see whether it works for you or not.

13
Floor-Standing Vertical Two-Shaft Frame Looms

These looms seem to me to be an obvious and logical development of the ancient Greek warp-weighted looms, and tomb illustrations show that they were certainly in use at the same time as the Egyptian horizontal ground loom. This latter is a type of primitive loom which, since it can if necessary be carried from place to place with the work in progress on it, is still used by semi-nomadic people in many parts of central Asia, the Near East, and North and West Africa.

The minimum requirement of a vertical loom is really no more than a pair of very strong (usually wooden) uprights, often set into the ground or fastened to the main beams of a house or hut. The top and bottom bars are then fastened to the uprights in a variety of ways and, with no more than these four main pieces, the weaver is in business. The intrinsic strength of the construction makes it eminently suited to the weaving of heavy weft-faced household textiles such as floor and wall covers, bags, bedcovers, and so on – which is what they have been used for all over the world. Only their non-portability somewhat restricts their use; you need to stay in the same place at least long enough to make the article. They are far too heavy, even if their construction allowed them to be dismantled, to load on to some poor camel – its protest noises would, with some justification, be even more peculiar than usual.

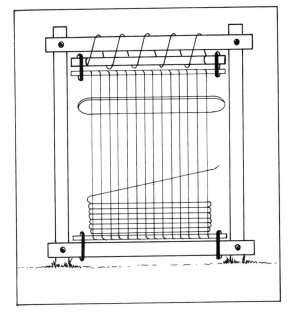

The Navajo loom.

Probably the best-known modern versions of these ancient looms are those used by the weavers of the North American Salish and Navajo Indian tribes. There is a nineteenth-century oil painting, reproduced in Eric Broudy's *The Book of Looms*, which delighted me when I first saw it some years ago. A Salish Indian woman sits at her loom weaving a blanket, while beside her is a small, rather cross-looking and obviously recently clipped white dog – very much of the spitz type that I was breeding and showing at that time. Since I occasionally used

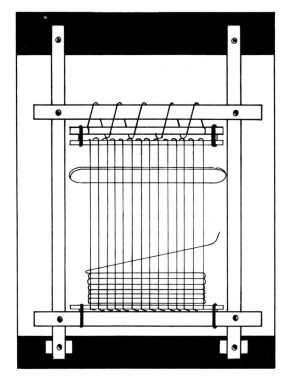

Designs for indoor looms – stayed on roof beam.

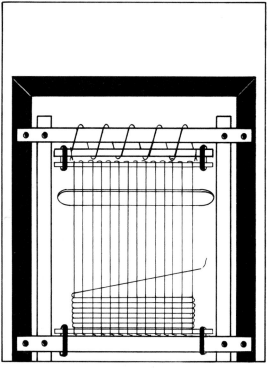

Design for indoor looms – and door frame.

to spin the fur combed from my dogs, I was most amused at the picture – and to learn that apparently the Salish used to keep these dogs especially for the soft hair they clipped off them.

Most of these upright looms are very similar in construction and although warping them varies a bit in detail it really falls into the two basic categories discussed in the last chapter – the on-the-loom and off-the-loom methods. Side posts are driven as far as necessary into the ground outdoors, or a couple of conveniently placed trees could be used. Alternatively, indoors, they are driven a short way into the earth floor of the hut, with the tops nailed or lashed to crossbeams in the roof timbers. In this

case, the sides of the loom can be made to slope away a bit at the top – the slight angle makes weaving more comfortable. Alternatively, while the roof beams are used as one fixing point, the bottom of the timbers are stayed to the wooden floor by being secured to large chocks of wood, or to a beam fastened down on to the floor. I have even seen it suggested that a door-frame serves as a good support for an upright loom – though how you get through the door once your work is on the loom I cannot imagine. To sum up, the main features of these looms are their strength, rigidity and steadiness – all of which can be reproduced in a home-made version. Perhaps they cannot be made quite so easily as the small hand-held weaving frames, but vertical looms are certainly not all that difficult.

MAKING YOUR OWN VERTICAL-FRAME LOOM

I think probably there are only two methods, and two materials, in which one can realistically set about this task; carpentry, using wood; and metalwork, using tubular (scaffolding) steel. Both methods will produce a loom which fulfils the criteria set out above – strength, rigidity and steadiness – so which method is used depends entirely on the maker and his or her friends who can be roped in to assist. (I do not honestly think that this is a job for just one person; perhaps I should say that it would be very much more easily completed with some help.)

However, for the purpose of this book I will stick to suggestions for a wooden version. Not only is it probably more user-friendly, since wood is the material from which most looms are made, but also it is the only one on which I can speak with any authority at all. I can do a little simple carpentry but I know nothing about working with metal.

When planning to build a wooden upright loom, anyone who is lucky enough to number among family and friends a really competent woodworker can put in warp and cloth rollers top and bottom, a pedal system of shaft lifting, and a batten to hold reeds of various sizes. All this helps to speed up work and would give a loom comparable to the best uprights money can buy. In fact, I think it would be even better because it would have been made to the individual weaver's specifications.

However, there is no reason why even a simple design of loom should not have at least some of these refinements so those of you whose woodworking knowledge is somewhat limited should not be discouraged: you will still end up with a valuable and useful tool, not to mention the satisfaction of having done it all yourself. Therefore, I will stick to the basics. Additions will suggest themselves to the more skilful woodworkers (you can always go and have a look at looms for sale, or send for illustrated catalogues, to give yourself ideas); the others, those with my level of skills, will, I hope, find something useful in my suggestions to get them going.

What Will you Weave on the Loom?

The first thing to decide is what you are going to weave on your loom. Until you have done this you cannot realistically make a decision on its dimensions. Unfortunately, the two main textile constructions likely to be woven on this type of loom may well be rather different: the wall-hung decorative tapestry, which is often wider than it is long; and the floor rug, which is normally longer than it is wide.

If you think you are going to weave both, but rugs more often than tapestries, you will want to make your loom higher than it is wide; but if the tapestries you intend to weave are likely to be fairly large ones, you do have a problem. There is a way round it, a way of weaving tapestries which are wider than the loom, and that is to weave them on their side. Although you weave up the length of the loom, the design that emerges on the face of the tapestry actually runs from one side to the other – that is, the width of the tapestry runs the length of the loom. This is in fact the traditional way the huge medieval tapestries were woven, and it is still the best way for certain designs, as we shall see in the next chapter, so you are doing nothing strange by adopting this method. And, of course, if you are making smaller tapestries whose width is not greater than that of the loom, there is no problem – you weave them whichever way suits the design.

Alternatively, if you think you are likely to be weaving only tapestries (or mainly tapestries, with just the odd rug), then make your loom wider than it is high. You can then comfortably weave tapestries, both large and small, either horizontally or vertically as your design suggests. If you do decide to weave a rug, you are not using the full width of your loom, of course, but that does not matter; and by warping off the loom you can weave a rug of whatever length you want – either nearly twice the height of the loom if you adopt the method demonstrated with the hand-held frame looms in Chapter 12, or as long as the clearance of your roller can accommodate if you incorporate one with the bottom beam (see below).

Where Will You Keep the Loom?

One more rather important point to consider whilst on the subject of the size of the loom frame is where the loom is going to live. It is a large item, and not too easy to move around the house. The perfect answer, if you are lucky enough to have your own workroom, is to build it in to the position you have selected for it. That way you get valuable extra rigidity, and can also organize other factors such as

positioning the lighting so that it falls properly on your work. If this is not possible and the loom is going to have to live *en famille*, then you have different problems. For instance, you will want to have it as near a wall as possible, or at least positioned so that it can easily be pushed back out of the way when not in use, to make sure that it is not too obtrusive. Considerations of height and, more important, width are also likely to figure even larger in your calculations.

A bonus point in the latter case is that work in progress on a loom is really rather nice to look at, and in fact can prove quite a talking-point with friends – not to mention perhaps bringing in some orders. So don't despair if the loom has to be in your living-room. Much as I like being able to spread myself in my workroom, I have to admit I rather enjoyed myself in the days when I wove in the living-room. The fire, the radio, the tape player and the television were all conveniently to hand, and family and friends passing through, commenting, making suggestions or just talking helped with what can sometimes, like so much other craft work, be rather a lonely business.

The Basic Construction

Having decided on the size of the loom, and where it is to live, you have in effect more or less decided on its construction. If it has to be free-standing, so that it can be pushed out of the way when not in use, then it needs to be made on a solid base so that it cannot fall over. If it is to be in a fixed position in the workroom then it is best to lengthen the side pieces beyond the bottom and top bars, and bolt these ends either to chocks or to a piece of timber securely fastened to the floor, and to a piece of wood attached through the ceiling to the beams above. If, however, the weaver likes working at a loom set back at a slight angle, and if the loom can be positioned close to a wall, then it can be angled back and the top bolted to a piece of wood attached to the wall. Really, the variations in constructional possibilities for a fixed loom depend entirely on where you are putting it, and also to the construction of your house – and, of course, whether you are allowed to start bolting bits of wood to floors, walls and ceilings.

Uprights, Top and Bottom Beams and Crossbars

The timber used for the sides depends on how you want to fasten top and bottom beams and crossbars to these two main uprights. If you choose to have a series of holes or slits in the uprights through which the top beam, and perhaps the crossbar, is fitted, then you must use timber of deep but narrow dimensions – about 20 × 5cm. The crossbars can either be hollow tubular steel or timber not quite as big as the side pieces, say 10 × 3cm. The important thing is that they do not bend when the warp is put on under tension.

The benefits of this method are that it gives a good deal of flexibility as to the actual height of the loom. For large projects the top bar can be put into the highest holes; for smaller ones it can be set so as to be at a comfortable height in front of you as you sit working at the loom. The

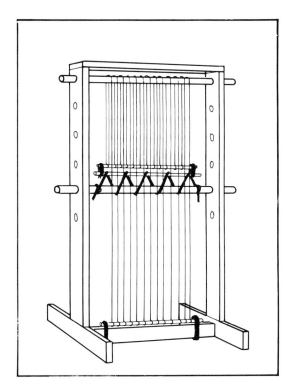

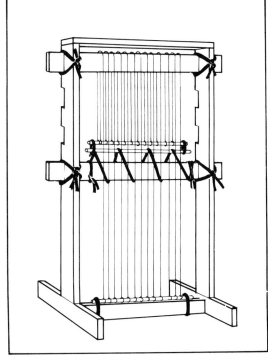

Designs for free-standing upright looms with crossbars supported in holes in the side beams . . .

. . . and in notches in the side beams.

snag is that because the weaving face, which is determined by the position of the top and the bottom beams, is set rather far back you will have to allow a really good gap between the side of your weaving and the sides of the loom, otherwise you will have difficulty in inserting your shuttles in to the shed (the same problem as with the card looms and the hand-held frames made from artists' canvas stretchers). This, in effect, means making the loom frame wider than it needs to be.

The alternative method of fastening the top beam to the uprights, and a crossbar too if you wish, is by notching the uprights so that the cross members fit in and can be lashed into place. Alternatively, bolt uprights and beams together or stay them with metal plates and slot just the crossbar. In the latter case, I would suggest that the beams are fastened to the face of the side uprights, as we did with the small home-made frame, so that they stand proud of them. This does away with the problem of the weaving face being set uncomfortably far back.

Both these designs give some choice of weaving lengths and positions so, all things considered, this is the loom construction I would go for myself. In fact I have the timbers ready for it – its just a question of finding the time. Where, I wonder, did I hear that cry before?

Warping Methods

If you have made the main frame, the sides and the top and bottom bars – perhaps in a doorway or stayed to the roof beams – but have not made provision for a crossbar, there are other options, and you need to decide before going any further how you will usually be warping up the loom, on or off the loom. Then you

can decide on your choice of refinements to the basic construction you have made.

The first warping option is to wind the warp in a figure-of-eight configuration straight on to the top and bottom beams – in fact, exactly as with the smaller frames described in the last chapter. This is assuming that the height of the room allows you to make the frame large enough to take the full length of your work, for example with top and bottom bars set 2 metres apart, which would give enough space to weave an average-sized rug 1.85 metres long. An alternative, if you have a long enough wall, is to set the uprights 2 metres apart and the top bar only 1.25 metres from the bottom bar. On this version of the loom (which is, in effect, the rug loom set on its side) you can weave your tapestries since they will not normally be more than 1.1 metres high, and can be up to 1.85 metres wide.

This method of warping, though simple, has a snag: it is not easy to keep a good tension on the work, and with a large loom it is not really possible to use tensioning strips, as I suggested doing with hand-held frames. So, instead of warping actually on to the top and bottom bars, I would advise trying one of the following methods.

Wind the warp off the loom, thread thick dowelling sticks through the loops at each end, spread it evenly across the sticks and lash them to the top and bottom beams. If the warp stretches or contracts as work progresses, it is an easy matter to tighten up the lashings to re-tension the warp.

Alternatively, warp on the loom but with a tensioning bar secured to the top beam with long bolts and springs, as described for the larger frame looms in the last chapter. The warp is wound in the usual figure of eight between the tension bar and the bottom crossbar, and the bolts can be tightened up or slackened off as necessary to tension the work.

Leaving aside considerations about the length of the project, and of making proper tensioning arrangements, there is another problem to take into account when warping direct to the top and bottom beams, or to sticks lashed to them, and that is the fact that the level at which you are weaving, the fell of the work, cannot be adjusted. This means that you have to work out a method of raising yourself to the level of your weaving as the work progresses.

Here are two possibilities. The first is to raise whatever it is you are sitting on – a telescopic chair would be a comfortable, if rather expensive, solution. The second is to raise yourself; first sit on the floor, then on stools of varying heights and finally stand to weave. If these options do not attract, you will have to make an arrangement, as with the small frames, that allows you to move the warp round the frame to reposition it at a comfortable level for weaving as you sit in front of it.

This can be done quite easily, in fact. Try winding the warp off the loom and slipping two extra crosspieces into the end loops; either thick dowel (broomhandle thickness) or 4.5 × 2cm timber should be strong enough to prevent bending. These crosspieces are then lashed together at the back of the loom, as with the small frames.

Alternatively, there is the warping method using the extra crosspiece secured either through holes or notches in the uprights. The warp is wound as shown in the diagram of the Salish Indian method of warping their looms. Each pass starts and finishes at the extra crosspiece,

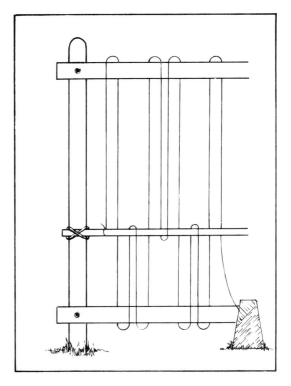

The Salish loom (warping detail).

and goes backwards and forwards between it over the top and the bottom beams. To adjust the level at which you are weaving, just release the crosspiece, slide the whole warp round the loom, and tighten up again in the new weaving position.

A final design option to consider is a cloth roller used in conjunction with the bottom beam. A circular piece of wood is preferable and one of about 5cm diameter is the minimum for a large loom; a piece 5cm square with four slats screwed the length of each face to round it off would do. It should be cut to a length just less than the distance between the sides, with bolts set into each end and threaded through the side bars just above the bottom beam. (It would be a good idea to bring the face of the bottom beam forward, by bolting on an extra piece of wood. This gives more clearance for the roller.) A ratchet and cog wheel on one end can be used to lock the roller into position, or a wooden handle which is lashed to the side beam is another possible method of securing it.

When using a roller, warp off the loom and slip crosspieces into the end loops. One of these is secured to the back of the loom, in the slots or notches. The other is tied to the cloth roller. When the level at which you are weaving needs adjustment, loosen the crosspiece in its notch, and replace it one notch higher. Wind the slack of the woven fabric on to the cloth roller until the work is in the right position and the warp is well tensioned. Then lock the cloth roller and continue weaving.

Using the various warping methods suggested here, rather than warping directly on to the frame of the loom, will help to maintain a good tension on the warp while work is in progress. Additionally, these warping variations allow textiles almost twice the length of the loom to be woven, and to be quickly repositioned to a comfortable weaving position as the work grows. Which version you choose is, as always, up to you.

SOME USEFUL WEAVING TOOLS

There are various tools which are generally used for weaving on frame looms. Admittedly, you can lift warp ends and insert the weft with your fingers alone or, at most, with a darning or upholstery needle, but it might get a bit tedious after a while – especially on a big frame. So, as with everything else, the choice of tools used is something about which each weaver makes a personal decision.

There is, nevertheless, no real harm in starting to collect up some small tools, quite a few of which can be home-made, and many of which will serve a whole range of weaving projects. (I often find it quicker to use some of my small *stick shuttles*, rather than the more usual *roller* or *boat shuttles*, when I'm weaving narrow loom-controlled inlays in several colours on my dobby floor loom.) More expensive aids to weaving can be left until later, when experience will have shown exactly what is likely to be most useful. Also, many weaving courses will be able to lend looms and tools to students.

Probably the most useful tools are *pick-up sticks* and *shed sticks*, and stick shuttles. All these can be bought either from craft shops or mail-order suppliers. They are made from hardwood – usually beech – and can be bought in a great number of sizes and designs at no great cost. However, they can equally well be made from lengths of softwood lath cut, shaped and finished by the weaver to his or her precise requirements. Width, thickness and length really depend on the frame with which the shuttles are to be used, and can range from 2–3cm wide and 4–5mm thick for sticks and shuttles suitable for the smallest frames up to 5cm wide and nearly 10mm thick for shuttles to use with a full-size rug loom.

Shed sticks and pick-up sticks need to be a little longer than the width of the frame they are to be used with. If you are using the frame for fabric weaving rather than for tapestry, the shuttle length needs to be at least the width of the piece being woven, so that it can be put through the shed in one pass. Trying to pull through one that is too short is fiddly. (Big, heavy

Various weaving tools including stick shuttles, a pick-up stick, smaller shuttles, comb beaters, tapestry bobbins and threading hooks.

rug shuttles of this length would be rather unwieldy, though, so you may find them rather shorter. But using a bigger loom, with its bigger shed, means that you can usually pass the other hand through and grab the end as it comes across.)

However, if you are doing tapestry weaving things are different. This technique involves what is known as a *discontinuous weft* – one in which each weft pass does not consist of a single thread extending the full width of the weaving, but of several threads of different colours linked together across the width of the work.

There are various ways of packaging the weft yarns, considered in detail in the next chapter. Usually, what are known as *tapestry bobbins* are used. These are not so easy to make unless you have wood-turning tools, although at a pinch small lengths of thin notched dowelling will do. Alternatively, you can make a tool with a hook at each end out of lath and use this to pull the weft threads through the shed. Odd lengths of the same thin dowelling you can use for tapestry bobbins are also useful as *leash sticks*, and this is considered at greater length in Chapter 15.

Netting shuttles, which also do very well as small weaving shuttled, can be bought from ship's chandlers or from shops selling yachting supplies. Being made nowadays of a synthetic material (nylon, maybe, I'm not really sure), they are nice and smooth, and come in a variety of sizes which will suit most frame looms.

Finally, you need some sort of tool with which to beat your weft down on to the fell of the work as you weave. When you are weaving a tabby-weave fabric right across the width of the loom you can usually do this by using the shed stick or a pick-up stick. With tapestry techniques woven in a weft-face weave you really need something heavier, but it can be quite narrow because usually you are weaving backwards and forwards across small areas of pattern rather than right across the full width of the work. With small frames, a fork from the cutlery drawer is the favourite beater of a lot of tapestry weavers; mine is what is often known as an 'Afro hair-comb' and can be found in most chemists amongst the brushes, combs and hair clips. They are usually very smooth, are wider than a fork and have a nice, chunky, comfortable handle.

As well as these cheap and easily available versions there are, of course, many variations on the beater theme which can be bought from suppliers – from small wooden ones with metal teeth for light work through larger wooden metal-teethed ones weighted by an iron inset for medium-weight beating right up to heavy, beautiful and extremely expensive metal (often bronze) ones for beating down thick tapestry-weave or warp-faced rugs. But, at least to start with, something cheap and simple is probably the best answer.

14
Introduction to Tapestry Weaving

Tapestry is a word readily recognized as referring to a textile, but nevertheless there is often confusion between tapestry in the embroidery sense – a form of surface patterning by means of stitchery on a loosely woven cloth base, usually canvas these days – and woven tapestry, in which the base (warp) and the pattern (weft) are constructed together.

I have a suspicion that tapestry is a well-known textile today largely due to the popularity of canvas work rather than to familiarity with the woven form, particularly in this country, where the craft of the handweaver is so little considered. However, my *Pocket Oxford Dictionary* still defines tapestry as 'a thick textile fabric in which coloured weft threads are woven (orig. by hand) to form pictures or designs; embroidery imitating this, usu. in wools on canvas', so I think we have good authority for saying that our tapestry came first. Actually, this makes sense when you think about it. The closed shop operated by the male-dominated medieval weavers' guilds would have prevented women making these household furnishings for themselves (women were only allowed to do the spinning – hence *spinsters*) so it would have been quite logical for those who could not afford to buy such expensive luxuries to find a way of getting the same effect without weaving.

F.P. Thomson's definitive book *Tapestry – Mirror of History* tells us that tapestry 'has been called "the elegant art" . . . the "mirror of civilisation" – [whose] origins extend back . . . to the time when man's ancestors were learning to make tools'. He goes on to say that elegance with popularity attracts imitation so the name was borrowed to describe other, often inferior, textile constructions. True tapestry is defined by the structure of the material, and in the strict sense is only to be used for 'a hand-woven material of ribbed surface resembling rep, but into which the design is woven during manufacture, so that it forms an integral part of the textile'.

Egyptian tomb paintings dating from *circa* 3000 BC clearly show weavers working on a vertical tapestry-type loom, with much the same tools as we use today. The biblical Book of Exodus, Chapter 26, has the earliest written records of woven fabrics, and appears to refer to a tapestry-type fabric; while it is assumed that, because the Latin name for tapestry (*tapetium*) is taken from the Greek, the Greeks taught the Romans how to weave tapestries. Greek vase illustrations dating to about 500 BC show the warp-weighted upright loom being used by women to make what are evidently wall hangings which appear, from the tools illustrated, to be tapestry-woven. (It seems that wall hangings predated floor rugs. All these old illustrations show floors decorated with tiles, mosaics, and the like, while the textiles decorate the walls.)

Archaeologists have found evidence of very early weaving in the Americas as well. In North America spinning and weaving tools have been dated to about 5000 BC; some of the fabrics woven may well have been of a weft-faced tapestry type, judging from the loom remains found. In South America the finds from archaeological digs have confirmed that weaving without looms goes back to 4000–3000 BC, and that the backstrap loom was in common use by some 3,200 years ago. Actual textile remains – tomb textiles being particularly notable – have been well preserved by the hot, dry climate of the coastal plain and show a very considerable degree of manipulative and technical ability. Tapestries are relatively rarer than other forms of weaving, but some of those found are of incredible fineness: the thinnest of handspun thread was woven, for instance, at over 60 weft picks per centimetre. Finally, dating from the thirteenth century up to the Spanish conquest of Peru in 1532, there are the woven textiles of the Incas, whose empire included parts of present-day Peru, Colombia, Chile and Argentina. They were technically no more expert than the earlier work but extended the range of symbolism and colour in the designs used.

Apart from these American textiles probably the most famous of early tapestries are the Coptic (Egyptian Christian) ones – maybe because many Western museums with textile collections have examples. But over and above this there is a technical point which singles them out too. Coptic tapestries are the first in which we see the weft being laid not at right angles to the warp but crossing it obliquely so that curved forms can be woven without the edges being 'stepped', as happens when the weft is laid horizontally.

(This is one of the tapestry techniques we will look at in Chapter 16.) Most Coptic tapestries can be dated to between AD 200, when the early Christian church was first centred in Alexandria in order to try to escape Roman persecution, and AD 641, when Muslim Persia overran Egypt. Although richly patterned articles of clothing were woven, a great deal of what has come down to us is tapestries of religious origin, some being church furnishings and vestments, some grave goods.

In Europe, the Dark Ages succeeded the Roman Empire and it is fair to assume that with Roman civilization went tapestry weaving and the other decorative textile crafts. So it was not until the Moorish invasions of Spain around AD 710 that tapestry weaving returned to Europe. The Coptic tapestries made after the Islamic conquest of Egypt have lost much of their variety of pattern, due to the conquerors' religious beliefs, which forbade the representation of human or animal forms. But the highly developed Islamic civilization continued and extended the tradition in other ways, and so became the link between the tapestry of the ancient world and what was probably the craft's greatest flowering – the medieval secular and religious tapestries of France and the Low Countries and, to a lesser extent, of Germany, Italy and other European countries.

It would really take up far too much of this book to give even the briefest information on these tapestries, so I can only suggest that anyone interested should read Francis Thomson's book. From it they will undoubtedly learn all there is to know, and it is his scholarly and interesting work that has been the source of a good many of the facts contained in this brief run through the history of tapestry.

THE LOOMS

European tapestries have traditionally been woven on one of two types of loom: the *haute lisse*, or high-warp loom, which is an upright loom with the warp running vertically; and the *basse lisse*, or low-warp loom, where the warp lies horizontally and the shafts, as with other floor looms, are operated by foot pedals. Both these types of loom are still available to tapestry weavers, and which is used is simply a question of the preference of the individual weaver. Both were traditionally two-shaft looms (all that are needed for tapestry weaving) and normally the upright versions still are, although there is no reason why a weaver should not use four or more shafts to weave tapestries.

In fact many weavers, if only for reasons of expense, work on the same loom whether they are doing cloth weaving or tapestry weaving. However, this does rather narrow the choice to a horizontal loom because, although it is possible to weave tapestries on any of the normal models of table or floor loom, it is not really feasible to weave cloth on an upright two-shaft tapestry loom. The most one can say is that it is possible to weave both tapestries and rugs on the larger vertical looms.

Much the same applies to small hand-held frame looms. These are often described as tapestry looms and that is because although you can weave cloth on two-shaft looms it is more usual today, if only for considerations of speed, to do so on four or more shafts. So, to sum up, it makes sense, if you are purely a tapestry weaver, to weave on two shafts only, because that is all you actually need – and what is the point of lifting more shafts than you have to?

WEAVING POSITIONS

Traditionally, European tapestries were woven back to front, with the weft ends hanging on the front facing the weaver – which was the wrong side of the work. A mirror, together with the cartoon, was placed at the back so the weaver could see the progress of the work on the right side and check it against the cartoon. As the weavers were copyists rather than creators, perhaps it did not matter to them that they spent their time looking at the wrong side of their work. But most of today's designer-weavers prefer to work from the front. Apart from being able to see more clearly how the design is developing, textured stitches and effects can be used which would be impossible otherwise.

Before sitting down to weave it is a good idea to organize what you think is going to be the most suitable position for this. Often a comfortable high-back chair drawn up to a small table – on which you can keep your design work, weft yarns and tools – is the best option. (The problem with using the dining-room or kitchen table is that you have to clear away each time a meal is due.) Place this work space in such a way that the maximum of daylight, and a source of adequate artificial light, is available, and tell the family that this is *your* space, and on pain of your most vigorous displeasure nothing is to be touched without your permission. Then relax and sit down with the loom on your lap, leaning against the table edge at a comfortable angle. (Put a cushion on the table to lean the frame against, if this helps to angle it comfortably – I have a triangular polystyrene-bead-filled one for supporting work on my lap, and this doubles as a useful frame

Linen and cotton warp yarns, including a ball of cotton string from the local supermarket.

support.) You are now ready to start collecting everything together for weaving.

WARP YARNS

Tapestry warp yarn should be a strong *corded* or *cabled* yarn (these are plied yarns which are folded together again for greater strength). Although wool and silk are used to fulfil particular requirements such as flexibility, linen and cotton are the most commonly used warp yarns. Linen, however, is liable to shrink and stretch according to changes in humidity, which does terrible things to tension, so many weavers stick to cotton.

Suppliers will usually offer warp yarns in a variety of thicknesses and strengths,

so to start with a good, all-purpose medium yarn, about 15/9s (15-ply of 9s cotton, if you remember), is what you should look for. This can be doubled up if you are going to weave something heavier on a large frame loom – a rug, for instance. Most weaving yarns are sold by weight – 250 or 500 grams, or 1 kilo – on *cops, cones* or *cheeses*, although some rug weft yarns are sold by weight in hanks.

A quick tip here, although I know some weaving friends who consider this to be absolute heresy: if the worst comes to the worst and you cannot lay your hands on any warp yarn, and are longing to get started, then go out and buy a high-twist, strong, smooth cotton string and use this until you are able to get the correct yarn.

Berber yarns.

WEFT YARNS

Suitable yarns for heavy tapestries and other weft-faced fabrics are the 2- or 3-ply yarns usually plied from 9s singles, often in a wool-nylon mixture for extra wear. These are listed by suppliers as rug or tapestry yarn, and weave up at about the 3 ends per centimetre we are using for this first tapestry sampler project. For a finer weave, at 4.5 e.p.cm, I use a strong wool, worsted-spun from the fleece of a long-wool breed such as the Cheviot, at about 2/16s. This needs a finer cotton warp (about 6/9s) or even the Cheviot worsted itself – it is quite strong and smooth enough to do the job. This type comes in a variety of colours, for those weavers who do not want to dye their own.

Both these types of yarn are equally suitable for the thickest floor rugs – double them up until the required e.p.cm is reached. In fact, I like to work this way, even to the extent of using a fine 16s singles Cheviot. As a dyer, I can then combine a number of different tints or shades of singles yarn in any one pick and in this way I get a much more lively colour than the flat effect of a rug-weight yarn which has been dyed in the one dye mix. Alternatively, if I am weaving a design in which I want the colour to move along the pattern, I can get a very subtle effect by combining, say, five singles of the first hue with one of the second for as many picks as required, then moving to three singles of the first and three of the second, and finally to one of the first and

125

five of the second – or whatever combination I want. It gives me a great deal of control over the colour in my work, and since colour is very important to me I find I am happiest working this way.

Another class of yarns which are very suitable for tapestry and rug weaving are the *Berber* yarns. These were originally spun by the North African tribesmen of that name from the long, rather coarse and naturally coloured wool of their own sheep, and were used for all the strong weft-faced textiles which their nomadic way of life made necessary. Nowadays they are machine-spun in Europe, but still come in a range of natural colours from very dark brown through intermediate fawns and greys to natural off-white. When dyed, colours are usually a muted range similar to those obtainable from plant dyes. They are not sold by the yarn count system but come in an excellent range of thicknesses from reasonably thin tapestry-type wools up to thick cabled yarns more like rope than weaving wool. Just send off for samples and order the ones you need.

PACKAGING THE YARN FOR WEAVING

The various colours of weft yarn needed for tapestry weaving must be organized properly if they are not to get into a terrible tangle. With a small frame, a *butterfly* of yarn is easiest to push through the weft with your fingers. Make this by winding about a metre of yarn (depending on thickness, of course) round thumb and little finger in a figure of eight, secured round the middle with a half-hitch. Pull out from the beginning of the yarn length, the bit round your thumb, as you weave.

Alternatively, wind the yarn on to little pieces of card, and finish with a half-hitch; with these, you pull out the yarn from the half-hitch. The same winding method is the one used with the true tapestry bobbin. Providing the half-hitch is correctly tied you need never undo it – the yarn slides out easily for use as you weave, and the knot holds the bobbin suspended from your weaving without unravelling.

THE CARTOON

The cartoon may be anything from a general indication of a design roughed out on

A cartoon for one part of the Stourhead gardens triptych in place on a floor-standing tapestry loom. The warp is tied to the top and bottom rollers; it is a short one, but enough extra has been made to allow it to be adjusted to keep it at a comfortable weaving position.

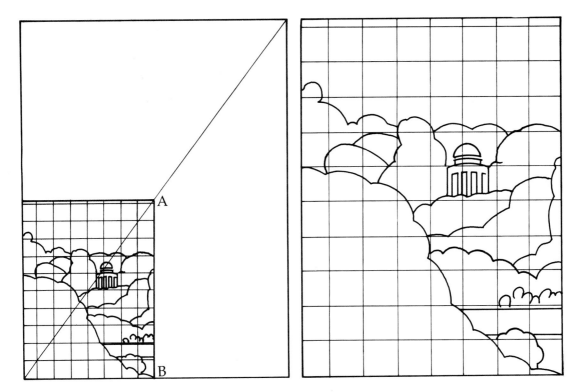

Scaling-up a design. Trace the design and place it in the corner of a larger sheet of paper. Extend the bottom line to B by the sizing-up factor (in this case × 3). Draw in the diagonal from bottom left to top right. The vertical line from B to the intersection with the diagonal at A gives the size of the scaled-up rectangle. Draw a grid over the tracing, and the same grid, but proportionally larger (here × 3), on the paper. Using the grid as a guide, transfer the main elements of the design from the tracing to the paper. This is now a cartoon three times the size of the original design.

paper to a full-scale painting of what the finished work will look like. Weavers all have their own ideas about this. Some like to have an accurate drawing of exactly what they intend to weave; others merely put down a very general outline of the main features of the design so that, as they see the work developing, they can respond to it, and vary colour, pattern or shape as they wish. As with so many other aspects of weaving, each individual arrives at the method which suits him or her best. Either way, though, the cartoon does need to be full size, so enlarge it on a photocopier or by means of the simple squaring-up method illustrated. Keep the

original art work pinned up near your work so that you can refer to it for colour changes.

Whatever method is finally adopted, to begin with a reasonably definite idea of what is to be woven is undoubtedly a good idea. There are so many other things to think about and the new weaver does not really want to have to worry about the design as well. So, before starting to weave, it helps to mark the warp threads with the main outlines of the design. To do this, lay the design cartoon – the full-size version – on a table, and put the frame, face up, on top of it. With a water-proof pen, mark each warp end at the

An overshot weave designed on point paper, with two versions woven from it, with different lifts used for each (Jo Tether).

point where the end crosses a line of the design. Make sure each warp end is inked all round as they do tend to swivel as you weave.

DESIGNING ON GRAPH PAPER

For some types of design – abstract and geometrical ones based on tribal rugs, for instance, or designs such as the ones for the 'sampler' house and garden tapestry in Chapter 8 – it is probably easier to work out the shapes on graph paper rather than freehand. This can be done with coloured pens or pencils, or in black and white with a key linking the symbols in the squares to actual samples of the yarns to be used.

Ordinary graph paper, where each square on the paper is actually square, as high as it is wide, is not really suitable for designing weft-faced weave patterns, because the half-pass of weft over a warp end is not as high as it is wide. In fact, even a full pass is barely so if the fabric is heavily beaten down, so there is always some distortion when working from designs drawn out on graph paper. A paper such as those sold for knitters, in which the vertical lines are twice as far apart as the horizontal ones, is the best one to use and will give a reasonably accurate idea of what the finished design will look like.

Shetland ewes (© Norwood Farm).

A group of Soay sheep (© Norwood Farm).

Samples of cloth woven in wool, cashmere and silk, emphasizing the classic, subtle charm of natural colours.

Colour and shape design references in a collage . . .

. . . and in the 'eye' in the tail of the peacock.

Dyed silk cravats woven in loom-controlled inlays.

Silk and cashmere cloth samples.

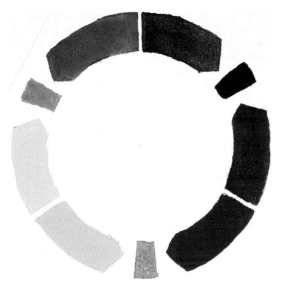

The colour wheel.

Colour harmony (colours adjacent on the wheel) and colour contrast (those opposite each other on the wheel).

Atomic colour mixing, and two methods of visual colour mixing (dashes and stripes).

Colour mixing and matching – clear greens using Cerulean Blue and Lemon Yellow, with shades (mixed with black) and tints (mixed with white) below – and dull oranges using Alizarin Crimson and Cadmium Yellow, with shades and tints below.

The plumage of tropical birds, photographed for use as colour references.

A colour extraction exercise based on parrot colours.

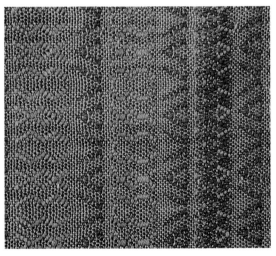

Detail of loom-controlled inlay woven with silk yarns dyed to this theme.

An orchid photographed at Kew Gardens.

A corner of one of the tropical houses at Kew Gardens.

A silk cravat and purse with both colour and shape references to the photographs.

INSPIRATIONAL PICTURE SUGGESTING LIGHT SHINING THROUGH TREES WITH WATERFALL

...GE DEPICTING COLOURS & SHAPES FROM 'INSPIRATIONAL' PICTURE

WRAPPING SHOWING COLOURS & YARNS

A free tapestry interpretation of a waterfall, by Jo Tether.

Clematis flowers suggesting colour and pattern for a stylized picture using overshot weaves, by Jo Tether.

Tapestry woven on a ring in curved and distorted weft techniques, and displayed with its artwork, by Jo Tether.

A weft-face rug woven in double-faced weave, using three colours, by Jo Tether.

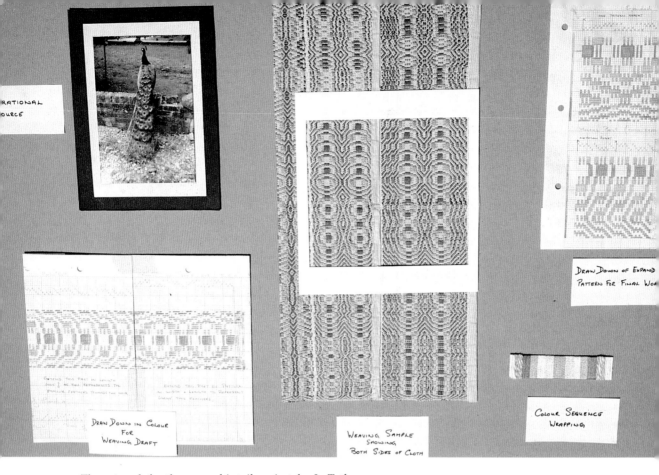

DRAW DOWN OF EXPAND PATTERN FOR FINAL WOR

DRAW DOWN IN COLOUR FOR WEAVING DRAFT

WEAVING SAMPLE SHOWING BOTH SIDES OF CLOTH

COLOUR SEQUENCE WRAPPING

The artwork for the peacock's tail project, by Jo Tether.

A weft-faced rug woven in double-faced weave in three shades of peacock blue, by Jo Tether.

15
Dressing the Loom for Tapestry Weaving

WARPING ON THE FRAME

To start warping, after deciding how many ends per centimetre you want by the warp-wrapping method described in Chapter 11, wind off the cone what you calculate will be approximately the length of yarn you need and tie the end firmly to the bottom bar of your frame on the left-hand side. Your weaving should be centred on the frame, so work out where you need to begin winding in order to spread your ends across evenly.

Now start to wind your warp, reasonably firmly, up and down the length of the frame in a figure of eight – down to the bottom of the frame, over the bottom bar, round it and under it, up to the top of the frame, over the top bar, round and under it, and so on. This figure-of-eight configuration not only keeps the ends in order but also gives you a natural shed for weaving, formed by the thickness of the frame. As you warp, try to space the ends out as evenly as possible across your marked ruler. Remember that each figure of eight you wind represents two warp ends – one over the bar, one under the bar – so count as you wind across and when you have wound enough ends tie off firmly at the top of the frame and rearrange the ends so that they are correctly spaced. By the way (and this applies to warping any type of loom), if you come across a knot in your warp yarn you must

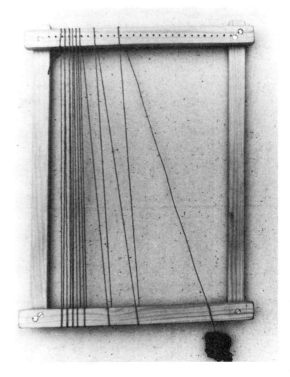

Winding a figure-of-eight warp directly on to a small frame.

make sure that the join comes at one end or the other of the frame, not in the middle, even if it means cutting and rejoining it and thus wasting some yarn. As you can imagine, it would be impossible to beat the weft down properly if there were knots in the warp.

Before you actually start weaving, the last two steps in warping up a small tapestry frame are, first, to put in any laths

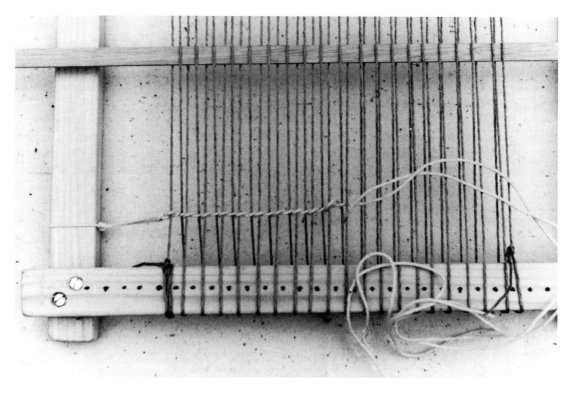

Twining a heading cord.

you need in order to tension the warp correctly. These are best slipped under your rulers and the whole bundle tied in place at either end. It is worth leaving the rulers in as you weave, as they act as a useful check on the spacing of your warp yarns. Second, put in a *heading cord*, to give you a firm base on to which to start your weaving.

You can do this by *twining* with a length of warp yarn, about six times the width of the frame. Tie the centre of the yarn near the bottom left-hand side of the frame and then start twining the two ends of the yarn in a figure of eight over and under each warp end until you reach the right-hand edge. Before you tie the two ends securely round the frame, in order to keep the twined heading level and firm beat

the row of twining down as near as you can to the bottom bar of the frame. This type of heading will help in spacing your ends, as well as giving a really firm base against which to beat down your weft picks. You can also make a heading by weaving the two ends of yarn through the warp in a simple plain weave, over and under alternate warps, and then securing the ends round the opposite side of the frame in the same way as with the twining method, but I do not think this is so secure. Nor does it really help in keeping your warp ends properly spaced.

One more aid to good-quality weaving on a small frame – at least for the first few projects, until you become more practised – is to have a guide, or stretcher, on each side of the work, measuring out the distance between the last warp end and the frame and so helping to keep the edges of the work straight. These guides are pushed up above your weaving as it grows upwards, and will alert you instantly if the weaving starts to *pull in* (something which it tends to do if one is not very careful). Tie each length of yarn in a fairly loose double knot round the selvedge warp on each side, just above the twining thread, and then knot firmly against the inside edge of the frame, wrap twice round the frame – don't pull too hard; you need to be able to slide it up the frame – and tie with another firm knot. Then push each guide up a couple of inches, and the warp is wound and ready for weaving.

WARPING OFF THE FRAME

The type of tool used to wind warps depends very much on the type of warp you want – that is to say its length. Short warps for tapestries and small articles such as cushion covers, bags and the like can easily be made with a couple of *warping posts*. These can be bought at a reasonable cost or, again, are not too difficult to make and, secured with G-clamps to a table edge at the measured distance apart, are fine for a short warp. (As you have to walk between the posts as you wind on your warp, you will appreciate why winding on a very long, very wide warp would be an exhausting business – although no doubt good for the figure for those trying to slim.) However, if you are making a long warp on posts, you can get a number of single ones and place them strategically on the sides of a table – in effect making your own warping board, which can be dismantled each time after use.

With a *warping board* longer warps, up to 8–10 metres, can be made comfortably. Whether hung on a wall or laid on a table

A warping board, warping posts and G-clamps.

(the position in which it is used is, as always, a question of the user's personal preference), this type of warping board fulfils the needs of most weavers. Only production weavers of cloth lengths are likely to find it insufficient; they need to have a *warping mill*. This is a large cylindrical slatted wooden drum set vertically on a revolving central axis, round which the warp is wound. Like any major item of equipment it is not cheap and no beginner need, or indeed should, consider buying one, so we will leave it at that – just as a mention that such things exist for those whose work justifies it.

Calculating Length and Width

Whether I am using the warp on a two-shaft frame loom or on a horizontal loom with four or more shafts, my method of making the warp is the same. I beam on to the back roller before threading the warp through heddles and reed (the method is explained in Chapter 18) and make only one *cross*, at one end of the warp skein. (Some books illustrate warp winding with a cross at each end. Do not be alarmed; it is just yet another instance of the weaver's individual preference in methods of working.)

Before starting to wind on, you have decided the length of the piece you intend to weave, and its width, and the number of ends per centimetre you need. Let us use as an example the tapestry sampler which you will find as an exercise at the end of Chapter 17. It is being woven on your smallest 50 × 40cm frame, but you want it to be an overall 55cm long by 20cm wide – that is to say, it is longer than your frame, which is why you are making the warp off the frame. This tells you that you must place your warping pegs 60cm

apart – 55cm plus about 10 per cent allowance because you cannot weave right up to the ends. To calculate the width of the warp, wrap the two-ply tapestry yarn on a ruler. Six wraps gives 2 ends per centimetre – well spread out for a weft-faced weave. So, for a finished tapestry 20cm wide you need to wind on 44 ends (20 × 2 ends = 40 ends, plus 10 per cent because the work will inevitably pull in). In other words, this exercise project requires a warp 60cm long, consisting of 44 ends.

Using Warping Boards or Posts

Warping boards are usually arranged so that there are at least two or three pegs at top and bottom set about 20cm apart, with others similarly spaced out on the two sides of the board. If you use warping posts you will need at least two: a double or triple peg one to start you off and a single to finish on. The cross at the end of the warp is made between the first and second pegs on the board, or between the pegs of the double-peg post if you are using warping posts. I mark the base of my warping board to show the route the yarn must take on the outward journey, and on the return, in order to make the cross. This ensures that I follow the right path and so make the cross correctly, which is essential, particularly in the case of a wide warp with many ends, because the entire warp-winding process can be ruined if the cross, and therefore the order of the ends, is done wrongly.

Measure out your warp in the following ways. Using warping posts, clamp the first, double-peg, post in position, then clamp the second, single post the required warp length away from it (in the case of the tapestry sampler, 60cm). On a warping board, the first thing to do is to cut a

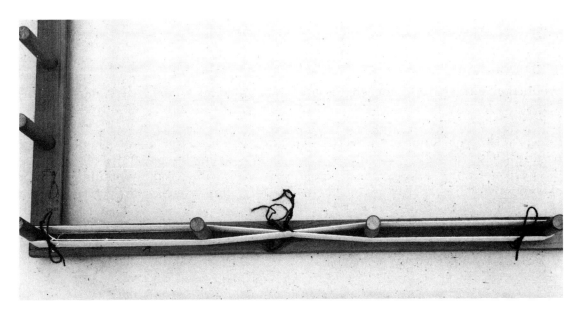

Winding a short figure-of-eight warp on the warping board (above) and a longer
warp on the board (below). It is quite a wide one of 140 ends of 2/16s cotton, so has
been wound in two halves.

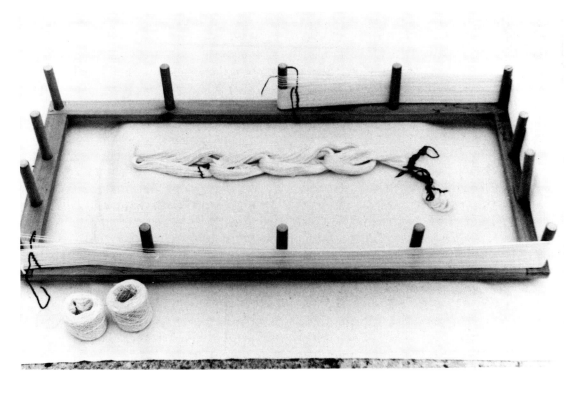

Using two chairs as an emergency warping board.

piece of string to the length of the warp you are winding. This is to help you to work out the best path for winding on. So, for this sampler, plot a course with a 60cm piece of string. Always settle for a bit more, rather than less, if it does not work out exactly. It helps to leave the string in place to act as a guide as you start to wind the warp, particularly if, as happens with longer warps, the path you have taken zigzags from side to side and is therefore a bit complicated. At this point, make a final check that all the posts are securely clamped and/or the pegs firmly set into the frame. If the pegs bend off the vertical, your warp will get shorter and shorter as you wind it.

One last point: if you have not yet bought or borrowed warping posts or a frame, but are anxious to get on with this first project, try using a couple of suitable straight-backed chairs, placed the warp length apart. Weight them down well so that they cannot 'travel' as you wind on. It is not, of course, an entirely satisfactory way of warping, and certainly is no good for a very long or wide warp, but it will at least get you started on the sampler and similar short warps until you can organize things on a more permanent basis.

Winding the Warp

This really is quite simple but it does need to be done carefully if you are not to waste time and yarn by losing the order in which the warps are threaded on the loom. This is not a total disaster when making a warp for a small frame, as with this sampler, but it most certainly is if you are winding a long, wide warp for a multi-shaft loom. So, since the method is the same, I find it helps to practise on short warps; then, by the time you get on to making the more complex ones you are quite confident, everything goes smoothly and no problems arise.

Tie the warp yarn in a secure, fairly

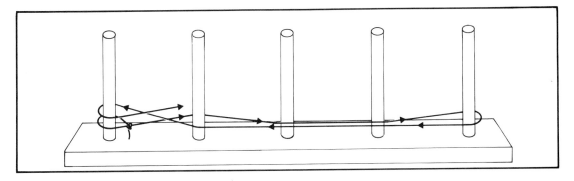

A diagrammatic representation of warp winding.

loose loop round the first peg – where your guide string started. Put the yarn down by your feet, or in some position where it can run smoothly off the cone, or, if you have wound it into a ball, put the ball into a container so it doesn't run around all over the floor. (The type of ball winder which allows you to feed yarn from the inside of the ball is a good investment for a weaver, just as it is for a machine knitter. Both need to have smooth-running yarn.) Then take the yarn in and out of the first two pegs, follow the guide string to the end, loop round the final peg and return on the exact path you came out on until you get back to the first pair of pegs. To finish your cross, return round these two pegs the opposite way to the route you took on the outward journey, and loop round the first peg. You have now wound on the first *two* ends, and are ready to start again, winding on ends three and four, by following exactly the same route out and back as you did with ends one and two.

Two things should be noted here. First, wind your warp smoothly, not jerkily, using even pressure, firm but not too tight. (This is why it helps to have the yarn feeding smoothly off the cone or ball.) And ensure that the warps do not overlap each other as you round the pegs at each end, and do not let them pull in tighter and tighter as you wind further up the pegs, which they have a disconcerting habit of doing if you are not careful.

Second, it helps to put in a counting thread at intervals as you wind. A contrasting colour is best, so that you can see it clearly. This is particularly important, of course, when winding a wide warp with a large number of ends, but even with a small warp it helps to keep track of the number of warps wound. With this sampler, which has 44 ends, I would divide the warp into groups of six ends – that is, cross over the threads of the counting thread every three times you wind the yarn out and back again ($6 \times 7 = 42$, plus a final 2 ends). Then, by doing a quick count of the number of groups of ends, you can clearly see when you have reached the end of the warp winding. It is usual to put the counting tie beyond the cross, so that every end is included. If you put it beside the first peg remember that only every other end is included, because each thread turning round the peg represents *two* ends. Finally, tie the yarn in a loose loop round the first post, as you did at the start – *but do not under any circumstances take the warp off the pegs yet.*

135

Securing the Cross

The final thing to do before you take the warp off the board (and without it all your work is for nothing) is to secure the cross. There are different ways of doing this, but here is my method. I take a long thread, a little more than double the width of the warp I am making, and tie the cross carefully, making sure that the first and last threads particularly are pushed over to the correct side. (Because of the way they are tied in a loop round the end peg, rather than wound round it like the others, they tend to slip sideways, so watch this.) For the moment, I finish

securing the cross with a fairly firm double bow to keep the long ends of my tying yarn neat and tidy. An additional security measure, particularly if you are going to store the warp, rather than use it straight away, is to put a firm tie round the loop at each end of the warp. You can now take it off the pegs and hang it up somewhere until you are ready to use it.

When you are ready to put the warp on the frame, slip a couple of dowelling rods through the loops at each end of your warp. Make sure one piece of dowelling is through the small loops tied at the ends of the first and last threads too; it is worth checking at each stage of warping up that

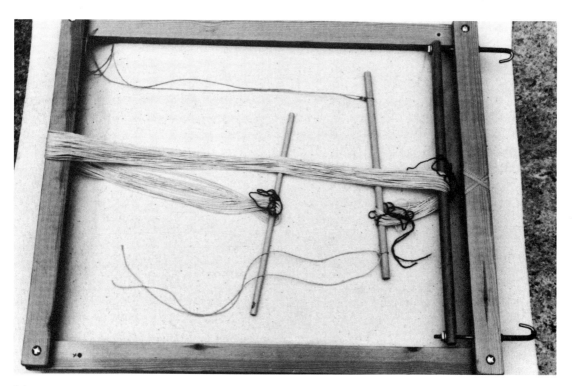

(a)

Putting an off-the-loom warp on a frame. (a) The frame is laid face down on the warp, with dowels threaded through each end of the warp. (b) The dowels are lashed together at the back of the frame. (c) The warp has been pulled round the frame, ready to start weaving, and the shed stick is in place.

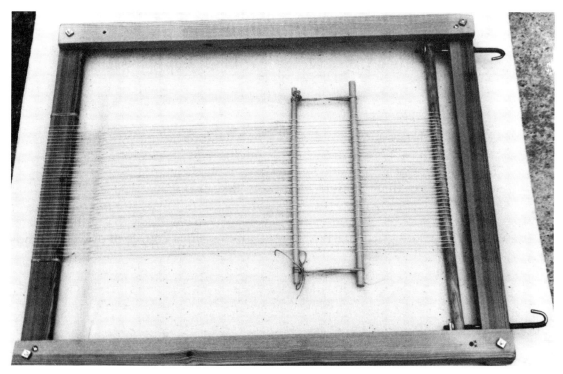

(b)

(c)

137

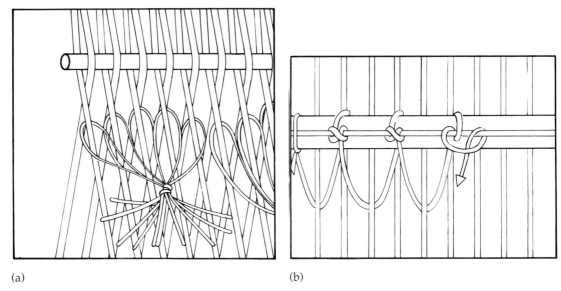

(a)   (b)

Tying various leashes. (a) Groups of leashes. (b) A leash bar. (c) Leash bar in profile (the temporary stick in the warp helps to ensure that all leashes are tied the same length).

these are included. Loosen the yarn securing the cross so that the ends can be spread out as wide as necessary, in this case, 21cm wide, lay the frame face down on the warp, bring the dowels to the back and lash them together – not too tight, until you have spread the warp out evenly and put in your twining cord to hold all in place. Then you can give a final tensioning to the two rods and you are ready to make the leashes which open the sheds, the last stage before weaving.

FORMING THE SHEDS AND MAKING THE LEASHES

Straighten out the long tie securing the cross, and into the top of the cross, along the line of the thread, place a shed stick – a piece of thin dowel, or a flat narrow piece of lath, just longer than the width of your frame. Once you have secured the

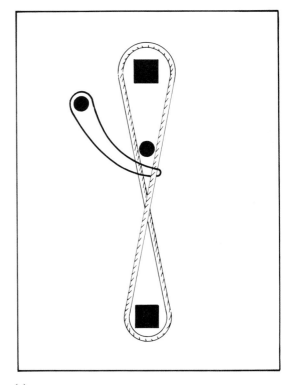

(c)

shed with the stick you can pull out the tying thread. Weaving on a small frame, this is all you need to do. The shed stick stays in place all the time during weaving: the *open shed* or *stick shed* is formed by lifting it or, if it is a flat stick, by turning it on its edge; the opposite shed is made by pushing the stick up to the top of the frame, out of the way, and then lifting the ends which come out from under the shed stick with your fingers.

On a larger frame it is easier to combine the stick shed with *leashes* to operate the opposite shed. These can be even-sized loops of warp yarn, or a slightly thinner cotton yarn, tied round every other end (the ones not being lifted by the shed stick) and then grouped together. A pull on them opens a section of the second shed. Or you can use the Navajo method, in which a long length of cotton yarn is looped evenly and continuously round every other end, and a stick threaded through the loops to enable you to lift across the whole width of the second shed. An added refinement on a larger frame would be blocks of wood, grooved to fit the shed and leash sticks, and then clamped to each side of the frame. Moved up as you work, they can be used to support the sticks, thus keeping the whole of either shed open while you work in it.

Various leashes – a shed stick turned on edge, and opening the opposite shed with the fingers.

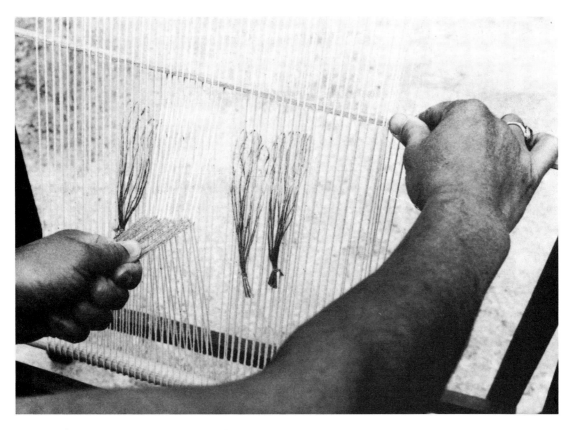

Groups of leashes to open the opposite shed.

Also, a hinged stand to support the frame on the table top might be a comfortable option with larger frames.

On the very largest floor-standing frames the traditional method of securing the leashes to operate the opposite shed is slightly different again. A round shed stick is put into the natural shed, and is kept just above a flat *leash bar*. This leash bar is clamped to the sides of the frame, projecting out about 15cm, and is kept at a comfortable level above the fell of the work (the level at which you are weaving). Strong cord is tied tightly along the leash bar and secured to the clamps – not to the frame, otherwise you cannot move the leash bar when this is necessary. A

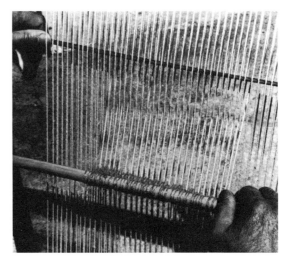

A Navajo heddle stick.

A leash bar, with the leashes pulled down by hand to open the shed.

length of cotton yarn, about three times the width of the frame, is secured to the leash bar cord on the left of the frame, and then goes round the first warp end in the open shed (an end coming from behind the shed stick and so not being lifted by it). It is then brought up and round the leash bar, and tied in a double hitch round the leash bar cord. Then the thread is taken round the next but one warp end (the next one behind the shed stick) and back up and round the leash bar, and tied in another double hitch on the leash bar cord. Continue across the loom in this way from left to right, making sure you include every other warp end in the leashing system, and then fasten off. Make sure also that each leash is the same length, and reasonably slack. This leash shed is operated by putting your hand behind a group of the leashes and pulling down on them to open the shed.

Now you are ready to actually start weaving – did I hear someone say 'At last'? I know it all seems an endless fiddle, but dressing the loom, even with relatively simple two-shaft looms, is accepted by most weavers as being quite the worst job in weaving. At least it is now finished, for this project anyway.

16
Tapestry Weaving Techniques

SECURING THE YARN

Because you are likely to be working with many different colours of weft yarn, each of these need to be secured properly at start and finish. The problem here is that weaving them in can produce an un-sightly bump or ridge, especially in the case of thick yarns. You may therefore decide to darn the ends in at the back to anchor them. If so, I suggest doing them as you go along, rather than leaving them all to the end: it somehow does not seem quite such a chore that way. However, if

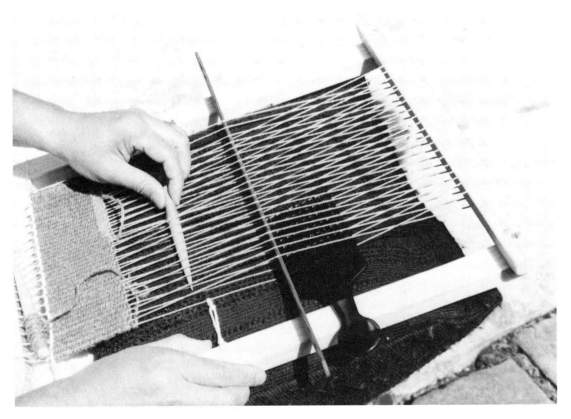

Tapestry-weaving techniques – weaving with the frame supported on an angled cushion.

you can weave them in without affecting the face of the tapestry, that is the best way to do it. For articles which will be lined, a length of yarn can be left hanging at the back, so a single twist round just one warp end will prevent it pulling through. For rugs, which need to be equally tidy back and front, weave the end in and out of three or four warp ends and, if you can, split the tails of yarn so they are not quite so bulky. They can then safely be trimmed off short and neat. This is all made easier if several finer yarns are being combined in the weft, rather than just one thick one, as some of these can be dropped as the weaving-in progresses, to give a less bulky join.

WEAVING GEOMETRICAL SHAPES IN DIFFERENT COLOURS

Vertical Joins

If the design being woven is made up of vertical lines there are various ways of making vertical joins. The first is the *slit technique*, often known as Kelim as it is the method used in these North African flat-woven rugs. Each different coloured pattern element is woven separately. The first colour of weft yarn comes across, turns round a warp end and returns in the opposite shed. The second colour starts from the next warp end, travels across

The vertical (Kelim) slit.

143

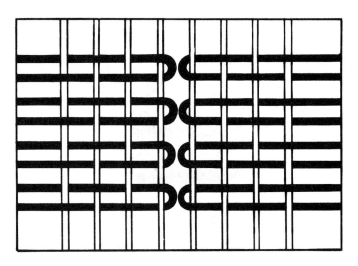

Tapestry techniques – Kelim slit.

and then back, and so on. Each shape is built up separately until its required height is reached. This technique gives a nice clean line between the individual parts of the pattern and, if the slits are too long, you can sew them up at the back without blurring the line. However, left unsewn, the distortion and the hard edge they cause can be an interesting feature of the design.

Do this discontinuous weaving (the same applies to the other techniques we shall deal with below) in one of two ways. For the first, turn the shed stick on its side to open its shed, and then weave the first *half-pass* (the name given to a pick by tapestry weavers, so two picks equal one *pass*) of each different colour across each shape. Leave the butterfly of yarn hanging down at the front as you move on to the next shape. When the half-pass is completed, beat the shed down, push the shed stick up out of the way and thread another stick into the opposite shed. Open this shed by turning the stick on its side. You then weave the return half-pass in this shed, threading the various weft yarns through the ends for each separate shape, and leaving the tails of yarn hang-

ing as before. In this method the various colours of weft yarn all move in the same shed, one after the other, to the left. They then return in the opposite shed, one after the other, to the right, completing one full pass.

In the other method of discontinuous weaving, the true tapestry technique, weft yarns move independently of each other, meeting and parting in various joins. In this way design elements can be built up separately. The shed is opened with fingers and/or shed sticks and weft colours weave back and forth, beaten down as they are laid in, until a change of colour is required. Whole areas of the design can be built up in this way, quite separately, provided that the join between them is a vertical slit or an angled dovetail rather than some of the other interlocking joins described below.

The next two methods of making a vertical join between shapes are both versions of the *dovetail*. In the first, the weft yarns from adjacent shapes turn round the same warp end before returning; in the second, one or two passes (depending on the thickness of the yarn) are made round the same end, working on alternate

Vertical dovetails.

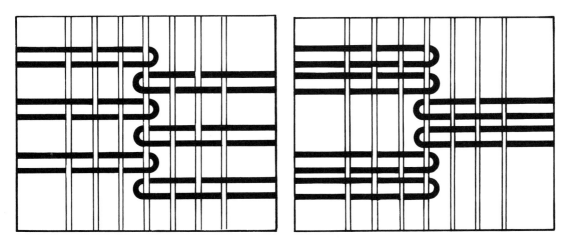

Tapestry techniques – dovetails.

Angled dovetails and interlocks.

shapes. Both these methods give textured and jagged joins which can add interest to a design.

Finally, *interlocking* is a technique which can also be used to make a vertical join. In this, two adjacent wefts are woven towards each other, looped round each other and then returned in the opposite shed to complete the pass. If the interlock is done on every pass it will form a noticeable ridge. This may suit the design; if not, the join will be quite secure and less noticeable if the interlock comes every

second pass, alternating with a dovetail join. Take care with weft tension at the point of the join between the adjacent shapes when you are combining techniques in this way.

Diagonal Joins

For diagonal joins use the *angled dovetail*, in which the wefts meet, butt up against each other and turn on adjacent warp ends, as with the slit technique. However, because these turns are staggered diagonally, no slit is formed. In another version of the angled dovetail, which gives a more textured join, the wefts meet and pass each other before turning on the same warp end. In a third version the wefts meet, pass, and turn on adjacent warp ends. This gives an even more textured and defined join because the weft colours intermingle.

In any dovetailing the angles can be varied. If a steep angle is wanted, two or three passes can be turned round the same two warp ends, then the next two or three passes can turn round the adjacent warp end, and so on. To get a less angled

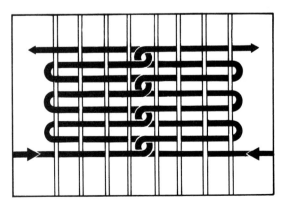

Tapestry techniques – interlocking.

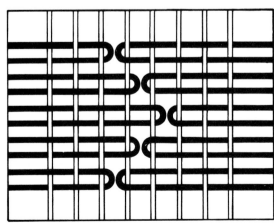

Tapestry techniques – diagonal joins.

146

effect, the turn round the warp ends on each pass can be done not on adjacent ends but at two or even three ends removed.

The interlocking weft method (described above) can also be used for an angled join. Carefully tensioned so that the interlock falls exactly between the warp ends, it makes a neat and interestingly textured join. Take care to ensure that the interlock is done in the same direction each time. With these various joins it is usually easier to see which end the weft should turn round if a full pass is completed for each colour/shape before going on to the next one.

TWO WEFTS IN THE SAME SHED

When building up different coloured shapes separately take care not to end up with the wefts of two adjacent shapes in the same shed. This happens when the place where wefts meet changes position (in weaving a stepped design, for instance) and the fault must be corrected, otherwise it will not be possible to beat

the weft down so that the warp is completely hidden. The large loop at the back in the first method does not matter if the tapestry is to be lined but, if it is a rug which requires a neat and strong back, use the second method. The extra turn round the warp should cover it adequately – if not, make one more turn round it with the weft yarn.

WEFT TENSION

It is also important to ensure that you do not put in the weft yarn too tightly, or your shapes will pull in; or too loosely, because this will cause ugly loops where the colours join, especially at a slit. If you are weaving across a large single-colour area, for instance in a border or frame, it is wise to adopt the method used in any weaving where the weft yarn travels the full width of the work. Lay the yarn into the shed either in a diagonal, in an arc or in waves (if you are doing very wide work), and then beat down from the end you entered the shed towards the other side.

This method, which lays in extra yarn, allows the weft to travel over and under

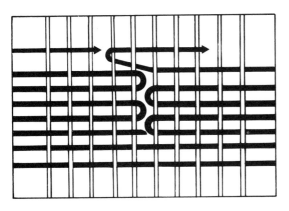
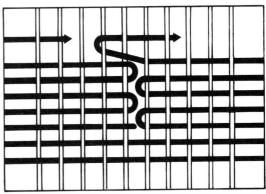

Two wefts in the same shed.

the warps without pulling them out of true, which is particularly important if you are to keep a straight selvedge, but distortion from the parallel can also occur with the warp in the main weaving area.

WEAVING LARGE AREAS OF ONE COLOUR

In tapestry weaving it is very important to remember that if the design demands a large area of one colour in the centre of the design, the yarn should never be taken right across but rather built up in small shapes. These are linked with the smoothest version of the angled dovetail, the one in which the wefts meet and turn on adjacent warp ends – though even this join shows in marks on the fabric which are known as *lazy lines*. The technique is used in order to prevent the work from distorting, which is what will happen if some areas are woven full width and other parts are broken up into discontinuous patterning.

UNDERCUTTING WHEN WEAVING DIAGONALS AND TRIANGLES

As with the diagonal lines, the angle of the triangle can be controlled by the number of weft passes made round the same warp end, or by the number of warp ends left between each turn at the end of each half-pass. When working on diagonal and triangular shapes be careful not to undercut these as you build up areas of work. Meet-and-return, as in interlocking, is the correct way, rather than weaving shapes separately.

HORIZONTAL JOINS BETWEEN COLOURED AREAS

Horizontal joins between shapes would seem to be easily made just by changing colour between passes. But this very simplicity (as opposed to the more complex problems of vertical joins) brings us back to one important aspect of tapestry weaving, which was touched on in Chapter 13. This is the question of which way a tapestry is woven: from the bottom upwards or on its side.

The reason why the large medieval tapestries were woven on their side was their sheer weight. If they had been woven from bottom to top the pressure of the weaving as it built up would have forced the weft passes lower down the work to slide closer and closer together on the warps, thus distorting the design irretrievably. This fact is still an overriding consideration for those weaving studios, such as West Dean in Sussex and the Dovecot in Edinburgh, whose clients are often large commercial or institutional organizations requiring large-scale works – and of course for individual designer-weavers working on a similar large scale.

There is, however, one other aspect of design which has a bearing on which way the tapestry is woven, and this applies whether it is a large or a small piece of work. Because it is easier to change colour on a horizontal join than on a vertical one, a design with a preponderance of vertical lines – for instance, one based on tall city buildings – would obviously be woven more easily from side to side rather than from bottom to top.

The straight-line techniques demonstrated so far are used particularly in tapestry and rug designs based on geometrical

A montage of tall buildings in a city – a possible design source for strong shapes and lines to translate into a pattern of abstract geometrical shapes for tapestry weaving. Treated in a more figurative way, this is the type of design which would be better woven on its side.

This montage of a Georgian cityscape might well be a source of ideas for a
tapestry using dovetailed circles and curves, or eccentric-weft techniques.
Making up collections of photographs and magazine cut-outs on themes that
attract you is a good way of building up source material for reference purposes.

shapes: modern abstract designs, maybe, or those derived from tribal and ethnic work – Kelim rugs are an example we have already looked at. And, although they are also needed in the weaving of pictorial tapestries, for more natural forms weavers will need to extend their repertoire of joins into curved ones.

WEAVING CURVED SHAPES

Dovetailing

When working with a construction like weaving, which is made up of vertical (warp) lines and horizontal (weft) lines, it is obviously difficult to achieve a satisfactorily curved join between shapes. However, an easy way round the problem, is to use a simple dovetailing technique round adjacent wefts. The curve is achieved by varying the depth of the steps where the wefts meet and turn.

There are three points to note here. The first and most obvious one is that the finer the tapestry work being done (that is to say, the thinner the weft yarn and the greater the number of ends and passes per centimetre) the better the effect will be. So, weaving at the 2 e.p.cm of the sampler in the exercise at the end of this chapter, it will not be possible to get a really smooth curve.

Curved weft techniques. A circle woven with dovetail joins.

The second point to note is the need to transfer the line of the curve really accurately from the cartoon to the warp threads, and to keep carefully to this line as you weave. Remember also that as the wefts pack right down, a few passes below the fell line, this affects the accuracy of the curve. But do not worry; as in so many aspects of craft work, practice will perfect the technique once the basics are known. Again, the way it is done is really a matter of personal preference. Some weavers like to build up large areas of the background (but beware of undercutting) and then start to weave with the pattern colour; others prefer to weave all parts of the curve or circle simultaneously in order to make sure that the background and the shape it contains remains even, level and in the same pass as the work grows.

The third point is that the ease of following the line of the curve is considerably affected by which way the weft turns round the warp yarn: whether in a *high pass* or a *low pass*. The high pass is best for a curve going up to the right, while the low pass gives the smoothest edge to a curve running up to the left. It is therefore good weaving practice to place curves in the design so that this factor can be taken into consideration, if this is possible.

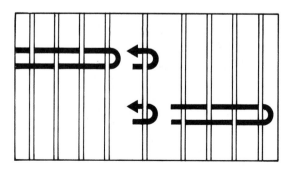

High pass and low pass.

Eccentric Weft

Coptic tapestry weavers are generally thought to have been the first to use this technique. When woven not horizontally but at eccentric, oblique angles and curves, the stepped effect of dovetailing can be avoided. It is a good technique to use in pictorial weaving, particularly of natural scenes and objects – nature tends to be curvy, as often as not. However, there is one problem: extreme care must be taken or the weaving will 'bubble' and distort badly, making it impossible, unless it is steamed, stretched and mounted very carefully, to get a smooth finished work. So, if you hope to simply line and hang your tapestry rather than mount it, beware of this method.

The technique is also used by Navajo weavers, and is sometimes called *wedge weaving*. This is because most Navajo designs are geometric, wedge-shaped ones rather than curved, so the effect obtained is somewhat different even though the method used is similar. The Navajos manipulate the weft into a triangle at one selvedge and the diagonal line this gives is extended until it forms a basis for all-over chevrons and zigzags.

However, this method of weaving diagonal joins between colours is not so popular with the Navajos as dovetailing. One of the reasons for this is that weak points appear in the weaving line where the chevrons meet; the two weft ends looping round adjacent warps – although similar to dovetailing – are on the diagonal rather than the horizontal and therefore distort the warps into quite an obvious series of holes. An old or worn textile may well tear at this point. Also, the formation of triangles of eccentric weft at the selvedge gives a scalloped edge to the blanket

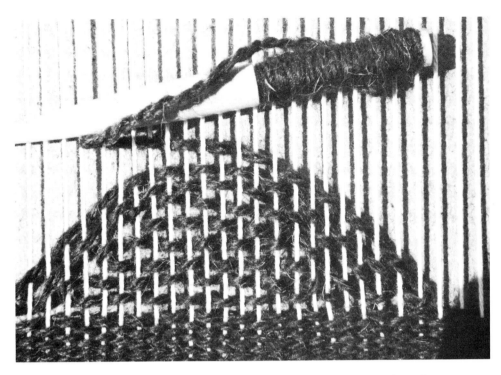

A detail of weaving curves with an eccentric weft (not beaten down, to show the method of laying in wefts).

A detail of wedge weaving, starting with a triangle at the selvedge.

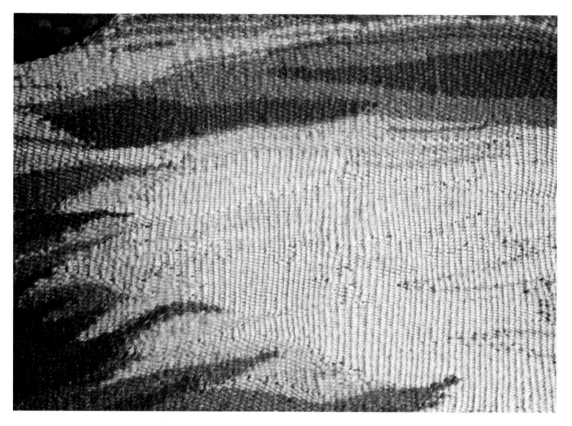

A detail of a tapestry in curved and eccentric-weft techniques.

which, to weavers who are used to judging the worth of a piece of work by the straightness of its edge, appears to be all wrong.

However, for a weaver looking for 'dazzle-effect' designs to use on a decorative, rather than a utilitarian, piece (where the instability of the construction will not matter so much), the exciting movement in the pattern makes this a technique worth remembering. And the distortion of the warps which occurs if the technique is used alone can be corrected by putting bands of horizontal plain or textured weave between the wedge-woven sections.

So, in any form of eccentric-weft weav-

ing, whether the aim is to achieve straight or curved lines, the first necessity is to lay in a base against which the obliquely laid wefts can be beaten down. But remember, whether started on the selvedge or in the centre of the design, this technique does have a tendency to distort the warps; and, the steeper the angle at which you are weaving, the greater the bubbling and buckling that will take place. However, used carefully, and particularly in the interpretation of natural forms, the technique can give a particularly lively sense of movement to a design – an effect which it is impossible to achieve from the more prosaic and plodding stepped curves of dovetailing.

WEAVING ON A DOUBLED WARP

This technique allows the weaver to achieve much greater detail in parts of the design where this might be useful – in faces and hands, for example – or where a very complex shape is wanted, one whose edges and details will be more clearly defined in a finer weave. For instance, with the 2 e.p.cm of the sampler tapestry in the exercise at the end of this chapter, details could be woven at 4 e.p.cm using a double warp – a big enough difference to give a good deal more flexibility and definition in the design.

This technique starts with the warping up of the frame. With two cones or balls of a finer cotton warp yarn (9/9s would be fine, if the original warp is 15/9s) the warp is wound in the usual way, either on or off the frame, but because it is wound from two cones each warp end is a double one. All the preparations for weaving, such as twining the head cord (see 'Warping on the Frame' in Chapter 14), putting in the shed stick and making the leashes, are done in the normal way, but with each warp end being, in fact, a pair of ends. When weaving starts with the main weft yarn, it is also done with each pair of ends treated as one end.

When a more detailed area of work is wanted, separate the pairs of ends and weave the weft through each individual end – thus doubling the number of available warp ends. In order not to distort the work, a weft yarn which is about half the thickness of the main yarn is needed for this area. Either split the main yarn, if this is possible, or find another suitable yarn. (My preferred method of using a number of fine singles as my weft, rather than one thick yarn, makes this easy to do.)

COLOUR-MIXING TECHNIQUES

One of the simplest ways of mixing colours in your work is to weave with multiple wefts – a number of different fine yarns in each weft pass rather than one thick yarn. Handspinners can vary the effect even more: a light twist to the bundle of fine yarns will give the effect of diagonal flecking (particularly interesting if one yarn is a metallic one); laying in the yarns untwisted gives an interesting shaded effect as random lengths of different colours surface or are covered. The technique, while hard to describe, is well worth experimenting with on a card loom sampler. The unexpectedness of the way the yarns behave is quite surprising and exciting.

Hatching was the technique used by medieval tapestry weavers to shade and blend colours. It is a form of dovetailing, but the penetration of colour from one block into another is done in a more haphazard manner, giving a more gradual naturalistic merging of the colours.

Stippling is another colour-shading technique. One half-pass of a colour interspersed amongst full passes of another will give a flecked effect which can be increased or diminished by the number of half-passes woven between each stippling line. (Alternating half-passes of two different colours gives vertical stripes – see 'Pick-and-Pick Colour Weaving' in the next chapter.)

SUPPLEMENTARY WARPS AND WRAPPED WARPS

Both these techniques are ways of building up extra surface interest on the face of

155

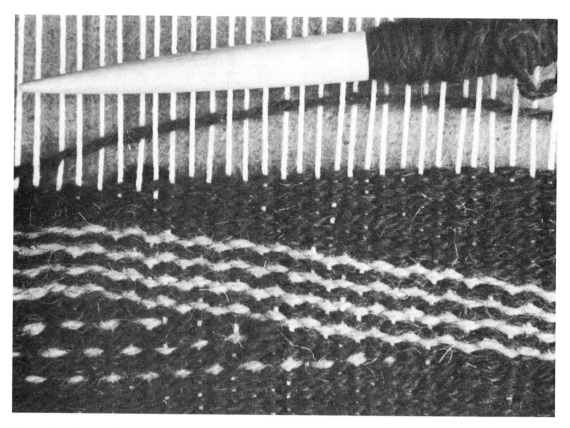

A sampler showing hatching and stippling on an eccentric weft.

the design. In the former, extra warps are brought through to the front of the work at the point where the extra layer of weaving is wanted. Depending where this is, the supplementary warps can be temporarily anchored either to the frame itself or to a rod tied to the back of the frame, and the ends secured neatly when the work is finally finished. These supplementary warps are tensioned by slipping the fingers through them, or use a short rod to pull on if you run out of fingers. It is usually easier to weave with a large needle.

Wrapping is normally done over a supplementary core of thicker yarn if it is to sit free on the surface of the work – piping cord, for instance, or a group of weft yarns if a decorative tassel or pompom is wanted on the end. Alternatively, it can form an integral part of the tapestry and be done round a group of the main warp threads. Wrapping, and *partial weaving* techniques such as the use of supplementary warps, can and inevitably will become a prominent feature of any design, so consider emphasizing them even more by using a coloured warp instead of a white cotton one, parts of which can be left uncovered, or only partly covered by, say, loose half-hitches. In this way a much lighter, more open design can be achieved, incorporating a very free use of the various tapestry techniques. And the

A detail of a tapestry showing partial weaving on supplementary warps ('Burning stubble' by Jo Tether).

Wrapped warps and other textured effects on a ring-woven tapestry (detail of 'Four Seasons' by Jo Tether).

interpretation of a theme in this way can result in a very abstract, personal and, to my mind, exciting piece.

THE NECESSITY OF CAREFUL SAMPLING

Particularly when trying out new or complex techniques such as these double and supplementary warps, it is a good idea to do a small sample, perhaps on a card loom, to make sure that the tension is right and the effect is as you want it. This is much easier than experimenting on the work itself, finding that you are not

happy with what you have done, and having to undo it all. Undoing weaving is an awful chore and I do my very best to avoid it.

Both the basic techniques themselves and all the variations and embellishments possible in and on the surface of the work are the reason why tapestry, although a much slower technique than some other forms of weaving, is so popular with so many weavers: it allows a degree of manipulative skills and the direct tactile control of the work which loom-controlled techniques do not give.

Another attraction of tapestry is that it

lends itself to the fairly exact reproduction of a design, and there is certainly a place, and a demand, for such pieces, often copied from actual scenes or derived perhaps from traditional European pictorial tapestries or from ethnic fabrics. Many weavers like making them, and their clients are more than happy because they recognize them as being traditional and familiar and find them comfortable to live with.

But sticking to this way of working, rather than a free and more abstract, more interpretative 'lets break the rules and see what happens' approach, can sometimes produce really rather dull work. So, as confidence grows, it is certainly worth trying out some experimental pieces to see if you enjoy these freedoms; admittedly, not everybody does.

The worst that can happen is that the experiment fails, in which case you can always hide it away and tell nobody. (But don't forget about it yourself. You should always use all work, whether or not it is successful, as part of the process of learning the craft.) And you never know – in a few years time you may well come back to the idea. Perhaps your first efforts were made before you were artistically or technically ready for that particular way of thinking and making.

But if what you achieve as a result of throwing away at least parts of the rule book does seem to have possibilities for you, then I suggest that it is well worth while continuing to develop it. You may well be starting down a path which leads to somewhere very special.

WEAVING EXERCISE 1

A small decorative wall hanging with vertical and diagonal tapestry joins for a design based on the patterns derived from a cityscape, and developed in Design Exercise 3.

You need:

- small tapestry frame at least 25 × 35cm
- cotton warp yarn
- tapestry yarns in the colours of your design

Using the wrapped-ruler method, calculate the required ends per centimetre for the warp.

Warp up the frame, using the figure-of-eight method. Put in heading cord and guides.

Lay the frame down on the A4-sized cartoon, and mark the warp ends with the main elements of the design. Keep the cartoon by you as you weave, to refer to.

Using weft-faced plain weave and vertical and horizontal joins, weave the project.

When finished, cut off the loom, and finish with tassels, beads, or the like, as you please. Depending on your colourway, this could look very ethnic, like a Turkish Kelim carpet, or very modern and abstract, like the North African townscapes painted by Klee.

(This design could be scaled up ×4, and given a plain border, to make a small weft-face rug to weave on a larger frame.)

17
Two-Shaft Weaving with a Rigid Heddle

Other than frame looms, probably the best-known and most useful small two-shaft loom on which to learn the techniques of continuous weft fabric weaving (as opposed to the various discontinuous-weft techniques used in tapestry weaving) is the *rigid heddle loom*. Although they are two-shaft looms, a pick-up stick allows the weaver to open more sheds and so extend their use into very complex pat-terned and inlaid designs; the quick change-over from shaft to shaft makes them faster to weave with than anything but a pedal-operated frame loom; and, either clamped to a table or held on the lap and braced against a table, they are sturdy enough for weaving both warp- and weft-faced fabrics. Altogether they are a most useful tool, one that costs only about one-third the price of the equivalent

A rigid heddle loom.

four-shaft table loom, and which can even be home-made.

The rigid heddle loom has a roughly square box-like frame about 15–20cm high and is made in various sizes to give a weaving width from about 25 up to 50cm. At the back is a warp beam with, below and behind it, a warp roller. In the front is a similar cloth beam and cloth roller. About two-thirds of the way back, raised in two positions – level with the line from warp roller to cloth roller, and above this level – is a notched support for the rigid heddle itself.

Rigid heddles are the only part of the loom which has to be bought; it is not really realistic to try to make them oneself, although traditionally they were hand-carved from bone, wood and ivory. Like lace bobbins, I am sure some must have been love tokens, they are so beautiful. The rigid heddle has been, and still is, the shed-making mechanism for many forms of simple weaving device; the way it is normally used now, with a purpose-made frame, is a fairly modern idea. In the past it has been used singly (or severally, for multi-shaft brocaded weaving for example) with all manner of narrow cloth looms such as the backstrap, the North American Indian braid loom, and the South American and West African ground looms.

Nowadays the rigid heddle is usually made of enamelled metal or a tough, smooth man-made material. They come in various lengths to suit the loom width (or in short sections of about 10cm which can be combined to the length required) and are made in various *dents*. The dentage of the heddle matches the ends per centimetre at which the weaving is done – so a different number of ends per centimetre equals a different heddle. Three heddles

of 3, 4 and 5 dents per centimetre would give a reasonable range, useful for two-ply rug/tapestry wool, a finer 2/14s–2/16s worsted or similar cotton, and a fine Botany wool, cotton or silk at around 3/18s–2/27s.

A warp of the required length is made off the loom, in the usual way as described in Chapter 15. The cross is secured and a flat stick – the *apron stick*, which is attached to the back or warp roller – is threaded through the loops at the cross end of the warp. The warp is then brought over the back beam and laid down. Spread the long tie securing the cross in the warp (which should lie just in front of the back beam and behind the heddle) and put in two cross sticks, behind and in front of the cross, to hold it in place. Remove the yarn tie and spread the warp out to its required width. You can then suspend the cross sticks from the heddle uprights; this will keep the warp level with the eyes of the heddle as you thread it.

Do this by first finding the centre pair of warps and threading their loop through the slit in the centre of the heddle. Pull it right through until it is taut and lay it down. Then, working alternately from side to side (and keeping an eye on the cross to make sure the ends are in the right order), continue to thread each pair of warp ends through the slits in the heddle, pulling them right through as you go. When you reach the final single warp ends they go through the final slit on each side. You are now ready to *beam on*.

This is the process of winding the warps, evenly and tightly, round the back roller. The fact that the warp ends run over the cross sticks and are threaded through the heddle helps to keep them properly spaced. A piece of stout brown

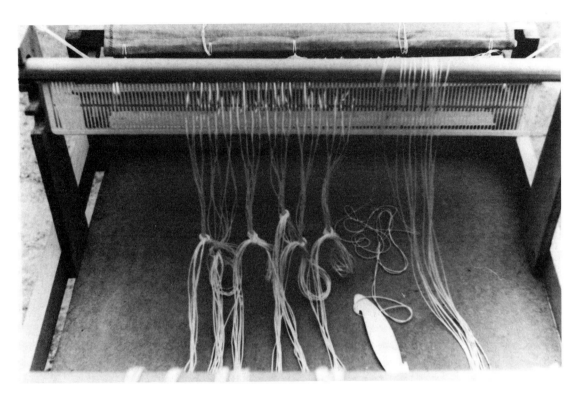

Dressing the loom – the warp tied on to the back apron stick and warp loops being threaded through the heddle slits.

paper rolled in with the warps will help to keep them evenly spread, which is essential if good warp tension is to be maintained. There are two ways of doing the winding on. The first is with two people, one standing at the front, holding the warp ends to tension them, the other turning the back roller to feed on the ends and their paper interlining. Alternatively, if you are single-handed, you can do it by yourself. Give the roller one full turn and lock it; then come round to the front of the loom and pick up groups of warp yarns in sequence across the width of the warp, giving them a series of sharp, even tugs to tighten them on the roller. Repeat the rolling and tugging until the warp is fully wound on – that is to say until the ends

just about reach the front beam. The one-man method is a little slower, but I find it makes a much better and more even warp and so I always use it now.

Having wound the warp, bring the front apron stick over the beam and into position for tying on. Then cut the loops, pull every alternate end back out of the slit in the heddle and rethread it through the next-door hole. As you do the re-threading make sure, by keeping your eye on the cross, that all the ends in one shed are rethreaded through holes, and that all the ends left in the slits come from the other shed. Then, to change to the opposite (the *rising* or *up* shed) all you do is to lift the heddle frame up into the higher of the pairs of notches.

161

After beaming on, re-threading the warp through the heddle eyes.

Tying groups of ends on to the front apron stick.

The warp has been tensioned, tying on completed and a few picks of heading woven.

When all the ends have been re-threaded tie them, in groups of four or six, on to the front apron stick. Take each group of ends over the stick, divide it into half, bring the halves up on either side and tie them together in a single knot. Continue like this, working outwards from the centre on alternating sides, until all the groups of ends are tied on. Check that the warp tension is even right the way across the width (the first ends to be tied will probably need pulling up) and then finish the tying on by securing each group of ends with a bow or a reef knot.

All that remains now is to weave a few picks of heading. Use a length of any different-coloured yarn for this, about double the thickness you will be weaving

with. The heading evens out the warp ends. Also, if there are any mistakes in the threading they will be seen now, and can be rethreaded.

TEXTURED EFFECTS

There are two methods of achieving textured effects: either by using textured yarns, particularly in the weft, or with various techniques such as knotting and looping, which produce a decorative textured surface to the work. These techniques are rooted in the early history of ethnic and tribal weaving, particularly of rug weaving, and have been enthusiastically adopted and freely adapted by

163

Weaving on the rigid heddle loom with a pick-up stick to open a shed.

Beating down the weft with a comb beater (using the rigid heddle as beater is seldom enough with weft-faced fabrics).

modern rug and tapestry weavers as a means of decorating the surface of their work.

The use to which a piece will be put has considerable bearing on the suitability of decorative yarns and techniques. While floor rugs, bags and other utilitarian articles require strong yarns and hard-wearing weave techniques to withstand household wear and tear, a purely decorative piece can be made with fancier yarns, longer floats and loops and even found objects.

Textured Yarns

Using fancy yarns such as bouclé, slub, loop and multi-coloured yarns in order to mimic natural textures and colours can be most effective, but care has to be taken when using yarns of different types and thicknesses that they do not distort the work. Careful sampling is, as always, the name of the game: using a double warp, with the pairs separated for the smooth, fine yarns, the medium yarns woven over the doubled ends and the thickest yarns taken over and under two ends at a time, might be worth trying out, for instance. All in all, textured yarns can be used to introduce a considerable variety of surface textures and effects into the simplest plain weaves.

Twining

This is thought to be one of the oldest textile-making techniques. Used by basket makers, it probably predates woven textiles. The fact that it needs to be interlaced

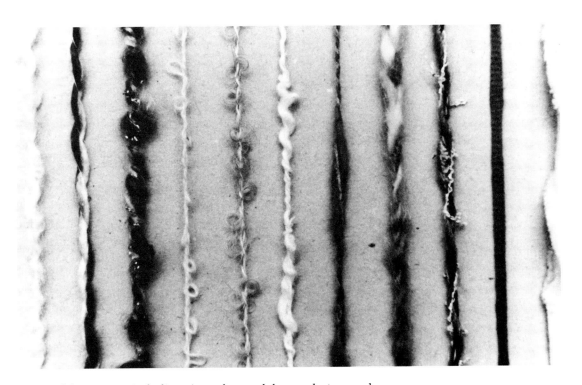

Textured fancy yarns including gimps, loops, slubs, snarls, tape and rag.

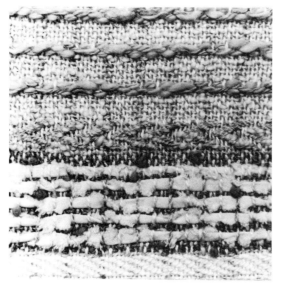

A plain-weave sampler with textured yarns.

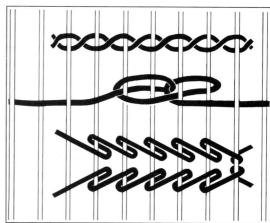

Textured weaves – twining, chaining, soumak.

on a firm framework suggests that it may well have been the forerunner of weaving. It is, of course, the same method as the one used to make a heading at the start of frame-loom weaving, so the fabric produced by twining techniques is firm and strong, as well as interestingly textured. Variations in the colours of the yarns and the direction in which they are intertwined can produce combinations of both pattern and texture.

Chaining

This technique gives a series of interconnected loops on the surface of the work, not unlike chain stitch in embroidery. Because it is not very stable it needs to be alternated with at least one pick of plain weave to hold it in position, and since it sits on the surface of the work it can be done with a different, perhaps thicker, yarn than the weaving weft yarn. When using a different yarn it is best to darn the

end in securely at the start of the pick. Then take this chaining weft yarn behind all the warps and lay the butterfly or shuttle down so that the yarn can feed out freely. With your fingers (or a crochet hook if the ends are closely sett) pull out a loop off the weft from under the second warp end and lay it over the next end, then pull another loop of weft through the first loop, and so on. Carry on chain-making like this across the full width of the work, making sure that the loops are evenly spaced and sized.

Soumak or Sumak

This is another weft-wrapping technique. Named after Sumak in the southern Caucasus, it is a central Asian textile technique which is still used in Turkish flat-woven rugs and sacks. As with twining and chaining, it is often alternated with plain-weave areas for contrast; and because it has a slight degree of instability, since it passes over and under more than one warp end at a time, it is a good idea to lock the soumak picks into place with one or two picks of plain weave. The same yarn can be used for the plain-weave weft and the decorative soumak weft, or they can be different; for instance, a thick wool yarn can be used for the soumak while a much finer, stronger cotton one makes the plain-weave locking pick. In this way, the latter will not show at all on the right side of the work – it is there merely to give stability to the fabric. If two different weft yarns are used it is once more a good idea to darn the soumak weft end in straight away at the beginning of the pick, as this gives a firm start against which to tension the soumak loops.

The soumak weft yarn is passed over at least two warp ends (and up to four if the weaving is finer) and then goes round and behind one (or two) ends. It then comes back to the front, and the second and subsequent loops are made in a similar manner until the full width has been covered. As with twining, the angle of the soumak can be varied by the direction in which it is looped; likewise, a single row of soumak can immediately be followed by a second row, looped in the opposite direction. This *double soumak* gives an interestingly textured herringbone effect. An article woven entirely in soumak is much more flexible than one woven in a weft-faced plain weave, but the Turks consider it equally strong and use it for carrying and storage sacks.

Vertical Soumak

In both single and double varieties, vertical soumak can be very decorative. The single version is often used to outline tapestry-woven motifs; this gives extra emphasis and textural interest, and is known as *raised-outline technique* in Navajo weaving. In Turkey, the slit

formed between the stepped designs in Kelim rugs is sometimes filled in with a single weft of vertical soumak, to close it. The vertical double soumak technique forms an interesting surface decoration on a firm weft-faced plain-weave fabric.

Weft Inlay

This is yet another technique from central Asia, which the Turks call *cicim*. It is woven with two different weft yarns in alternating picks – a thicker or different-coloured inlay weft yarn and a finer or neutral-coloured *binding weft* yarn – and gives an effect like satin-stitch embroidery. Because of the instability of the inlay, which can pass over quite a number of warp ends particularly at the back of the design, it is necessary to alternate every pick of inlay with a pick of binder. For rugs, the designs need to be organized so that there are no long *floats* on the back, but in purely decorative pieces, or articles

Weft inlay.

167

that are to be lined, this is not so critical. Very intricate surface decoration can be achieved using this technique.

Single-Warp Inlay

I have given the technique this name for want of a better. I had not met the technique before we went to Turkey, where they call it *sili*, and even Peter Collingwood's definitive work *The Techniques of Rug Weaving* does not seem to mention it. (The Turks appear to use the term warp-wrapping to describe *cicim* and *sili*, although we tend to think of soumak and chaining as warp-wrapping techniques, and these as warp-overlaying, or inlay.) This pattern-making technique is also done with an inlay yarn and a binder, the former usually a thicker wool and the latter the same much finer yarn, often a strong, coloured cotton, as the one used for the warp.

The different coloured motifs are built up over every end in the first pick of dis-

Single warp inlay.

continuous weaving, as in the tapestry technique, leaving all the different coloured ends of the woollen weft yarns hanging down the back. The return pick is done in the opposite shed with the fine cotton binder yarn, and goes straight across the width of the work. Weaving continues in this way, alternating inlay and binder picks while building up the individually coloured pattern motifs. The finished effect is an interesting mix of a heavy, vertically ribbed weave across areas of both pattern and background, each rib alternating with a fine vertical line made by the cotton weft thread locking round the warp. In other words, this is not a true weft-faced weave because every other warp is visible.

It seems to me that single-warp inlay would be woven more easily from the back than from the front, as with the traditional tapestry technique, although I have not tried it this way myself. The fabric is, after all, reversible and the pattern can easily be seen from the back. The simple geometrical designs could be worked out on graph paper, so that the number of ends to be covered in each pick by the different colours of weft yarn could be counted off. The benefit of working back to front is that the weft ends are on the side of the work facing the weaver and so can easily be picked up and dropped as needed.

KNOTTING AND LOOPING TECHNIQUES

Knotted-pile rugs and carpets are of very ancient origin. Like so many other textile techniques and processes, they followed the routes out of central Asia taken by succeeding waves of nomadic tribesmen:

east into China, south into India, west into Persia, Turkey and North Africa and thence finally into Europe via Spain. Naturally, slightly different knotting methods evolving during the course of their travels.

Knotting allows the maker to design and weave patterns of great intricacy and delicacy, with none of the problems such as stepped edges that we have seen with flat-weaving techniques. The use of varying types and thicknesses of yarn (usually wool or silk) can enhance this pattern making by varying the density of the knotting – from a relatively coarse 16 knots to the square centimetre through an average quality carpet at 40 knots to the finest 'court carpets' woven with about 140 knots. These latter were quite exceptional, though. In Turkey we saw ex-

quisite silk carpets woven at 100 knots to the square centimetre; even these take about three years to make and I imagine the young weavers, whose eyesight is never quite the same again, think that this is quite enough.

Traditionally the knots are cut (though the uncut loop gives an interesting variation) and the pile is then scissored down uniformly to give a smooth, velvety finish. In China the pile cutting is done to different levels, adding a sculptured element to the pattern woven into the carpet. Some knotted carpets, however, have a very long, shaggy pile. Greek *flokati* rugs are woven like this, with a very loosely spun thick yarn like a pencil roving used for the knots, while for their *filikili* rugs the Turks actually knot with tufts of

A Greek flokati rug.

A rolag rug woven from the fleece of Jacob sheep.

unspun cut fleece. This is done so that the rug has the look and feel of a sheepskin but is easily washed and of a uniform shape and size.

These types of knotted rugs in which unspun, or virtually unspun, fibres are used need to be given a very careful and very hot soap-and-water scouring to shrink and set the knots into the woven base, otherwise they will shed the fibres and rapidly become bald. Having said that, I do think that they make a much more successful rug than the version that one tends to see more often in this country, known as the *rolag rug*, flat-woven from unspun woollen rolags or tops, usually in a plain weave. These seldom seem to be really all that stable, however well they are fulled.

Knots

The *Ghiordes* or *Turkish knot* is made round two warp ends, and is a strong, firm knot which is widely used in many rug-making areas of the world. As with all these knotting techniques, traditionally the weaver holds the butterfly or small ball of yarn in one hand, the scissors or knife in the other, and 'knots and cuts' across the weft, dropping one colour of yarn and picking up another as the design demands. After three or four rows of knots have been made and have been beaten down lightly, a heavy beater forces them well down on to the fell of the work, and the pile is trimmed off with angled scissors to the level of the previous knots.

However, certainly to begin with, it is probably easier to cut equal lengths of yarn, on the generous side, and make each knot individually. Then, after knotting across the width of the work, it is necessary to put in at least one or two picks of plain weave weft to hold them securely in place. The next row of knots is made round the alternate pairs of warp ends, to distribute the pile evenly. Alternatively, knotting can be done in the traditional method with an uncut length of yarn, but looped round a piece of dowelling. The loops can then be cut or not, as required. Because the knot ends are all of even length, no further pile trimming will be needed if a dowel of the right diameter is used.

The *Sehna* or *Persian knot* is the other classic knot. Because it is made round a single warp, with its ends coming out between every warp space, carpets made from it are denser, softer and more flexible, and have the most intricate patterning. So it has traditionally been used for the finest textiles, for court carpets, prayer rugs and wall and table rugs – those not subjected to too much wear. The Sehna knot can be made lying either to the right or to the left, which affects the lie of the pile; like the Ghiordes, it should be alternated with a pick of plain weave, and tied round alternate warp ends in each row.

The *Spanish knot* is another version of a knot tied round a single warp end, and on alternating ends in each row. But it differs from the Persian knot in that it is symmetrical, rather than lying to one side, and is normally locked in place with three picks of plain weave. This gives a looser, less dense pile to Spanish rugs.

The *Rya* or *Swedish knot* was used originally to make a double-sided textile produced as a warm bed covering, although

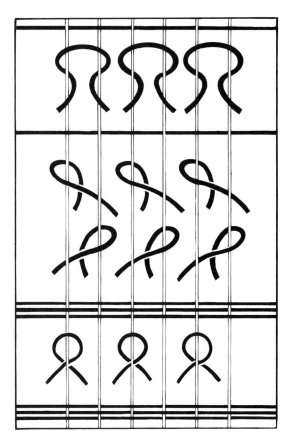

Ghiordes, Sehna and Spanish knots.

for floor rugs it is knotted on the one side only. The knots are made like the Ghiordes, but tied round the first and third warp ends, the second and fourth warp ends, and so on, while the pile is usually longer and shaggier than in other knotted rugs. Each row of knots is locked into place with at least three picks of plain weave, which means that there will only be about 2–4 knots per square centimetre. A thick yarn is therefore used for knotting, often made up of a variety of thinner ones to give interesting colour shading and blending effects.

It is always worth experimenting and techniques adapted from knotted structures such as macramé can be used to give very free, textured effects to tapestries.

SOME MORE PATTERN AND COLOUR WEAVES

Pick-and-Pick Colour Weaving

This is a weft-faced plain weave, with two colours alternating 'pick and pick'. Once the weaver understands the principle a number of different pattern combinations can be simply and quickly woven. As these are small patterns in themselves, the way colour is used in them can be critical. For instance, they can be made to look bold and definite by the use of strong colour contrasts – bright primaries against a dark background, or primaries woven pick-and-pick with their secondaries. Alternatively, by the use of more muted shades against a neutral background, or by a combination of closely related colours (those near to each other on the colour wheel), much softer, less assertive colour patterning will result.

Pick-and-pick patterns. Variations 1 and 2 give checks and dashes.

Using pick-and-pick patterns in combination with varying widths of stripes (the narrowest possible is two picks wide) enlarges the scope still more, while opening new sheds with a pick-up stick means that three or even more colours can be woven into the design.

Variations

I have found that the use of these small abstract and very controlled patterns contrasted with more figurative designs such as people, animals and natural forms can also be most effective. The patterning technique described below – Peter Collingwood calls it *skip plain weave* – is one used by North African flat-weave rug makers. It can be woven easily on two shafts, again using a pick-up stick, and although slow the method is quite simple. (From now on these pick-and-pick variations, and all the diagrams illustrating weaves, will be set out as a weave plan for clarity. The format is explained in Chapter 11.)

Variation 1 One pick colour A, one pick colour B, gives a series of vertical stripes. To form a chequerboard pattern, weave two picks of colour A at the point where you want to change colour, then continue one pick colour B, one pick colour A until the next change.

Variation 2 One pick colour A, two or more picks colour B will give a series of dashes. Odd numbers of picks of colour B (3, 5) will line the dashes vertically upwards; even numbers of picks of colour B (2, 4) will line the dashes diagonally.

Variation 3 Lift the first shed for the first pick, and working in the lower half of the

Variations 3, 4, 5 and 6 give stripes.

shed – *see* Variation 7 for an explanation – thread the pick-up stick under the even-numbered ends (2, 4, 6, 8 etc.) across the shed; insert colour A into this 'secondary shed'. Still with the first shed lifted, re-thread the pick-up stick under the odd-numbered ends (1, 3, 5 and so on) and insert colour B into this second 'secondary shed'. Now change to the opposite shed, and insert colour C. This will give you vertical stripes in three colours. By use of the pick-up stick, three or more colours can be introduced into any pick-and-pick variation.

Variation 4 Two picks colour A, two picks colour B and, if using three colours or more, two picks colour C, and so on. This gives fine wavy stripes.

Variation 5 Three picks colour A, three picks colour B – and three picks colour C, and so on, if required. This gives a thick/ thin line, rather like a chain.

Variation 6 Four or more picks of one colour give a solid, straight-edged stripe. Interesting effects can be achieved by varying stripe width and colour.

Variation 7 (simple skip-plain-weave tri-angles to try out the technique)   In order to keep the floats on the back of the work, all skip plain-weave patterns and others in which a pick-up stick is used must be done on the ends in the lower half of the shed – those which have not been lifted. Alternatively, as in North Africa, they can be woven with the back of the work to-wards the weaver. However, I prefer to see what I am doing, and have never found working in the lower part of the shed difficult.

In the first shed, and counting always from right to left, with the pick-up stick lift ends 3–9–15 and so on in groups of one end all the way across. Lay in the pat-tern colour A. Withdraw the pick-up stick

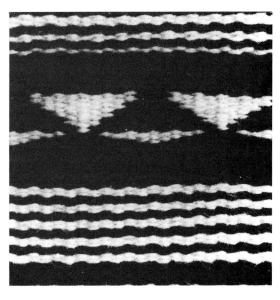

Variation 7, triangles in skip plain weave. The second, steeper-sided one is woven by repeating each pick a second time.

A weft-faced-weave wall hanging 'A coat for Tansy' in pick-and-pick and skip-plain-weave patterns.

A shoulder bag 'Spin a Shetland' in weft-faced patterned weave.

and reinsert it to lift all the remaining ends, 1, 2 – 4, 5, 6, 7, 8 – 10, 11, 12, 13, 14 and so on in groups of five ends across the shed. Lay in the background colour B.

These two picks have now covered every end in the first shed (this is most important) so you can now change to the opposite shed. To make the second complete pick, and the second row of pattern, and again counting from right to left, thread the pick-up stick under ends 2, 3 – 8, 9 – 14, 15 and so on for pattern colour A, and then rethread the pick-up stick under ends 1 – 4, 5, 6, 7 – 10, 11, 12, 13 and so on for background colour B. For the third pick, in the opposite shed, first lift ends 2, 3, 4 – 8, 9, 10 – 14, 15, 16 and so on and lay in the pattern colour A. Then complete this full pick by covering all the remaining ends (5, 6, 7 – 11, 12, 13 and so on) with the background colour B. The fourth pick covers first ends 1, 2, 3, 4 – 7, 8, 9, 10 – 13, 14, 15, 16 and so on, with pattern colour and the remaining 5, 6 – 11, 12 and so on with background colour. The fifth and final pick to complete the triangles will

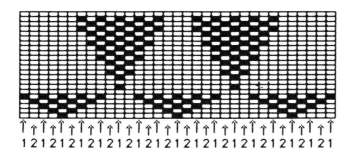

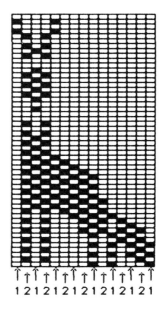

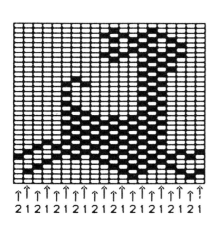

Skip-plain-weave patterns drawn out on graph paper (alternating shafts marked 1 and 2) – triangles and hare and fox from detail of 'A coat for Tansy'. They illustrate the possibility of adapting other graphed designs (Fair Isle knitting and so on) for skip plain weave.

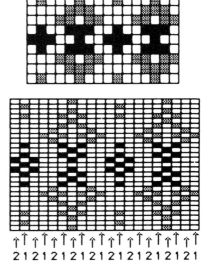

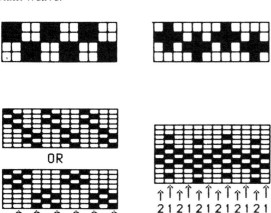

A detail of hare and fox motifs in skip plain weave.

cover ends 1, 2, 3, 4, 5 – 7, 8, 9, 10, 11 – 13, 14, 15, 16, 17 and so on with pattern colour A, and then lay background colour B over all the remaining ends (6 – 12) and so on to the end.

Even a simple triangle seems very complicated written out like this, so I hope that a look at the graph pattern will simplify this string of figures. In fact, once the first complete pick is laid in for the triangles the next comes automatically because it is obvious that the two ends to cover with pattern colour are the ones on either side of the first one. You don't in fact have to count them off, just build up the shape by eye.

One final point to watch when using a pick-up stick, particularly for complex skip-plain-weave designs is the length of the floats across the back of the work. As with inlay patterning, long floats are tolerable only on a piece that is going to be lined; they are not suitable for a rug to go on the floor.

The exercise at the end of this chapter is a shoulder bag made in weft-faced plain weave using pick-and-pick technique, with some simple skip-plain-weave patterns added. I always like samplers to be both decorative and useful, and I hope this will prove to be so.

WEAVING EXERCISE 2

A shoulder bag in weft-faced plain weave using pick-and-pick patterns based on the stripes derived from Design Exercise 2.

You need:

● either a rigid-heddle loom, or a frame loom large enough to weave at least one side of a 35 × 45cm bag
● cotton warp yarn
● tapestry yarn, and some suitable textured yarns to add interest to the stripes (strips of cotton rag, about 5–7mm wide, would be an interesting addition – or the whole bag could be woven with cotton rags used as the weft yarn)

Decide on a suitable background colour to complement, or contrast with, your chosen colourway. Use one of the stripe variations you designed in Design Exercise 2 as the basis of the pick-and-pick stripes (see variations 4, 5 and 6). Your figures (3, 4, 5, 4, 3) could be used to give the number of picks in each stripe, or their width – it rather depends how you did it in your original design in Exercise 2.

Work out (on graph paper, by cut-and-stick or by wrapping) how to arrange the groups of stripes over the whole surface of the bag; and, if you would like to try out one skip-plain-weave motif to give extra interest to the design, choose a simple, bold shape (such as a pet animal, a boat, a house, a flower), trace it, rub with HB pencil and transfer to suitable graph paper. (If possible, use the type of graph paper mentioned at the end of Chapter 14 to avoid distortion.) Alternatively, use a variety of textured yarns to give emphasis to your stripes. Remember, don't try to do everything at once, or the effect will be over the top. It is best to stick to *either* pattern *or* texture.

Having determined the e.p.cm required in the usual manner (ruler wrapping), warp up the loom or frame. When the weaving is completed, finish the fabric, seam the sides, line if necessary, twist a cord and trim as required.

18
Weaving on Four Shafts

Four-shaft table looms are really only smaller and simpler versions of the horizontal floor loom, or *treadle loom*, with its shafts operated by foot pedals. For thousands of years this was the ultimate in loom design, freeing the operator's hands for throwing the weft through the sheds and beating the pick down on to the fell of the work – in other words, considerably speeding up the process.

It appeared in Europe about AD 1000,

but its origin is undoubtedly Asian, and may well be at least three thousand years older. In his *The Book of Looms* Eric Broudy says that it was probably the use of silk and cotton as textile-making fibres in China and India that led to the development of the treadle loom.

The major difference between the table loom and the treadle loom is in the way the shafts are lifted. In the case of the former, the lifting is done by hand; with the

A four-shaft 24in table loom.

latter the feet are used. This variation in the lifting mechanism is also all that differentiates the four-shaft table loom from the two-shaft rigid heddle loom. In the case of the former, four heddle frames are lifted by hand-operated levers; with the latter, one rigid heddle is lifted into position manually. In other words, the main feature of the loom (a stout framework) is the same, because it has to perform the same basic function, which is to tension the warp threads. Refinements such as more shafts, and easier and speedier mechanisms for lifting them, are just that – refinements.

The other obvious difference between a rigid heddle loom and a table loom, and between a table loom and a treadle loom, is size and stength. Although a well-constructed small table loom can stand up to the considerable tension required of a warp for weft-faced cloth weaving, tensioning and beating down a thick, tapestry-woven rug is too great a strain

A 12in sample loom.

for anything but a large floor-standing loom – although small lightweight mats woven in strips and then joined together are perfectly possible on table looms. Nor is it really reasonable to expect to weave lengths of cloth on smaller looms. Not only will it take far too long to make commercial sense, but the warp rollers and more particularly the cloth rollers do not have enough clearance to accommodate more than a few yards of fabric. So use the smaller looms for short warps, the ones easily made on a warping frame, and for smaller projects – and, of course, for sampling work which will ultimately be woven on a larger loom.

THE CONSTRUCTION AND PARTS OF A FOUR-SHAFT LOOM

The parts and functions of a four-shaft table loom can be explained in almost the same way as those of the rigid heddle loom. Just as their construction is similar, much of the weaving which can be done on them is interchangeable. Many two-shaft weaves, ones that actually require only two shafts, are in fact often done on four; and, conversely, using a pick-up stick makes many four-shaft weaves perfectly feasible on two. So a great number of the weave patterns and techniques described from Chapter 11 onwards can be woven on other types of loom – it is largely a question of personal preference, convenience and, of course, what sort of loom you can afford.

The four-shaft table loom has a roughly square box-like frame about 20–30cm high and is made in various sizes to give a weaving width from about 30cm up to 75cm (30cm is usual for what is called a sample loom, 60cm for a general all-round loom). At the back is a warp beam with, below and behind it, a warp roller. In the front is a similar cloth beam and cloth roller. About two-thirds of the way back is a framework from which are suspended the four heddle frames or *harnesses*; these are lifted by means of pulleys and levers. In front of the harnesses is a *batten* or *beater* – a wooden framework enclosing a metal *reed*.

Accommodating and Supporting the Loom

Some table looms come with their own stand, which not only supports it firmly and steadily but also hold all the yarns, tools and so on needed for weaving. Otherwise, the ideal solution is to have a special table to keep the loom on, one to which it can be clamped permanently and which is big enough for all the necessary weaving accessories to be kept on it. The requirements for accommodating a table loom satisfactorily (and I include the rigid heddle loom in this category) are much the same as finding a working space for a frame loom: a good source of both daylight and artificial light is essential as well as a degree of privacy. A work space of one's own is really a delightful luxury.

Tensioning the Warp

As with the rigid heddle loom, the warp runs between the apron stick on the back roller or warp roller (used for warp storage), over the back beam and thence to the front beam, over this, and then to the apron stick on the front roller (the roller used for cloth storage). Ratchets on front and back rollers are turned in opposite directions to tension the warp, and as weaving progresses the warps are rolled forward off the back beam and converted into woven cloth. This in its turn is rolled on to the front beam, thus keeping the fell of the work in an easy weaving position – approximately 10–20cm from the front beam is comfortable, I find. Too close to the beam and the beater cannot reach the fell; too far back towards the heddles and the shed is too small for comfortable weaving.

Making the Shed

As the warp ends journey from back roller to front roller each one is threaded through the eye of the heddles in the heddle frames to form the shed. These heddles, stretched between the top and bottom of the frames, are made from wire, or cotton or polyester cord.

Because the distance between the back and the front of the loom is greater in a table loom than in a rigid heddle loom – and becomes even more so with large floor-standing treadle looms – the shed is bigger. This is because the greater the length of the ends of warp yarn threaded through the heddles, the higher the lifting mechanism can raise the heddle frames, which in turn means that there is a larger gap between the warp threads lifted and the warp threads left in the level position. (Most table looms have a *rising shed*; that is to say, the warps are all on the same level as the back and front beams, and lifting the heddle frames raises the selected warps above this level to form the shed.)

Each heddle frame is connected to a lever by means of a cord and pulley. With heddle frames numbered from 1 to 4, reading front to back, there are fourteen

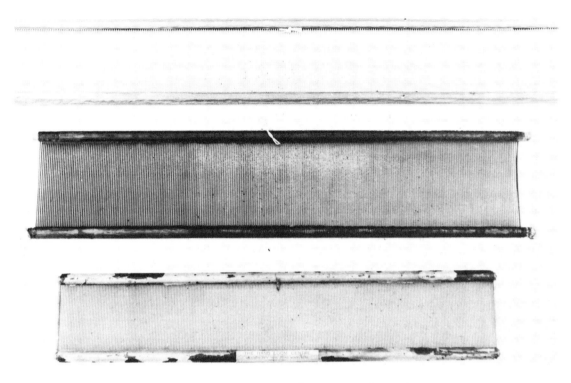

Three reeds – 8, 10 and 12 dents per 1in (2.5cm). Note the string marker at the centre of each.

different combinations of heddle lifts, and thus fourteen different sheds, given by a four-shaft loom. This shows why a table loom is such a useful and versatile tool: without rethreading (re-dressing) the loom – accepted by most weavers as being the worst job of all – a great variety of patterns can be woven. A four-shaft treadle loom has to be re-dressed for every new weave plan, because the heddle lifts are tied to the pedals and therefore only the predetermined lifts can be made.

So, when weaving on a table loom, what you lose in speed of weaving you gain in versatility – a fact which explains why weavers working on complex cloths needing, say, sixteen or more shafts will sometimes prefer to use a simple and light sixteen-shaft table loom rather than an admittedly faster but much heavier and more tiring to operate sixteen-shaft dobby loom. The reason why I have used a dobby loom in this comparison is that it works in the same way as a table loom: that is to say, individual lifts operate individual heddle frames. And please don't ask me, if four shafts give fourteen lifts, how many lifts sixteen shafts will give – my mathematics is just not up to it. Quite a few, I imagine.

Determining the Sett and Beating down the Fabric

Both these jobs are done by the batten and reed. The batten is a wooden framework containing a slotted metal reed – the best are made of stainless steel as it does not rust. It is set in front of the heddle frames and hinged either from top or bottom, normally from the botton in a table loom.

Reed threadings at ends per centimetre (e.p.cm)

Reed dentage (Dents per cm)	every other dent	every dent	Threaded 1, 2	1, 2, 2	2 in each
3	1.5	3	4.5	5	6
5	2.5	5	7.5	8.2	10
7	3.5	7	10.5	11.75	14

The warp threads, on their way from back roller to front roller, are each threaded through the slots in the reed after going through the eyes of the heddles and before ending their journey tied on to the front apron stick. Reeds come in various widths and depths to fit various sizes of loom, and they are graded in *dents* per centimetre (or dents per inch – 1 inch = 2.5cm approximately).

Reeds range from about 2 to 16 dents per centimetre (from 5 to 40 dents per inch) and are varied according to the ends per centimetre of the project being woven. They not only hold the ends in order but also space them, making the weaving of an evenly set cloth much easier than with the string heddles of a frame loom. Although they come in a wide range of dents per centimetre this does not mean that a weaver needs one of these expensive items of equipment for every cloth set. Particularly with a closely set fabric, more than one warp end can be threaded through a dent, dents can be missed out and a variety of ways of threading the reed can be used. In fact, the practice of *sleying* (threading) more than one end in each dent cuts down friction on delicate yarns such as silk and lambswool, while it is a good idea to sley fluffy yarns like brushed mohair one per dent to keep them separate and prevent tangles.

The main consideration when deciding on how to thread the reed is that the sleying should be done evenly across the width of the work. The table gives some ideas on how just three reeds can be used to weave cloth in a wide variety of setts, depending on how the warp ends are threaded through them – threaded every other dent, threaded every dent, threaded one end through the first dent and two through the second, and so on.

THE RECORD SHEET

As always, the first thing to do when starting a new weaving project is to decide on the piece being made, the yarn being used, the sett of the fabric to be woven and the weave plan. To help in this, I have designed a record sheet for myself. I find it serves as a most useful checklist and I use it for projects as well as sample work (in the latter case the record sheets, along with the actual fabric samples, are filed away for easy reference). For every project I try to keep at least a scrap of the fabric for future reference. If this isn't possible, say with a tapestry or a rug, a photograph of the finished work, including a close-up, serves as a valuable additional source of information. I also have various versions of the record sheet

RECORD SHEET

Project _____ Date (started (finished _____

Design source _____

Warp width

Threading & lifts

Warp length

e.p.cm.

p.p.cm.

Reed

Sley

Lifts

4 3 2 1

YARNS Warp	Source	Amount	Cost	Samples
Weft				

Cloth Sample	on loom	Lx	W	fulled	Lx	W
	off loom	Lx	W	felted	Lx	W

Sample

LOOM ALLOWANCES –

Width _____

to give _____

Length _____

to give _____

inc. hems:
    seams:
    pattern:

Sewing & finishing notes:

(a) The record sheet.

Project SAMPLER

Date (started ᴍ / ᴍ / ᴍ
     (finished ᴍ / ᴍ / ᴍ

Design source ' COLOURS OF NATURE '

Warp width

40 cm

Threading & lifts

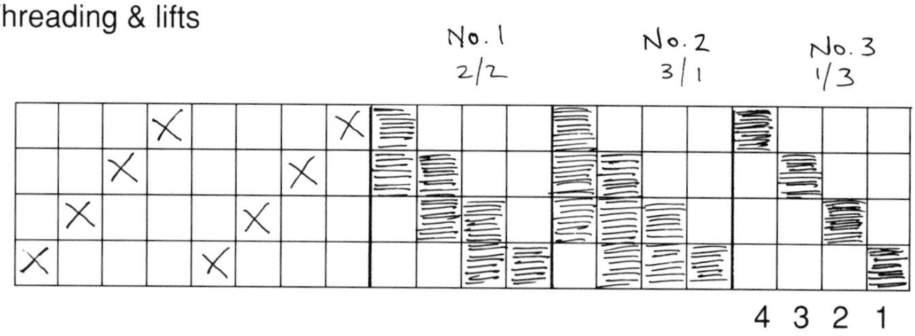

No. 1
2/2

No. 2
3/1

No. 3
1/3

Warp length

120 cm

e.p.i. 5

p.p.i. 5

Reed 5

4 3 2 1

Sley

EVERY

Lifts

YARNS Warp 4/16s CHEVIOT	Source Mirwla	Amount	Cost £ rrrrl per kilo	Samples
Weft				

(b) Filling it in for a project.

according to which loom I am using. The one illustrated here is for four-shaft weaving.

The calculations below are based on the decorative-weave sample featured in the exercise at the end of Chapter 19. The width to be woven is 40cm and since most of the yarns used will be wool, and for some of the weaves the weft will cover more than one end, the fabric can be expected to shrink widthwise more than the usual 10 per cent allowance – in fact, depending on the type of wool, it could lose anything up to a quarter of its width by the time the full finishing process is over. So this generous allowance will give a reasonably wide hanging of some 30–35cm.

The sampler is made up of five separate sections each 10cm long (total 50cm) with a decorative 2.5cm division between each (total 10cm). Add on the loom allowance (for the wastage of yarn in front of and behind the actual weaving – 45cm is about right for a medium-sized rigid heddle or table loom) and the shrinkage allowance, and the calculation for the warp looks like this:

50.00	5 × 10cm sections
10.00	4 × 2.5cm divisions
60.00	
45.00	loom allowance
105.00	
10.50	plus 10 per cent shrinkage allowance
115.50cm	

Rounding up the figure gives a warp length of 120cm.

The final calculation necessary is for the sett of the cloth. The yarn being used for the warp, and for most of the weft, is something like a 4/16s Cheviot – four 16s singles yarns in various 'tropical bird' colours plied together to give plenty of variety in the colour. Wrapping the ruler gives a count of 10 wraps per centimetre so, as this is to be a balanced weave, this means 5 e.p.cm. This calculation also decides which of the three reeds to use – the 5-dent one, sleyed every dent. So, with a woven width of 40cm, the warp to be wound is 200 warp ends, each 120cm long.

The final action necessary before starting to dress the loom is to make the warp, as described in the section on warping off the frame in Chapter 15. To recapitulate briefly: measure out 120cm on the warping frame, tie the 4/16s Cheviot warp yarn to the first peg, and start winding on evenly and smoothly, watching carefully that the cross is correctly wound. Since this is quite a wide warp of 200 ends, I suggest putting in a counting tie at both ends of the warp, not just at the beginning, to keep a track of the number of ends wound; use the counting tie to divide it into 25 groups of 8 ends each. (You might even decide to do the warp in two halves.) When you have finished winding the warp, secure the cross, and take the warp off the frame.

DRESSING A FOUR-SHAFT LOOM

Stage by Stage through the Three Vital Points

Dressing the loom is the job which no weaver really enjoys, but it really is critical. Ease of weaving and the quality of the resulting cloth depend entirely on how well it is done. As with the rigid-heddle loom, the first thing to watch is

The four-shaft loom.

that the warp is beamed evenly and tightly on to the back roller. Interleaving paper, extended well beyond the width of the work, helps here. The second point to watch is that the ends are threaded accurately through the heddles and then through the reed. This is done by checking against the order of the ends as they run over and under the two cross sticks, and is the reason why a properly wound and secure cross is so vital. The third point to watch is that the groups of warp ends are tied evenly and securely to the front apron stick right across the width of the work.

Beaming On

To start with, this is done exactly as for the rigid heddle loom. First the cross sticks are put in to the warp cross in place of the tie; then the warp is spread across them and the sticks tied together at each end, to stop the warp falling off them, and then to the top of the framework supporting the harnesses, so that they are level with the back beam. Then the apron stick is threaded through the loops at the cross end of the warp and re-secured to the back roller. (Looms differ as to how the stick is attached to the roller; most are tied to a canvas *apron* nailed to the roller. This is a better system than lengths of cord between roller and stick, which may stretch unevenly or poke through the rolled warps and distort them.)

From this point on, dressing the two types of loom varies a little. Whereas with the rigid heddle loom the heddle itself is used to control and space the warp ends

186

as they are beamed on, with a four-shaft loom an extra piece of equipment, a *raddle*, is needed. This toothed wooden bar with a removable top is used to spread the warp out to the weaving width, and is centred on the front beam and tied or clamped to it. The warp is then fed through to the raddle; the harnesses are not needed at the moment, so if they cannot be taken out then just push the heddles right over to each side of the frames to make room for the warp as it is brought through.

Checking with the cross as you go, to make sure they are in order, put bunches of the warp ends into the slots in the raddle, working from the middle out and distributing them evenly over the whole

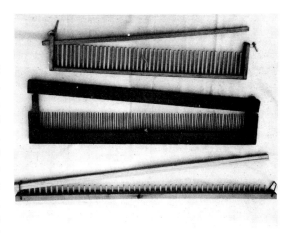

Raddles.

weaving width. (For instance, using a raddle with 7 dents to 10cm, and with 200 ends and a woven width of 40cm, 24 of

Dressing the loom – warp threaded on to back beam and ready to be spread evenly through the raddle.

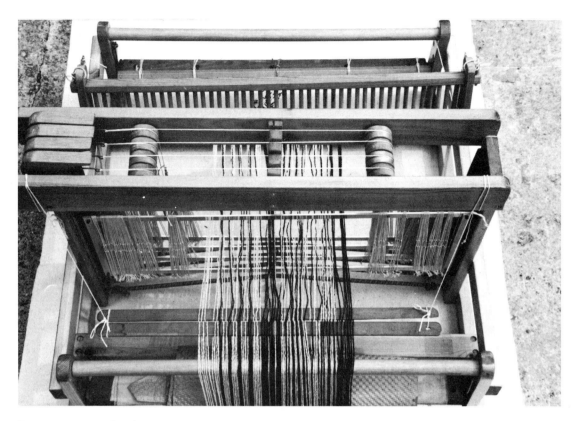

Beaming on completed.

the 28 slots of the raddle there will be bunches of 7 ends, with bunches of 8 in the 2 outside slots on each side.)

The warp is now ready to be beamed on and, as described for the rigid heddle loom in the last chapter, this process of winding it evenly and firmly on to the back roller can be done by two people or by the weaver alone. I find the cross sticks act as an extra tensioner, and help to feed the warp evenly on to the roller, when you are working alone; reposition them periodically by pulling them forward as they get dragged back. The warp is fully wound on when the ends just about reach the front beam. At this point, take away the raddle, cut the loops and loosely reknot each of the bunches of 8 ends separated by the counting tie, which you can take out as you go along.

Threading the Warp Ends through Heddles and Reed

This is done by means of special threading hooks. I use one which has a closed loop of wire at the end as it can be used for threading both heddles and reed (and rigid heddles too – in fact, it came with one I bought many years ago and is one of my most precious and useful tools). Other weavers have a small hook like an old-fashioned boot button hook for threading through the heddle eyes, and a larger, flat S-shaped metal one for pulling the ends through the reed.

Before starting to thread, count off the heddles needed on each harness, and move them towards the centre of the frame. (In this case, there are 200 ends to be spread evenly over the heddles in four

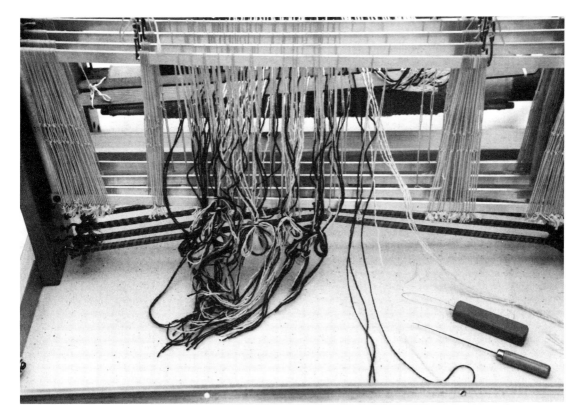

Threading warp ends through the heddles.

frames, so 50 heddles will need to be threaded on each frame.) Starting in the middle, work first towards the left. Pick up the first bunch of 8 ends, unknot it and, keeping an eye at all times on the cross sticks just behind the heddle frames to make sure that the ends are kept in order, take the first end and pull it through the eye of the first heddle on the back (number 4) frame. Then, take the second end and pull it through the first heddle on number 3 frame; take the third end and pull it through the first heddle on number 2 frame; and, finally, take the fourth end and pull it through the first heddle on the front (number 1) frame. Repeat these four threadings, from back to front heddle frames, with the final 4 ends in the first bunch. The first bunch is now finished, so check to make sure that

8 ends have been threaded through the eyes of the heddles on the frames in the order 4, 3, 2, 1, 4, 3, 2, 1 (string heddles have slots above and below the eyes and it is easy to mis-thread through these, so watch this). If all is well and no ends are crossed over each other or threaded in the wrong order, this first bunch of 8 ends can be loosely retied and dropped to lie in front of the heddle frames.

Working always to the left, the process of threading each bunch of 8 ends is repeated until all the 100 ends of the left-hand half of the warp are threaded. (This means that 12 bunches of 8 ends are threaded, then a final bunch of 4 are threaded 4, 3, 2, 1.) When this has been done, return to the middle and start threading again, this time to the right, until all the 100 ends of the right-hand half of the warp are threaded. But, and this is a very big but, the threading of each bunch of 8 ends is now done in the order 1, 2, 3, 4, 1, 2, 3, 4. A look at the drafting plan diagram will, I hope, explain this. If the order is not reversed a 'point' will appear in the centre of the woven fabric, and any diagonal weaves such as twills will come to a peak at that point, running away from it on opposite diagonals. This may well actually be what you want, and so we will come back to *point drafts*, as they are called, in the next chapter, but for the moment we are dealing with what is called a *straight draft*.

The drafting plan is a diagram of the order in which the heddles on the frames are threaded and, with the *lifting plan* (the order in which the heddle frames are lifted – different for each weave pattern, as we shall see in the next chapter) it tells you how to weave the cloth and gives you a diagrammatical expression, a weave plan, of the particular fabric being woven. For this project a straight draft threading is being used – this is in a sense the 'plain-weave' version of drafting plans and means that, by variation of the harness lifts, a large number of different weave patterns can be done. And this is what we want for this sampler hanging – five different weaves in the five sections.

To finish off the threading, return to the centre and, again working first to the left and then to the right, untie each bunch of 8 ends and pull them, one by one, through the dents in the reed, according to the previously decided threading. (In this case, the reed is to be threaded one end per dent, so one bunch of eight ends threaded through the heddles is re-threaded through eight consecutive dents of the reed.) As each bunch of ends is re-threaded, check that they are in the right

Threading through the reed.

order and then tie them off loosely again to keep them secure. All this retying of ends is to prevent them from getting pulled back by accident through dents and eyes and thus destroying all your careful threading.

Tying the warp ends to the front apron stick

This is done in the same way as with the rigid heddle loom, but it might be a help to repeat the instructions. First, loosen the ratchet on the front (cloth) roller and bring the apron over the front beam so that the apron stick lies just forward of it. Lock the ratchet again to hold it secure as you tie on. Starting with the centre bunch of eight ends, bring it over the stick and divide it into two. Bring each half up on either side and tie them together in the first part of a reef knot. Continue tying like this, working outwards from the centre on alternating sides, until each group is tied on. (With the sampler project warp there are groups of four ends only at each side. As you get to these, give them an

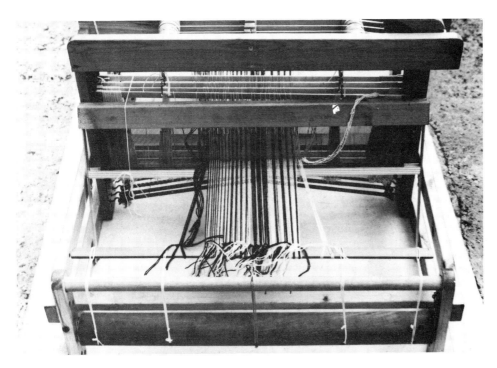

Tying bunches of ends on to the front apron bar.

Ends tensioned and secured to the front apron bar, and a few picks of heading woven ready to weave.

Weaving (below) – showing how the weft is laid in an arc (above).

extra hitch up to make sure the selvedges are nice and firm.)

To ensure that the warp tension is even across the full width of the warp, return to the centre ties and, working outwards again, pull up any slack that has developed and either complete the half reef knot or tie in a bow. I do the latter because I find it easier to undo if I have to do any subsequent tensioning. All that remains now is to weave a few picks of heading and the dressing of the loom is over. (However, if you would like a long fringe on the sampler I suggest putting in a couple of strips of cardboard, say 2.5cm wide, in alternate sheds and then weaving the half a dozen picks of heading. Together with the tied ends of the warp this should give a nice, generous 15–20cm of fringe to play with.)

VARIATIONS ON DRESSING A FOUR-SHAFT LOOM

Before starting to weave, I should like to say that the method described above makes no claim to be the correct one; it is just the method I use. There are probably as many ways of dressing a loom as there are weavers and looms, so I would suggest that those new to the craft should read up all they can about it, watch others working and finally make up their own minds. But everyone has to start somewhere and this way is the way I started and I have stuck to it.

One of the more obvious variations, only possible really with a short warp, is dressing the loom from front to back. The cross sticks go between front beam and batten, the loops at the other end are cut and the reed is threaded from the front. The heddles are then threaded from the back, and the ends tied in bunches to the back apron stick. Beaming on to the warp roller is then done as I have described it, and finally the ends are tied on to the front apron stick. (I have seen this suggested as the method to use for a warp-faced fabric designed to use up ends of many different colours and textures of yarn. The sett of the cloth can be varied to accommodate the differences in yarn thickness by varying the threading through the reed, and even short pieces of yarn, no more than the warp length, can be used up – in other words, the warp is not wound in the conventional way but literally threaded end by different end.

An intriguing idea, but one which I have not tried out myself.)

Another warping variation (used mainly with very long cloth warps) is done similarly to my method, but with a warp made with a cross at both ends. You will sometimes see these called the *porrey cross* and the *portée cross*. Before beaming starts the back cross is removed; it has served its purpose by guiding the threading of the raddle. When beaming on is finished and the second cross lies between the front beam and the heddles, the raddle is removed, the cross pushed up behind the heddles and cross sticks put in. After this, heddles and reed are threaded and ends tied on to the front apron stick as with my method.

Threading the heddles and sleying the reed can be done across the warp, rather than from the centre out, but the number of heddles needed on each harness must be carefully calculated so that threading starts in the right place and the warp is centred on the loom. Otherwise you may run out of heddles on one side or the other before all the ends are threaded.

You will sometimes see flat sticks or strips of card used to interleave the warp as it is beamed on. Some weavers feel that paper does not do the job properly. I can only say that I have found it satisfactory, providing it is of good, stout quality and that it is wide enough to extend well beyond the warp ends.

A final couple of tips. If you need an extra firm selvedge, say for a rug, wind one or two extra ends at start and finish when making the warp. These can then be threaded as doubles for strength. And if the warp you are making is very wide (even with fine yarn, I find 200 ends are plenty) then divide it into two, or even three, parts and wind each separately.

19
Weaves for Four Shafts

Up until now we have looked only at the weaves that can be done on two shafts – the over-and-under 'darning' action, the simple lifting of one set of warp ends, followed by the lifting of the alternate set of ends: that is to say, lift 1, followed by lift 2, then lift 1 again, and so on. But now we have four shafts to play with and the lifting options are considerably increased, although of course simple weaves can still be done. For instance, assuming that the heddles on the four harnesses have been threaded in a straight draft (see the previous chapter) a simple plain weave, whether it is a tabby, weft-faced or warp-faced one, can be done by lifting shafts 1 and 3 together for the first pick, then 2 and 4 together for the second pick, then back to 1 and 3 for the third pick and so on.

So having four shafts now allows us to do more complex interlacings without having to use a pick-up stick to help, even though they are still strictly speaking plain weaves. For instance, try the 2/2 hopsack (described under 'Plain Weave' in Chapter 11). For this, lift shafts 1 and 2 together for the first and second picks, and shafts 3 and 4 together for the third and fourth picks, and continue to repeat these alternating lifts.

Before looking in detail at some other weave options there is one aspect of planning the work that needs to be taken more seriously from now on, and that is the drafting of the weave plan, the weaver's way of illustrating weaves on point paper.

With simple two-shaft weaves drafts are not all that important, but with four shafts they become more necessary, so from now on each weave will be illustrated by its draft. Not only do drafts make it easy to recognize the construction of a weave at a glance, but the weaver can try out variations and combinations of lifts much more quickly and easily on point paper than on the loom itself. Note that it is the gaps between the lines on the point paper that represent the warp and weft threads, and whenever a warp thread goes over a weft thread and square is blacked in. It follows that, reading across a draft, the white squares indicate the path of each pick of weft.

COLOUR AND WEAVE

Although these variations can be done in tabby weave, and therefore woven on looms with only two shafts, I have left them to this chapter because the easiest way to design them is by drafting a weave plan. And if, instead of the method of the white and black squares, horizontal and vertical lines are used to represent the weft and the warp threads, the visual effect of the actual structure of the cloth is remarkably accurately shown.

This family of weaves is traditionally used to give various small patterns, formed when yarns of the same type but of two different colours are used in a balanced sett. Some are much used and

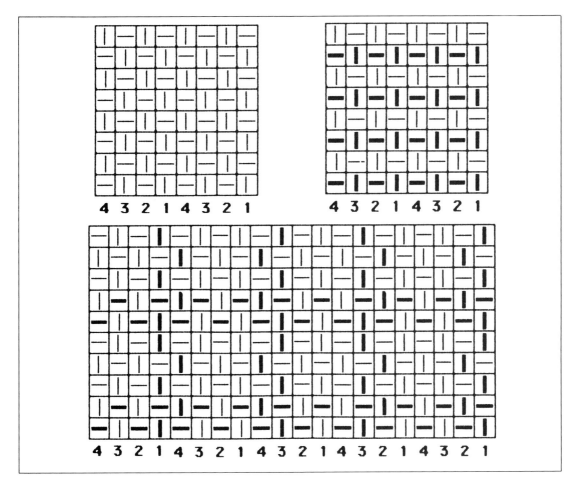

Colour-and-weave plans.

famous, such as dog-tooth check and Prince of Wales check, but in fact the variations that can be achieved are almost endless. The quickest way to do colour-and-weave drafts is to draw out a square of plain-weave interlacings (as in the first diagram), then take a thicker pen and draw over the threads which are going to be the darker colour. For a sampler it is best to keep a good contrast between the two colours being used in the actual weaving, and black and white is very effective.

The second diagram illustrates a cloth warped up in alternating ends of black and white and woven in alternating picks of black and white. The third gives a good visual indication of what a cloth is like when it is warped up in two ends black, three ends white, and then woven two picks black, three picks white. The result is a classic check. Try experimenting on point paper to see what patterns appear when the numbers of warp and weft threads in each of the two colours are varied.

A classic way of making a colour-and-weave sampler is illustrated here. It has 102 ends in 9 pattern blocks of 10 ends each, plus one of 12 ends. The warp is wound as follows: for the first block of 10 ends, wind all the ends black; for the next block of 10, wind one end black, one end white; for the next block, wind one end black, two ends white; for the next, wind two ends white, two ends black; and for the next, two ends black, three ends white; then four ends black, one end white; five black, five white; three black, four white; four white, two black (12 ends); and finally, for the last block of 10 ends, all white. Then weave the same number of picks as there are ends, and in exactly the same order; that is to say, the first block of 10 picks are woven in black, the next block is woven one black, one white, and so on until the final block which consists of 10 white picks.

Undoubtedly a sampler like this is an interesting exercise in finding out what patterns various colour-and-weave combinations will give, but the truth is that a neatly drawn series of weave plans will do virtually the same thing, and in a fraction of the time. So I would suggest that drawings, followed by a development of the original weave designs (still on paper) – maybe trying out combinations of patterns which look interesting, and perhaps introducing a third colour or a different texture, the dots in the final diagram – might well give some original and exciting possibilities which can then be translated on to the loom.

One final point: all these (and this has only been a very brief look at the great variety of possible colour-and-weave patterns) need not be done in plain weave alone. In fact, most of the famous tweeds such as Prince of Wales check are twill-woven, while other combinations of colour-and-weave with, for instance, undulating twills can produce the most exciting fabrics. And while on the subject of variations and combinations I must also mention Ann Sutton's book *The Structure*

A colour-and-weave sampler being woven.

of Weaving. Not only has it the essential feature of any really useful technical book, that of being easily understood, but all weavers, whatever their standard of competence, will find it a help not only in improving their technique (and we can all do with that) but also in feeding their imagination. It really is a must.

TWILL WEAVES

Twills are one of the most important weave constructions, and are probably second only to plain weave in their usefulness to the cloth weaver. Because the wefts pass over more than one warp end twills give a supple yet firm cloth with the good draping qualities required for fine-quality wool tweeds. Equally, woven at a close set in crisp cotton they produce the ultimate in strong work-wear fabric, denim (called, incidentally, after a town in France: de Nîmes = Denim). Twills are extraordinarily versatile in other ways, too. The diagonal patterning which distinguishes them can be a mere

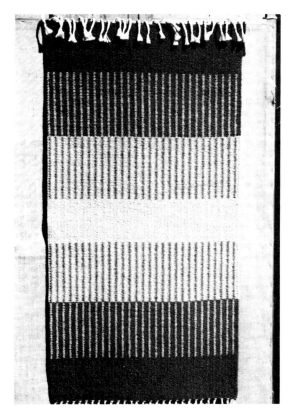

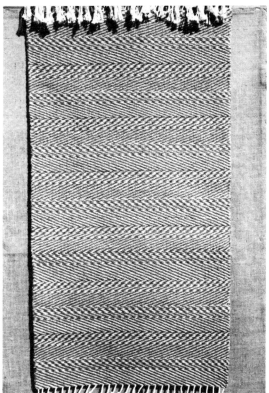

A rug in a Norwegian weave called *krokbragd* (crooked path); a three- or four-shaft variation which gives colourful abstract patterns (Jo Tether).

'Dazzle' – a rug in weft-faced reverse broken twill (Jo Tether).

shadow on the surface, or if the yarns are varied it can be accentuated so that it becomes in effect an inlay. It can be made steeper or more shallow; it can be zigzagged or undulated across the face of the fabric; in fact, it can be made as much (or as little) of a feature of the cloth design as the weaver wishes.

Whereas plain-weave fabrics can all be woven on two shafts, twills, because of their construction, require at least three (this is the number used to weave denim, in fact – it is a 2/1 twill on one face of the cloth, a 1/2 twill on the other). And the more shafts a loom has, the more intricate and interesting are the twills which can be woven on it. However, four shafts are usually the minimum used by hand-weavers, and they give a good choice, with six different ways of weaving the two basic twills: 2/2 and 3/1, plus all the variables which can be introduced by way of the yarn, by combining twills, and by combining twill with other weaves. So four shafts really do give a weaver plenty to be going on with. (By the way, twills are expressed like this: 2/2, 3/1, 5/3. Adding the two numbers together gives the number of shafts needed to weave that particular twill: that is to say, 2/2 and 3/1 can be woven on four shafts, but 5/3 will need eight.)

Even Twills

A 2/2 twill is an even twill. This means that each pick of weft goes over and

197

under the same number of warp ends – two – and the same amount of warp and weft shows on each face of the fabric. However, the diagonal line of the twill runs in a different direction on each face. Using this twill as an example, let us look at five different variations of twill weaves.

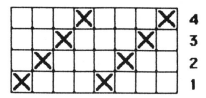

Twill weave plans. (a) A straight draft for the following twills (b) – (j).

1 For *plain* or *regular twill* (called this because the shafts are lifted in a set and regular sequence and the diagonal line of the twill is unbroken), lift shafts 1 and 2 together; then 2 and 3 together; then 3 and 4 together; and finally 4 and 1 together. Repeating this progression of lifts makes the 2/2 twill run up the cloth at an angle of 45 degrees, with the weft skips moving along one end each pick. A 2/2 twill is used particularly in the weaving of traditional wool tweeds. A singles yarn is used in the weft and the direction of the twist in the yarn is the same as the direction of the twill diagonal. When the cloth is

4 3 2 1 4 3 2 1

(b) 2/2 twill.

fulled this finishing process causes the two twists, in the yarn and in the weave construction, to lock into each other, giving the required firm yet supple fabric. This property of 'bedding in' – or, if opposing twists are used, separating – is one which is worth exploiting in twill design, whether with singles or plied yarns.

2 For an example of a *fancy twill* (the term fancy is used in weaving to describe any variation on the basic weave being used at that time) try one which gives a steeper angle of twill and thus a firmer fabric: one pick of 2/2 twill, woven with the lifts as in plain twill, is alternated with one pick of plain weave (12, *13*, 23, *24*, 34, *13*, 41, *24* – the lifts in italics are plain weave). This is the same technique as the one used to stabilize inlay weaves – see 'Textured Effects' in Chapter 17.

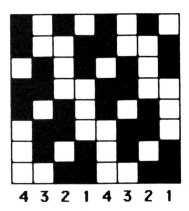

4 3 2 1 4 3 2 1

(c) 2/2 twill alternating with plain weave.

3 With *undulating twill*, varying the number of picks done over and under the same two warp ends before moving on to the next warp end produces an uneven, wavy diagonal. In the diagram, a simple undulating twill has been woven using lifts 12, 23, 23, 34, 34, 34, 41, 41; these eight lifts are then repeated again from the be-

Twill weaves – 2/2 twill: tussah silk warp, Botany woll and cashmere weft.

ginning. As with the example of fancy twill above, to give added stability and to vary the angle of the undulations try alternating the twill picks with picks of plain weave. For this weave, the lifts read 12, *13*, 23, *24*, 23, *13*, 34, *24*, 34, *13*, 34, *24*, 41, *13*, 41, *24* – again, the lifts in italics are the plain weave. This twill can be particularly effective if different yarns are used for the twill picks and the plain-

4 3 2 1 4 3 2 1

(e) Undulating 2/2 twill alternating with plain weave.

Undulating twill: Botany wool warp, cashmere and silk weft.

4 3 2 1 4 3 2 1

(d) Undulating 2/2 twill.

199

weave picks – for instance a space-dyed silk for the twill, so that the colour 'moves' up the undulations, with a fine mercerized cotton for both the warp and the plain-weave picks. A good way of getting what appears to be a silk fabric even though the expensive yarn makes up only about one-third of the total.

4 For a *granite weave* or *broken twill* the sequence of lifts is varied so as to break the continuity of the diagonal line. To illustrate: lift shafts 12, 23 then 41 and finally 34; then return to the beginning and continue to repeat the four lifts in the same order.

4 3 2 1 4 3 2 1

(g) Reverse 2/2 twill.

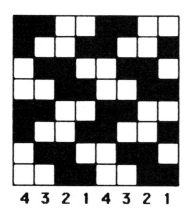

4 3 2 1 4 3 2 1

(f) Broken twill.

5 For a *reverse twill*, the direction of the diagonal is reversed at intervals. For instance, weave four lifts in the sequence 12, 23, 34, 41. On reaching 41, reverse and repeat the lifting sequence thus: 34, 23. Then reverse again, lifting 12, 23, 34, 41 again, then 34, 23, and so on. You will see (and this is most important) that on reaching the end of each angle, and when reversing direction, the 41 and 12 lifts are not repeated. If the *point* of the twill was woven twice (that is, 12, 23, 34, *41, 41,* 34, 23, 12 and then repeat from 12), these two

picks of weft floating over the same two warp ends would give instability at the point. To avoid this we weave 12, 23, 34, 41, 34, 23, and then repeat from 12. Similarly, there is a degree of weakness

Reverse 2/2 twill: tussah silk warp with cashmere weft.

4 3 2 1 4 3 2 1

(h) Broken reverse 2/2 twill.

Reverse undulating twill: Botany wool warp, Shetland and cashmere weft.

where the weft end floats over the three warps 343 just under the point. This can be overcome by breaking the lifting sequence so that it reads 12, 23, 34, 41, 23, 12, 41, 34 and then repeats from 12 again (see the remarks on the *herringbone* and *chevron* or *point twills* in the next section).

Uneven Twills

Uneven twills are those where the weft ends pass over and under larger or smaller numbers of ends: with four-shaft looms, 3/1 and 1/3. A 3/1 twill, where the warp goes over three picks and under one pick and so shows more on the surface of the fabric, is (somewhat obviously) called a warp-faced twill (lifts 123, 234, 341, 412 and repeat); the reverse, a 1/3 twill, where the warp goes over one pick and under three (lifts 1, 2, 3, 4 and repeat)

is a weft-faced twill. For the former, the weaver has to lift three shafts for each pick – quite heavy work, particularly with a large floor loom – so it is usual to weave this twill back to front. In other words, weave a 1/3 twill, and then use the reverse of the fabric as the right side. But remember that the diagonal will run in the opposite direction on the reverse, and this may matter in your design. (Lifting

4 3 2 1 4 3 2 1

4 3 2 1 4 3 2 1

(i) 3/1 (warp-face) and 1/3 (weft-face) twills.

201

shafts from front to back, from 1 to 4, gives a diagonal from left to right on the front, and right to left on the back.)

The variations on the even 2/2 twill weave described above apply equally to uneven twills. The diagonal line of a regular twill, whether woven 3/1 warp-faced or 1/3 weft-faced, can be accentuated by using yarns with either colour or textural differences as the warp and weft – a dark warp will show up the fine diagonal stripe of the weft-faced 1/3 twill, or alternatively the thick stripe of the warp-faced 3/1 twill. Even with a regular twill, and even more so with fancy twills, these uneven twills with their long skips give a most effective and quick-to-weave inlay-type patterning. For instance, the weft-faced 1/3 twill might be woven pick-and-pick with plain weave, using a softly spun silk weft over fine mercerized cotton for the warp and the plain-weave picks (1, *13*, 2, *24*, 3, *13*, 4, *24* – plain weave picks in italics again).

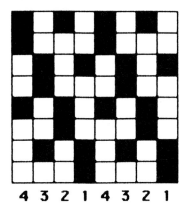

4 3 2 1 4 3 2 1

(j) 1/3 twill alternating with plain weave.

With undulating twill the inlay effect can be even more accentuated; also, combining even and uneven twills (Ann Sutton calls these *shaded twills*) gives added scope for designing exciting undulations

– for instance, using the same soft silk (perhaps space dyed) with mercerized cotton, the lifts 123, 234, 234, 345, 451, 12, 23, 23, 34, 34, 34, 41, 41, 1, 2, 2, 3, 3, 3, 4, 4 repeated as required would give a varied and interesting undulation across the face of the fabric. An added bonus is that the reverse effect on the back might well suggest combining the two fabric faces into an interesting mix-and-match cloth from which to cut out a garment. A quick tip here: I find if I am weaving with a complicated sequence of lifts like this it helps if I write them out clearly and pin the piece of paper to the frame of the loom. I can then read them off easily and make sure I keep to the correct sequence.

There are other ways of achieving the effect of undulating twills, of which I have to admit a particular fondness. For instance, if different thicknesses of warp yarn are used in stripes across the width of the warp, the twill will appear to undulate because the diagonal stripe is thicker where the warp ends are of thick yarn, and thinner where they are of fine yarn.

This is really a variation of the *crammed and spaced* warp technique. Using warp yarns of different thicknesses but sleying them through the reed at the same dentage means that the thick ends will be closer together in the fabric and the thin ends further apart. Alternatively, the same thickness of warp yarn can be used but the dents per cm varied – if, for instance, the main part of the fabric is sleyed at one end per dent, then stripes of warp ends can be sleyed at two ends per dent, and others at three ends per dent, giving a similar visual effect of variations in the width of the diagonal stripes.

As with the other variations, broken twills and reverse twills can both be designed

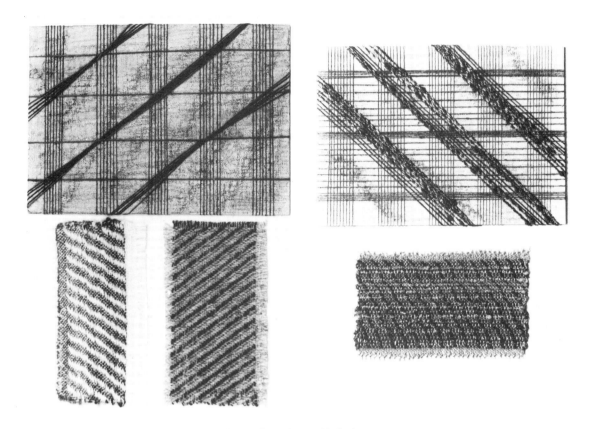

Design work, including wrappings and sampling, for twill cloths.

using the straight draft and uneven twill lifts. But we have not so far mentioned a final and famous twill – *herringbone*, and its close cousin the *chevron* or *point twill*. These bring us finally to the other way of constructing twills – upside down, as it were. So far we have threaded the harnesses on the loom in a straight draft (as I said before, what might be termed the 'plain weave' of threading) and got our fancy weaves by varying the lifts. This is a threading system which gives great flexibility – a single tedious session dressing the loom gives the weaver the option of a great many weaves of different patterns, simply by varying the lifts. It does have one major snag, however. As we saw above with the combination of uneven/ even undulating twill, the sequence of

lifts can be long and complicated to follow. This may not be too critical for a scarf, or a metre or two of fabric, but it would drive one mad over a jacket or dress length. The answer in these cases is to let the threading of the harnesses define the pattern of the weave, and then the lifts become the 'plain weave' – simply 12, 23, 34, 41 and repeat all the way.

Woven with the lifts 12, 23, 34, 41, the harness threading necessary for point or chevron twills is the point draft which was briefly mentioned in the last chapter. Compare the point twill threading (1, 2, 3, 4, 3, 2, 1 then reverse 4, 3, 2, 1, 2, 3, 4 and so on) with the straight draft, which was threaded 1, 2, 3, 4, 1, 2, 3, 4 and so on; then compare it with the reverse twill lifts (12, 23, 34, 41, then reverse 34, 23 and so on)

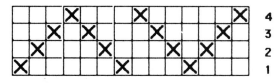

(k) Point draft.

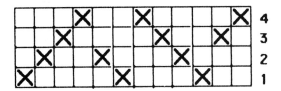

(l) Herringbone twill draft.

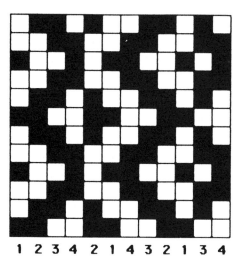

1 2 3 4 2 1 4 3 2 1 3 4

(n) Herringbone twill.

and I hope you will see why it is that this way of constructing twills was upside down.

As with the reverse twill, there is an area of instability at the point where the weft floats over three ends. This can be remedied by 'breaking' the point draft threading thus (1, 2, 3, 4, 2, 1 and 4, 3, 2, 1, 3, 4). Then, with the lifting sequence reversed periodically – 12, 23, 34, 41, 34, 23 and start again – you get the famous herringbone tweed pattern.

I hope that this explanation of how simple

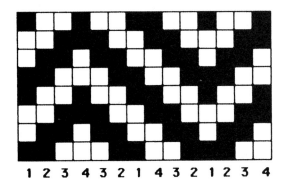

1 2 3 4 3 2 1 4 3 2 1 2 3 4

(m) Point twill.

it is to weave twills 'right side up' or 'upside down' – depending on which method suits the particular project – will start to suggest other possibilities worth investigating. For instance, why not thread a variety of twill drafts in bands across the width of the warp for a fabric? A combination of straight drafts, point and broken point drafts and undulating twills turned 'upside down' so that they become the harness threading rather than the lifting plan, might be interesting. Then alternating straight lifting sequences with reversed and broken ones gives even more scope for variations in the weave pattern. Why not try some out in the exercise at the end of the chapter?

OTHER SUGGESTIONS FOR WEAVES ON FOUR SHAFTS

The basic weave techniques described in this book are those which I consider the most useful, but the possibilities of two- and four-shaft weaving are myriad and the following techniques are well worth investigating once the basics of weaving have been mastered.

Double cloth

At the end of Chapter 12 I talked about ways of weaving ready-shaped garments, either by means of a shaped frame or by using a discontinuous-warp technique with a garment-shaped cartoon as a guide. There is a third method of avoiding cutting into precious handwoven cloth and that is to weave a double cloth. This can be done on as few as four shafts, although only plain weave can be woven. Garment shapes can be woven to size, tubular or open on one side. Equally, if the double cloth is left open on one side, the width of cloth which can be woven on the loom can be doubled, or pockets can be woven into it, and stuffed as they are woven, and in this way an instant quilted jacket can be made.

Sampling for patterned double cloth woven on eight warps. Warping different colours in each layer reverses the colours on each side of the fabric.

A sampler trying out various overshot weaves for her 'Peacock' project (Jo Tether).

Overshot Weaving

This is an old and traditional method of producing extremely colourful and decorative pattern weaving. The sturdy fabrics produced were particularly popular in America for household textiles such as quilts and bedcovers. They are made not unlike some of the weft-inlay weaves discussed in Chapter 17 – particularly the Turkish sili technique, which I called single-warp inlay – in so far as they can have a fine warp and binder weft yarn, woven with a different yarn for the weft floats.

Leno or Gauze Weaves

These are the open, lacy weaves used traditionally for shawls and scarves. They can be made by the hand-manipulation of warp ends. These are twisted to lock the weft pick in well above the fell of the cloth. The way the twists are arranged

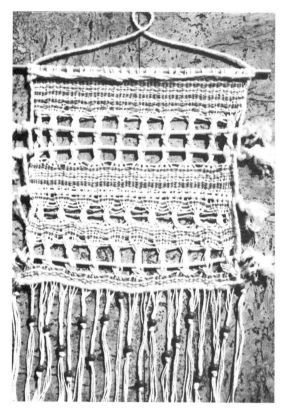

Decorative leno weave sampler in cotton yarns (Jo Tether).

forms the pattern in the lace. Alternatively, simple versions can be loom-controlled, even on four shafts, and alternated with areas of plain weave to give airy and light yet perfectly stable fabrics. Another use for them is in decorative pieces, where the twists can be used to lock fancy yarns or other materials into place.

There are many other classic weave techniques which weavers have found interesting enough to develop into work that is personal and applicable to handweaving today – which is really what trying out new techniques is all about. Something catches the weaver's eye and is tried out on a four-shaft loom, and from such

simple beginnings may well develop a way of working which ultimately becomes the basis for a thriving and satisfying handweaving business. You just never know until you try.

WEAVING EXERCISE 3

A decorative sampler in various twill weaves, using colours derived from Design Exercise 1.

You need:

- a four-shaft table loom
- 4/16s Cheviot or equivalent warp and weft yarn

Refer to the warping calculations in Chapter 18 and make the warp and dress the loom according to these. If you would prefer to have something useful rather than purely decorative, you could make the warp 30cm wide (150 ends) and multiply the length by 3 to give a scarf about 25cm wide and 160cm long.

Choose the five twill variations you like best and, using the colours from Design Exercise 1 as a basis for the colourway, weave the five strips of pattern. To keep the warp open for the divisions, put in a 2.5cm strip of card. Secure each with stitching as you go along, as described in the next chapter. Alternatively, you could weave in some much thicker yarn (perhaps cord made by twisting some of the Cheviot together) to give a variety in texture. If you are making the scarf, I suggest doing plain-weave stripes as the divisions.

After cutting off the loom, full according to the yarn used, and finish and trim according to which version you are weaving.

20
Finishing Techniques

I think there is a good deal of truth in the idea that an article, be it car or carpet, washing machine or woven textile, is only as good as its final finishing and quality control, and its after-sales service. Most of us, even leaving aside the expensive and sometimes near-disastrous effects of a 'Monday car' or a 'Friday washing machine', have suffered the equally irritating if not quite so costly experience of buying clothes which shed their buttons, stretch, shrink, lose their colour and even disintegrate at quite the wrong moment. So can I suggest, now you are going to be on the other side of the great divide, now that you hope to be the maker rather than the buyer, that it is well worth while taking finishing and after-sales care labelling seriously? That way you not only complement your own textile skills by presenting them to the market in the best possible way; you also have a satisfied client. And satisfied clients talk, and thus lead to other satisfied clients, and to increased sales and – need I say more?

What this means in fact is going back to basics, back to the very beginning of the project and to the first steps in the designing and making process. Back in fact to the checklist. Every project has to have a beginning, or several of them: What is being made and who is it for? Where are the design ideas coming from? What is it going to be made of and what is it going to cost? And is the final design idea suitable both for the construction method and the client? Then the project has to have a

middle, the actual making of it, and it has to have an end – the finishing, the testing and evaluating and, where necessary, the care labelling.

In other words, the finishing of the article is an integral part of the design process, one of the many technical considerations which have to be carefully thought out and as carefully executed. But, and this is the big but, it is also much more than this. Hours of work can be ruined by a lack of proper sampling to test fabric behaviour or the suitability of a weave technique, or by other forms of careless and sloppy finishing, and what the client sees and buys is the finished article, the article in its entirety – in other words, the way it is presented – rather than the design or technical skills which went into its making. (These, I am afraid, are more often than not taken for granted, except when they are not there.) Perhaps it should be a case of maker beware rather than buyer beware.

FABRIC FINISHING

Taking the Fabric off the Loom

This is simply a matter of cutting through the unwoven warp ends to release the fabric from the back apron stick, drawing the ends through heddle eyes and reed dents and then unrolling the piece off the front roller until the warps tied to the front apron stick appear. Either cut these

Cutting the colour and weave sampler off the loom, leaving warp ends bunched and ready to be retied to continue weaving.

between the heading woven at the beginning and the ties or, if the full length of warp is needed – for a long fringe, for instance – untie the bows securing each bunch of ends to the stick. Either way, leave the heading in until the fulling process is done.

With a loosely set fabric such as a leno weave or a lightly beaten brushed mohair, whether it is to be fringed or not, some weavers prefer to secure it by whipping or hem-stitching each end of the cloth while it is under tension on the loom, and then cutting it off. This means, of course, that the beginning of the fabric must be stitched when weaving starts. This is where putting in a piece of card, instead of a woven heading, can be helpful; if this is done, and a few centimetres are woven to hold the weaving before the card is withdrawn, a clear area of warp ends is left in which to stitch. Weaving is then continued until the piece is finished and

the final act before cutting the ends off the back apron stick will be to stitch them in the same way as at the beginning.

After the piece is cut from the loom, any loose or broken ends must be darned in, mistakes in the weave disguised or pulled through and rewoven with a needle, knots untied and the ends darned in, and so on. A zigzag machine stitch will do a good job of securing the raw ends of, for instance, a fabric length destined for cut-and-sew. It is then ready for the next stage of the finishing process.

Fulling

The piece of woven textile straight off the loom is in what is known as *loom state*, and, with some weave techniques at least, loom state bears very little relationship to its final appearance. Depending on the yarn which has been used, and to a slightly lesser extent on the weaving tech-

208

nique, various methods of finishing the fabric are employed. However, although wool and the hair fibres are usually those quoted as needing the shrinking and setting process that is known as fulling, in fact linen, cotton and other natural cellulose fibres and even some of the man-made synthetics also benefit from the treatment.

Wool and Hair Fibres

I do not think it is exaggerating to say that the treatment of wool and hair fibres, primarily in order to make them weatherproof, has always been the most important part of the process of turning these raw materials into a useful fabric. The felting of goat's hair by Central Asian tribesmen, to provide both wind- and rainproof cloaks and the material from which to make and furnish their yurts (tents), almost certainly predates weaving. Heavily felted woven cloths were a logical progression – just as dense and weatherproof but, being felted from a basis of securely interlaced threads, was both stronger and more hardwearing.

The process known as fulling is done in many ways. Fulling mills, powered by fast-flowing streams, were used in the part of the west of England in which I live. To produce the superfine broadcloth for which the area was famous for over five hundred years the rolls of loom-state cloth were taken to the fulling mill – Fuller is still a common surname hereabouts – to be pounded for hours in the running water by huge, wooden 'hammers' until the yarns were quite felted together and no fraying at cut edges was possible. In the islands of the Outer Hebrides, off Scotland, the tweed was fulled by *waulking* – a gathering of the

women would lay the newly woven lengths of tweed out flat, or fold them into large tubs, and, continuously applying water and lye (sodium hydroxide) or potash (potassium hydroxide), 'waulk' it with their feet or their pounding hands (the origin of the surname Walker). Nowadays weavers have been known to put newly woven cloth into the bath and, with careful additions of hot water and soap flakes, pound up and down in their wellies. (Using very hot water speeds the process but is rather hard on the feet – hence the rubber boots.) Another fulling method for modern handweavers is to use part, or all, of the hot cycle of a washing machine.

The reason for all this activity is to take advantage of the construction of wool fibres – the fact that they are formed with overlapping scales on the outside of each individual fibre – to set the cloth. The movement through the water, combined with the action of the lye or soap (or urine, if you want to be really traditional, but it must be stale to work properly, as in the dyeing process), causes the scales to open out and the fibres to contract. Thus the mass swells and tangles into a stable fabric. Another property of the strong alkali found in lye and potash is that it attracts greasy dirt and so the fulling process not only sets the fibres but also *scours* (cleans) them. This is fine for strong, coarse rug-type wools, maybe, but remember that the alkali damages protein fibres, making them dry and brittle if used to excess, hence the need to re-oil woollen weaving yarns after scouring. So it is a good idea to use a neutral, non-alkaline soap for fulling and washing yarns spun from fine protein fibres such as lambswool and cashmere, and also for silk.

As with all processes, proper sampling

Colour-and-weave sampler showing the difference between loom state (*top, left* and *right*) and hand-fulled fabric (*bottom, left* and *right*).

is absolutely critical. To weave a length of fabric only to find that fulling has so reduced the width that the jacket pattern you have set your heart on no longer fits is an expensive and avoidable disaster. (Before the invention of the flying shuttle in 1733 made broadloom weaving by a single weaver possible, most cloth was woven 75cm wide – it is not easy to throw the shuttle for a much wider cloth. This measurement is still used for traditional handwoven tweeds and, reduced to about

210

70cm after fulling, makes a cloth of suitable width for garment making.) So either weave a decent-sized sample beforehand or, and this is definitely second-best, weave at least 25 per cent more than you think you are going to need, and then a bit more, and use the bit more as your sample. This should be processed first, exactly as you intend to do for the finished cloth, so that it will give you an accurate idea of what to expect. The best way of determining the right degree of fulling for a particular fibre and a particular weave (remember, for instance, that a weave with skips such as twill will contract more than a plain weave) is to process the sample piece by degrees, taking careful notes of what you do.

Here are various methods of setting about this:

1   Measure the unfulled sample accurately (it should have been off the loom for about 24 hours at least, to allow the fibres to relax after the tensions of the weaving process).

2   Pin it out on a flat surface at slight tension, using brass or stainless steel pins, taking care to keep to the required size and shape of the finished article. Spray it with a fine mist of warm water and then leave to dry at room temperature. This is suitable for wool tapestries and rugs, and also for fine gauze-weave shawls and the like.

3   Press it for 2 or 3 minutes under a damp cloth or with a steam iron. Keep the iron just above the surface of the cloth, not touching or pressing on it. Measure and note the result, and repeat if necessary. Finally, if necessary, pin it out to size and shape and leave to dry naturally. This is suitable for fine fibres (cashmere, lambswool, Superfine Botany wool) and

for some man-made synthetic fibres, as well as for weft-faced fabrics distorted by eccentric-weft weaving.

4   In a bowl of hot water and soap flakes, lightly agitate or rub/squeeze the sample for 5 minutes. Remove it from the water, rinse, and roll it in a towel to absorb excess water, then pat it out flat, measure and note the result. Continue in this way with successive immersions in hot water and soap, for timed periods and using more agitation/rubbing if required, until the desired degree of fulling is reached.

The hand-fulling method can be varied in many ways right up to the action of the pounding wellington boot, or to a more modest degree by an adaptation of the waulking process using the hands. Alternating rinses of very hot and cold water also speeds up the contraction of the fibres. Remember that hair-fibre fabrics do not have the same construction as wool fibres and so do not shrink and felt so readily. This does not mean they need a more heavy-handed approach: they are delicate fibres and must be treated with care. Not-so-hot water and gentle pats to begin with are the order of the day. To sum up, the degree of hand-fulling depends on the type and weight of yarn, and the weave used. It is suitable for many fabrics, from fine Shetland-type tweeds to heavier cloths and those woven with oiled wools. Take care to check for colour-fastness, too, if you use very hot water. This applies equally to the next method.

5   Finally, if a really heavily fulled, almost felted cloth is wanted, the washing machine is the quickest way. But take care. Not only is the heat of the water in a hot cycle greater than anything likely to

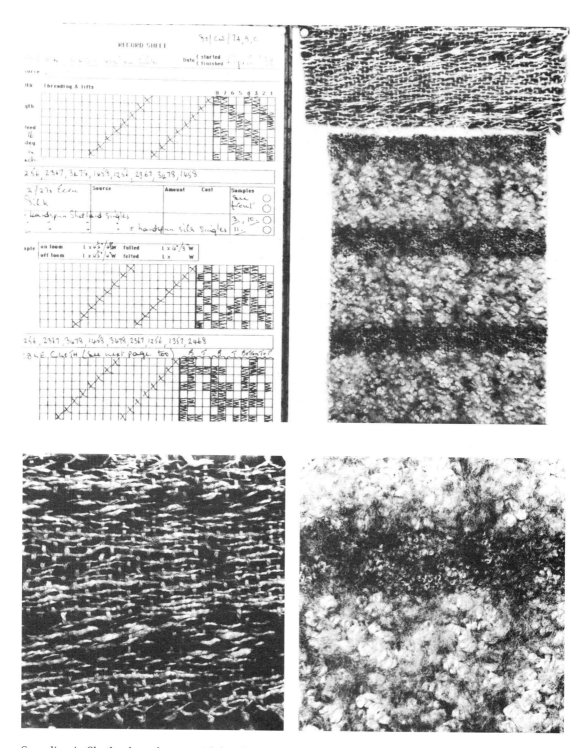

Sampling in Shetland wool warp with handspun Shetland and silk weft. Woven at a loose set and then heavily fulled (in the washing machine), the silk, because it does not shrink as much as the wool, forms 'poodle curls' on the surface of the cloth.

212

be used in hand-fulling, but even the action of filling and emptying the machine is agitating the water, and so contracting the fibres. So careful timing, and constant removal and testing, is necessary.

Another point about very heavily fulled cloths: it is easier to make these out of woollen rather than worsted-spun yarns, particularly ones that have not been preshrunk, scoured or re-oiled. (In fact, worsted cloths need very little fulling as they are usually closely woven from smooth, tightly spun yarns. A light treatment just to set them is all that is necessary.) For heavy fulling, a fabric containing a good mix of light woollen-spun or handspun yarn, say Shetland or Merino, particularly one which has been spun straight from the unscoured fleece, will felt better and more quickly than a fabric woven from coarser, commercially scoured and re-oiled fibres.

When I weave with my own handspun wools for cloth which is to be heavily fulled, I simply soak the skeins in hand-hot water – no soap, no agitation – just to float off the worst of the dirt before weaving. But if I want a normal degree of fulling, just enough to set the cloth, I pre-shrink the yarn; additionally, if I have dyed it myself, the process ensures that it is colour-fast by bleeding off any unabsorbed dye. I do this by putting the skeins into a bowl of soap and water hotter than I can bear to touch – no agitation whatsoever – and just letting it lie there for half an hour or so. I then rinse it very carefully in water of the same degree of hotness, again taking care not to agitate it. I find, even with fine fibres such as Shetland and cashmere, that this shrinks the yarn and sets the twist, but without felting it. This confirms that there has to be a combination of heat, agitation and soap to shrink

and felt yarn fully, and that some fibres react more to the process than others.

Cotton, Linen and Other Cellulose Fibres

With these considerably more robust fibres the best way is the washing-machine method. It depends very much, of course, on the yarn used. Soft-spun cotton or rayon fabrics require a good deal less processing to shrink and set them – possibly just a steam-ironing or a light hand-fulling – than ones in a natural linen yarn. Cloth woven from this somewhat unyielding fibre needs really hard *beetling*. This is the name given to a commercial process, very similar to the hammering action of a fulling mill, which gives the characteristic soft shine of well-washed and worn linen fabric. (When I grew up in India the only fabrics which stood up to the pounding the Indian dhobi, or washerman, gave our household textiles – slapping on stones appeared to be the least of it – were the Irish linen sheets and tablecloths.) To adapt the commercial process for the handweaver, using the hot cycle of the washing machine is probably the quickest and best way, followed, while the cloth is still wet, by rolling and pressing on a board – something like a rather heavy hand with the pastry is what is needed. Again, watch colour-fastness.

Silk

I think a lot of unnecessary alarm is provoked by tales of how difficult it is to care for silk. I have never found it so, except perhaps in the case of the very fine, loosely woven cheap Indian scarves. Their fine fibres have a tendency to catch on everything, and because the loose weave is so unstable it opens up and distorts however carefully it is washed. But normally, with a properly sett fabric, however fine the yarn from which it is woven, this should not happen.

Silk can be finished in the same way as fine wool, and in fact fabrics woven from the more robust yarns such as tussah or raw silk can be treated in much the same way as any medium-weight woollen cloth. One particular point to remember is that, like wool, softly spun or noil silks will felt if rubbed or washed in over-hot water. Also, silk needs to be handled while it is drying (out of direct sunlight, of course, as with wool); it should be pulled, snapped along its length and width, shaken, or whatever, to stop the fibres from drying as stiff as a board. Then iron it lightly while still damp. Heavier hand-woven silks may need no more than a steam iron held above the fabric, just to enhance the lustre.

If all this seems rather complicated (and, since the fulling process is irreversible, care obviously needs to be taken) craft magazines usually carry advertisements from firms willing to finish longer lengths of cloth for handweavers. Particularly if the cloth needs to be *brushed, napped* or *sheared*, processes to bring up or trim the surface, it is probably better to hand a precious length of cloth over to the professionals to finish rather than risk spoiling it by one's own amateur efforts.

FINISHES TO EMBELLISH TEXTILES

Particularly with some decorative and household textiles, such as tapestries and rugs, there are further processes before the piece is completely finished. Mostly these come down to making a feature of the necessary securing of wefts and warps to prevent the fabric unravelling, of joining or embellishing seams and selvedges, and of edging, binding, decorating and mounting.

Depending entirely on the design and style of the textile, fringes, which essentially protect the weft from unravelling, can range from the understated knotted finish of a cashmere shawl to the beaded macramé-knotted and tasselled trim of an ethnic hanging. A whipped or knotted fringe is simple and effective, as is the traditional way of edging woollen lap-rugs. This involves taking three or five warp ends and twisting each separately the same way as the yarn twists, then putting the tips together, giving a turn or two in the opposite direction to the whole bunch, and releasing. The group of ends will spring together into a nice tight twist which, in the fulling process, will felt into itself and never unravel. (Weavers who make twisted cords will recognize this as exactly the same technique, transferred from long pieces of yarn to short ends of warp.)

Finger-weaving is another simple way of securing fringes. Either the three-strand plait or a braid of four or more strands looks good, particularly if the yarn ends are of different colours and the colours can be arranged to enhance the pattern in the braid. Alternatively, consider a whipped fringe, the whipping taken down a certain distance, with the remaining ends fluffed up into little tassels. The twining method used in tapestry to give a firm edge against which to start weaving makes an excellent decorative binding to keep the first and last weft picks in place, as does chaining. The

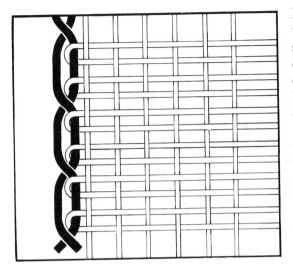

Navajo twining every four picks (two turns around the selvedge).

last few inches of the weft. They can be woven at the end of the piece and used to secure the hanging round a mounting bar, or at the beginning as well so that both ends have a similar decorative finish. Darn the warp ends in at the back to secure each tab.

A similar darned-in edge can be used, perhaps with a tapestry or rug, when the warp yarn is not attractive in itself. The ends can be darned up into the fabric at the back to form a false selvedge, and then fringes, tassels or the like in the weft yarn or yarns can be knotted or sewn on to the edges as required.

Weavers who are familiar with braid- and cord-making techniques – such as tablet and inkle weaving, Peruvian card braiding or Japanese Kumi-himo braiding – can contrive very attractive finishes for their textiles either by incorporating warps from the main fabric into the braids or by braiding with the same yarns and then using them as bound embellishments and edging trims.

Finally, it is sometimes necessary to join strips of woven fabric to form a wider piece – when weaving on a narrow loom, for instance. If a definite pattern, such as stripes, has to be matched, great care must be taken to beat the fabric down evenly so that there is no variation in the sett of the strips. This can be quite difficult, so needs watching.) Seams can either be 'invisible' or made an integral part of the design. In the latter case, for instance, Navajo selvedges butted together and joined invisibly on the back with a flat seaming stitch such as *loop stitch* can provide interesting additional surface decoration to the piece, or a flat loop stitch can hold the seam firm from the back while an additional decorative embroidery stitch (*Cretan stitch* or *feather stitch*) can be

fringe can then be left to hang free since it is quite secure. Incidentally, rather mean-looking fringes and tassels can always be enhanced by adding extra threads as required.

If integral fringed tassels are wanted on all four sides of a textile such as a shawl, they can be constructed on each edge during weaving, using a *gauge cord* (in effect, an extra and usually thicker and stronger warp end, set out the required distance from the selvedges). When the cord, which is threaded through the reed to maintain spacing, is removed, fringed ends similar to those at the start and finish of the work are formed. Another interesting selvedge finish is used by the Navajo on their rugs and blankets. This is also formed during weaving, and can be accentuated by the use of thicker or different-coloured yarns used in the twining.

A rather different finish, particularly useful for wall hangings, is the discontinuous weaving of tabs or scallops in the

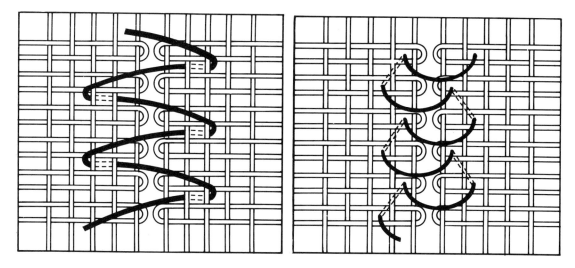

Seaming stitches – Cretan stitch and feather stitch.

worked on the face of the fabric. A decorative cord or braid can be *couched* over the seam to hide it, or knots can be used both to close and to give a decorative finish to a seam. In fact, really, there is no end to the possibilities for finishing and embellishing textiles. The problem, as always, is knowing when enough is enough. Which brings this section back to where it began, back to the need for a carefully considered design for each project. This is really the only way to solve the problem: designing is after all problem-solving, as we are all aware.

A FINAL FINISH – AND A LOOK TO THE FUTURE

And now I am faced with the same problem – how to find a satisfactory way of finishing off this book. Just as with my own textiles, those I weave and braid, and with my design and craft teaching, it is not all that difficult to get started. But finding the right way to stop is not quite so simple.

I think all I can really say is that when I began writing this book my aim was to introduce a rather complex subject in as simple a form as possible; and that during the course of writing I have tried, while setting out various ideas and techniques for woven textiles, to put over my feeling that not only do the arts and crafts still play a very real part in our lives but that craft makers themselves are as important today as they were before the Industrial Revolution; and that they are important whether they work purely for their own private satisfaction or whether they are trying to regain a realistic and sensibly commercial place for their craft in what can sometimes seem to be a hard and overmechanized modern world.

So my final wish is that we enjoy our craft, and that we all have that little bit of necessary luck, too – just to oil our looms for us.

Bibliography

Tools and Materials

* indicates recommended further reading.

Bridgman, Rosemary, articles published in *Home Farm*, 1984–5

British Wool Marketing Board, *British Sheep and Wool*

Broudy, Eric, The *Book of Looms* (Studio Vista, 1979)

Clabburn, Pamela, *Shawls* (Shire Publications, 1981)

Kolander, Cheryl, *A Silk Worker's Notebook* (Interweave Press, 1979)

Ladbury, Anne, *Fabrics* (Sidgwick & Jackson, 1979, 1985)

* Lorant, Tessa, *Yarns for Textile Crafts* (Van Nostrand Reinhold, 1984)

Morris, James, and Cave-Penny, Tony (eds), *Goats for Fibre* (The National Angora Stud, 1987)

Ponting, Kenneth, *Sheep of the World* (Blandford, 1980)

Ryder, Michael, *Cashmere, Mohair and Other Luxury Animal Fibres for the Breeder and Spinner* (White Rose II, 1987)

Storey, Joyce, *Dyes and Fabrics* (Thames & Hudson, 1978, 1985)

* Tompson, Frances, and Tompson, Tony, *Synthetic Dyeing* (David & Charles, 1987)

Ideas

* Bonfini Press, a series of reasonably priced biographies of artists, particularly Gauguin, Kandinsky, Klee, Matisse, Seurat, Turner and Van Gogh

Birren, Faber, *Principles of Colour* (Van Rostrand Reinhold, 1969)

Chevreul, M. E., *The Principles of Harmony and Contrast of Colours*, translated by Faber Birren (Van Nostrand Reinhold, 1981)

Dyer, Anne, *Dyes from Natural Sources* (Bell & Hyman, 1981)

Itten, Johannes, *The Elements of Colour* (Van Nostrand Reinhold, 1971)

* Rawson, Philip, *Creative Design: A New Look at Design Principles* (Macdonald, 1987)

Thomas, David, *J. M. W. Turner* (Medici Society, 1979)

Thurstan, Violetta, *The Use of Vegetable Dyes* (Dryad Press, 1979)

* Wilcox, Michael, *Blue and Yellow Don't Make Green* (Collins, 1989)

* Williams, David, *Design Graphics* (Blackwood, 1987)

* Varley, Helen (ed.), *Colour* (Marshall Editions, 1983)

Techniques

Beutlich, Tadek, *The Technique of Woven Tapestry* (Batsford, 1979)

Brown, Rachel, *The Weaving, Spinning and Dyeing Book* (Routledge & Kegan Paul, 1979)

Clark, Hazel, *Fibres to Fabrics* (Batsford, 1985)

* Collingwood, Peter, *The Techniques of Rug Weaving* (Faber, 1968)

Tod, Osma Gallinger, *The Joy of Handweaving* (Dover, 1977)

* Halsey, Mike, and Youngmark, Lore, *Foundations of Weaving* (David & Charles, 1986)
* Pegg, Barbara, *Weaving Without a Loom* (A. & C. Black, 1986)
Pekin, Ersu, *Turkish Flat Weaves and Carpets* (Minyatur Publications, Turkey)
* Phillips, Janet, *The Weaver's Book of Fabric Design* (Batsford, 1983)
* Sutton, Anne, *The Structure of Weaving* (Hutchinson, 1982)
* Sutton, Ann, Collingwood, Peter, and St Aubin Hubbard, Geraldine, *The Craft of the Weaver* (BBC Publications, 1982)
Reichard, Gladys A., *Weaving a Navajo Blanket* (Dover, 1974)
Thomson, Francis Paul, *Tapestry – Mirror of History* (David & Charles, 1980)

Useful Addresses

General Suppliers

Dryad
PO Box 38
Northgates
Leicester LE1 9BU
(looms and accessories, weaving
equipment, dyes)

Fibrecrafts
Textile Crafts Supplies
Style Cottage
Lower Eashing
Godalming
Surrey GU7 2QD
(looms and accessories, weaving
equipment, dye systems and equipment,
dyes and mordants, plans for DIY
equipment, yarns, fibres and books)

Handweavers Studio & Gallery Ltd
29 Haroldstone Road
London E17 7AN
(looms and accessories, weaving
equipment, fibres and yarns)

Dyes

Wood & Wool (Frances and Tony
Thompson)
2 High Meads
Wheathampstead
Herts. AL4 8DN
(dyes of all sorts)

Yarns

Craftsman's Mark
Tone Dale Mill
Wellington
Somerset TA21 OAW
(natural-coloured weaving yarns in pure
new wool; also undyed cotton/linen/
jute/sisal)

T.M. Hunter Ltd
Sutherland Wool Mills
Brora
Scotland KW9 6NA
(dyed weaving yarns, including
Shetland, Harris-type, Cheviot)

Jamieson & Smith Ltd
90 North Road
Lerwick
Shetland Isles ZE1 OPQ
(dyed Shetland yarns)

Lodge Enterprises (Angela Lodge)
56A Ayres Street
London SE1 1EU
(Filoni specialist yarns)

Norwood Farm Shop
Norwood Farm
Bath Road
Norton St Philip
Bath BA3 6LP
(Mrs Catherine Mack)
(some fleeces and wools, as well as
information on rare breeds of sheep and
goats)

Texere Yarns
College Mill
Barkerend Road
Bradford
West Yorkshire BD3 9AQ
(dyed and undyed yarns – including
machine knitting yarns, which can be
used for weaving – in wool, silk, cotton
and man-made fibre mixtures)

Wingham Wool Work, Freepost
70 Main Street
Wentworth
Rotherham
South Yorkshire S62 7BR
(a wide variety of hand-spinning
supplies and some yarns)

Index

A £15.95   M11690 (1498) ALBION — BA.